Charles Gore

**The Incarnation of the Son of God**

Charles Gore

**The Incarnation of the Son of God**

ISBN/EAN: 9783337062866

Printed in Europe, USA, Canada, Australia, Japan

Cover: Foto ©Lupo / pixelio.de

More available books at **www.hansebooks.com**

# THE INCARNATION

OF THE

# SON OF GOD

BEING

## *THE BAMPTON LECTURES*

### *FOR THE YEAR 1891*

BY

## CHARLES GORE, (M.A

PRINCIPAL OF PUSEY HOUSE ; FELLOW OF TRINITY COLLEGE, OXFORD

Tu ad liberandum suscepturus hominem non horruisti Virginis uterum

## London

### JOHN MURRAY, ALBEMARLE STREET

1891

THE INCARNATION

# EXTRACT

## FROM THE LAST WILL AND TESTAMENT

### OF THE LATE

## REV. JOHN BAMPTON,

### CANON OF SALISBURY.

——" I give and bequeath my Lands and Estates to the
"Chancellor, Masters, and Scholars of the University of Oxford
"for ever, to have and to hold all and singular the said Lands or
"Estates upon trust, and to the intents and purposes hereinafter
"mentioned; that is to say, I will and appoint that the Vice-
"Chancellor of the University of Oxford for the time being shall
"take and receive all the rents, issues, and profits thereof, and
"(after all taxes, reparations, and necessary deductions made)
"that he pay all the remainder to the endowment of eight
"Divinity Lecture Sermons, to be established for ever in the
"said University, and to be performed in the manner following

"I direct and appoint, that, upon the first Tuesday in Easter
"Term, a Lecturer may be yearly chosen by the Heads of Col-
"leges only, and by no others, in the room adjoining to the
"Printing-House, between the hours of ten in the morning and
"two in the afternoon, to preach eight Divinity Lecture
"Sermons, the year following, at St. Mary's in Oxford, between
"the commencement of the last month in Lent Term, and the
"end of the third week in Act Term.

"Also I direct and appoint, that the eight Divinity Lecture
"Sermons shall be preached upon either of the following
"Subjects—to confirm and establish the Christian Faith, and
"to confute all heretics and schismatics—upon the divine
"authority of the holy Scriptures—upon the authority of the
"writings of the primitive Fathers, as to the faith and practice
"of the primitive Church—upon the Divinity of our Lord and
"Saviour Jesus Christ—upon the divinity of the Holy Ghost—
"upon the Articles of the Christian Faith, as comprehended in
"the Apostles' and Nicene Creed.

"Also I direct, that thirty copies of the eight Divinity Lec-
"ture Sermons shall be always printed, within two months after
"they are preached; and one copy shall be given to the Chan-
"cellor of the University, and one copy to the head of every
"College, and one copy to the mayor of the city of Oxford, and
"one copy to be put into the Bodleian Library; and the
"expense of printing them shall be paid out of the revenue of
"the Land or Estates given for establishing the Divinity Lecture
"Sermons; and the Preacher shall not be paid, nor be entitled
"to the revenue, before they are printed.

"Also I direct and appoint, that no person shall be qualified
"to preach the Divinity Lecture Sermons, unless he hath taken
"the degree of Master of Arts at least, in one of the two Uni-
"versities of Oxford or Cambridge; and that the same person
"shall never preach the Divinity Lecture Sermons twice."

# PREFACE.

BAMPTON Lectures are addressed necessarily, at least in modern Oxford, to a general rather than to a specially theological audience. It is natural therefore to endeavour to keep within limits the discussion of points of technical theology.

Thus in the present volume of lectures—which are printed as they were delivered, with not more than verbal changes and occasional expansions—I aim at presenting the subject of the Incarnation rather to the general reader than to the professed theological student ; and I hope to have the opportunity of preparing another volume which shall appeal to a more strictly theological public, and deal with some subjects which are necessarily alluded to rather than discussed in these pages, such for example as—

(1) The conception entertained in early Greek theology of the supernatural in its relation to nature (see pp. 41–44 and notes).

(2) The relation of Ebionism and Gnosticism to the theology of the New Testament and of the 2nd century (pp. 83–87 and notes).

(3) The conception of the Incarnation at different epochs, patristic (p. 163 and note), early mediaeval

(pp. 163–5), later scholastic (pp. 151–2). This is said, however, only to explain what would otherwise appear to be the deficiency in the annotation to these lectures, not in any way to deprecate the criticism of theological experts on anything that is contained in them.

It is my hope that these lectures express throughout the same intellectual principle :—the principle namely that all right theory emerges out of experience, and is the analysis of experience : that the right method of philosophy is not *à priori*, abstract, or external, but is based in each department of enquiry upon a profound and sympathetic study of the facts.

As Christians of course we desire that the moral and spiritual facts, with which our religious life is bound up, should be appreciated as from within, before they are criticized ; and should be allowed fair opportunity to tell their own tale, and justify their claims at the bar of reason by their power to interpret and deal with experience as a whole. But it is not only in the case of critics of Christianity that we have occasion to deprecate the abstract, external, *à priori* method. Within the area of Christianity this false method is frequently intruding itself.

Thus in current discussions as to the nature of religious authority it is remarkable how seldom the appeal is made to the actual method of our Lord, and how small is the force allowed to indisputable facts of Church history in limiting and conditioning abstract general statements. And in the highest subject of all, the doctrine of the being of God, abstract statements of the divine attributes—infinity, omnipotence, immutability—frequently take the place of a careful estimate of what God has actually manifested of Himself in nature and conscience and Christ. The religion of the Incarnation is preeminently a religion of experience and fact. We know what God has revealed of Himself in the order of the world, in the conscience of men in general, by the inspired wisdom of His prophets, and in the person of Jesus Christ; and the best theology is that which is moulded, as simply and as closely as may be, upon what has actually been disclosed.

I am at a loss in expressing my obligation to others in the preparation of these lectures : in part because it is indirect : in part because it is obligation to so many persons. My indirect obligations to many writers will be apparent ; not least to the writers of Essays i, ii, v, vi, in *Lux Mundi*. I have contracted obligations to many persons, because the common enemy, the influenza, made it necessary for me to prepare these lectures for press at a distance from libraries, and thus made me dependent upon much external assistance, which I can only gratefully acknowledge.

WIMBLEDON,
*St. Bartholomew's Day*, 1891.

# SYNOPSIS OF CONTENTS.

———•———

## LECTURE I.

### *WHAT CHRISTIANITY IS.*

## LECTURE II.

### *CHRIST SUPERNATURAL YET NATURAL.*

## LECTURE III.

### *THE SUPERNATURAL CHRIST HISTORICAL.*

## LECTURE IV.

*THE CHRIST OF DOGMA THE CHRIST OF SCRIPTURE.*

## LECTURE VII.

### _CHRIST OUR MASTER._

## LECTURE VIII.

### *CHRIST OUR EXAMPLE AND NEW LIFE.*

b

# APPENDED NOTES.

## LECTURE I.

## LECTURE II.

## LECTURE III.

## LECTURE IV.

## LECTURE V.

# THE

# INCARNATION OF THE SON OF GOD.

————

## LECTURE I.

### WHAT CHRISTIANITY IS.

*We know that the Son of God is come, and hath given us an understanding,
that we know him that is true, and we are in him that is true, even in
his Son Jesus Christ. This is the true God, and eternal life. My
little children, guard yourselves from idols* —1 ST. JOHN v. 20, 21 (R.V.)

CHRISTIANITY exists in the world as a distinctive
religion; and if we are asked, ' What is the distinguishing
characteristic of this religion?' we can hardly hesitate
for an answer. Christianity is faith in a certain person
Jesus Christ, and by faith in Him is meant such un-
reserved self-committal as is only possible, because faith
in Jesus is understood to be faith in God, and union with
Jesus union with God. ' We know him that is true, and
we are in him that is true, even in his Son Jesus Christ.
This is the true God, and eternal life [1].'

### I.

That true Christianity is thus a personal relation
ship—the conscious deliberate adhesion of men who
know their weakness, their sin, their fallibility, to a
redeemer whom they know to be supreme, sinless, infallible— is shewn by the fact that it produces its charac-

[1] See appended note 1. p. 233.

teristic fruit only in proportion as it is thus realized. We can make this apparently obvious proposition more emphatic if we recall to our mind some of the many ways in which the true character of our religion has been, and is, distorted or obscured.

1. For, first, Christianity has brought with it a visible society or church, with dogmatic propositions and sacramental ordinances and a ministerial priesthood, and it has been easy so to misuse these elements of the ecclesiastical system, as to make Christianity no longer devotion to a living person, but the acceptance on authority of a system of theological propositions and ecclesiastical duties. When churchmanship assumes this degenerate form, Christianity is not indeed destroyed, nor does it cease to bring forth moral and spiritual fruit ; but the fruit is of an inferior and less characteristic quality, it is not the spirit and temper of sonship. At the lowest it even tends to approximate to what any religious organization is capable of producing, merely on account of the discipline which it enforces, and the sense of security which its fellowship imparts. To the true and typical churchman, on the other hand, all the ecclesiastical fabric only represents an unseen but present Lord. The eyes of an Ignatius, or an Athanasius, or a Leo, or a Bernard, or a Pusey, however much history may rightly identify these men with zeal on behalf of the organization and dogmas of the church, were in fact, as their writings sufficiently testify, never off their Lord for whom alone and in whom alone all external things had their value.

2. Again, the constant outlook of the soul of the Christian upon the person of Jesus Christ may be inter-

cepted by the undue exaltation of saintly intercessors. Thus there are districts of the church in which devotion to our Lord's mother has usurped such prominence in Christian worship as in fact to interfere with His unique prerogative, so that in some real sense there has been a division of territory effected between Him and her as objects of devotion. This statement may be justified by quoting from a writer who is specially representative of the attitude encouraged in the Roman communion towards the blessed Virgin—St. Alfonso de' Liguori. 'When she conceived the Son of God in her womb,' he writes, 'and afterwards gave Him birth, she obtained the half of the kingdom of God, so that she should be queen of mercy, as Christ is king of justice.' Thus, while the king must have regard to the interests of justice, the queen can be appealed to as unmixed compassion [1]. Once again, then, when Mary is thus exalted to a pedestal, which no one would ever have refused so utterly as she herself, the wine of Christianity is mixed with water. For the human character of Jesus, the historical character, combining the strength of manhood and the tenderness of womanhood in perfect alliance, is always strengthening to contemplate and to adore. In Him mercy and truth are met together, righteousness and peace have kissed each other; but the purely ideal figure of Mary, as it finds expression in all the weakly conceived images of the 'mater misericordiae' which meet our eyes so constantly in the churches of the Continent, appeals to a sentiment, a craving for a compassion unalloyed with severity, which it was part of the proper function of Christianity even to extirpate.

[1] See app. note 2, p. 233.

3. Once again, it is possible for our religion to lose its true centre by becoming what we may call unduly 'subjective.' Great stress may be laid on personal feeling, on the assurance of personal salvation. Questions may be freely asked and answers expected as to whether this or that religious emotion has been experienced, as to whether a person has 'found peace,' or 'gained assurance,' or 'is saved.' Now 'peace with God,' and 'joy in believing,' even assurance of a present state of salvation, are endowments of the Christian life, which God habitually bestows—which may be both asked for and thankfully welcomed. But they are not meant either to be the tests of reality in religion, or generally subjects of self-examination.

What our Lord claims of us is, first, service, the service of ready wills, then developing faith, and lives gradually sanctified by correspondence with Him. On these points we must rigorously examine ourselves, but the sense of the service of Another, of co-operation with Another, is meant to become so absorbing a consciousness as to swallow up in us the consideration of personal feeling, and at least to overshadow even the anxiety for our own separate salvation. By losing our lives in Christ and His cause, we are meant to save them; to serve Christ, not to feel Christ, is the mark of His true servants; they become Christians in proportion as they cease to be interested in themselves, and become absorbed in their Lord.

4. Once again; the enthusiasm of humanity may send men out using the name of Him who is the true liberator of man, but depreciating doctrine in the supposed interests of philanthropy. This inevitably results in the substitution of zeal for work for zeal for Christ. Where Christ

is really contemplated and meditated upon, it is impossible to be indifferent as to the explanation to be given of His person and work; in the knowledge of this lies the inspiration of labour and the ground of perennial hopefulness. When in fact this is ignored, the work becomes more and more the execution of the worker's own schemes, or the schemes of some one under whom he works, with less and less regard to what can truly and historically be called the purpose and method of Jesus. It becomes external or intellectual, it ceases to touch the springs of character; in a word, it becomes less and less a characteristic expression of the energy of Christian faith.

5. Once again and for the last time : the interests of a student may convert Christianity into a philosophical system, coloured intensely by the method and terminology of a particular phase of thought and very exceptional conditions of life. This was the case, more or less, with the Christianity of Clement of Alexandria ; it has been the case not infrequently, since his day, in academic circles. Where it is the case, a system becomes the object of interest rather than a person, and the real appeal of Jesus of Nazareth, whether to the heart of the student himself, or of those whom he may be required to teach by word or by writing, is proportionately weakened. Nothing, I suppose, can keep the Christianity of a theoretical student from deterioration, save the constant exercise of prayer, which is the address of person to person, and the constant and regular contemplation of the character in the Gospels, even as the apostolic writer bids us 'consider the Apostle and High Priest of our confession, even Jesus [1].'

¹ Heb. iii. 1.

I have specified these various ways in which Christians
of different tendencies may obscure, and have in fact
obscured, the true glory of the Christian life, because
it is important to throw into high relief, what is the
simple verdict of Christian history, that the characteristic fruitfulness of our religion—its fruitfulness in the
temper and spirit of sonship—varies with the extent
to which Jesus, the historical person, the ever-living
person, is recognised as the object of our devotion and
the lord of our life.   This is true equally of personal
religion and official ministry, for it is converse with the
perfect personality of Jesus, which gives the pastor his
power to deal with the various personalities of his flock,
and the preacher his power to move the wills and
consciences of his hearers.   It is devotion to Jesus which
has been the source of the enduring forms of Christian
heroism.   It is the same reality of personal relationship which touches the Christian's private life with
the brightness of sonship.   'To me,' says Paul the
prisoner, summarizing his religion, 'to live is Christ and
to die is gain,' for that too is 'to depart and to be
with Christ,' which 'is very far better[1].'   'Eighty and six
years,' says the aged Polycarp, again summarizing his
religion in response to the demand that he should
revile the Christ,—'eighty and six years have I been
His servant, and He never did me an injury; how then
can I blaspheme my king who is my saviour[2]?'

[1] Phil. i. 21–23.          [2] *Martyr. S. Polyc.* 9.

## II.

To recognise this truth is to be struck by the contrast which in this respect Christianity presents to other religions.  For example, the place which Mohammed holds in Islam is not the place which Jesus Christ holds in Christianity, but that which Moses holds in Judaism.  The Arabian prophet made for himself no claim other than that which Jewish prophets made, other than that which all prophets, true or false, or partly true and partly false, have always made,—to speak the word of the Lord.  The substance of Mohammedanism, considered as a religion, lies simply in the message which the Koran contains.  It is, as no other religion is, founded upon a book.  The person of the Prophet has its significance only so far as he is supposed to have certificated the reality of the revelations which the book records [1].

Gautama, again, the founder of Buddhism, one, I suppose, of the noblest and greatest of mankind, is only the discoverer or rediscoverer of a method or way, the way of salvation, by which is meant the way to win final emancipation from the weary chain of existence, and to attain Nirvana, or Parinirvana, the final blessed extinction.  Having found this way, after many years of weary searching, he can teach it to others, but he is, all the time, only a pre-eminent example of the success of his own method, one of a series of Buddhas or enlightened ones, who shed on other men the light of their superior knowledge.  Thus, in *The Book of the Great Decease* he is represented, in

[1] See app. note 3, p. 235.

conversation with his disciple Ânanda, as expressly repudiating the idea of the dependence of the Buddhist order on himself. 'The Perfect,' that is, the Buddha, he says, ' thinks not that it is he who should lead the brotherhood, or that the order is dependent upon him. Why then should he leave instructions in any matter concerning the order? . . . Therefore, O Ânanda, be ye lamps unto yourselves. Be ye a refuge to your-selves. Betake yourselves to no external refuge . . . And whosoever, Ânanda, either now or after I am dead, shall be a lamp unto themselves, and a refuge unto themselves, shall betake themselves to no ex-ternal refuge, but holding fast to the truth as their lamp, shall look not for refuge to any one besides themselves . . . it is they, Ânanda, who shall reach the very topmost height [1].'

It was plainly the method of Buddha, not the person, which was to save his brethren. As for the person, he passed away, as the writer of the Buddhist scripture re-peatedly declares, ' with that utter passing away in which nothing whatever is left behind,' living on only metaphor-ically in the method and teaching which he bequeathed to his followers. We are touching on no disputed point when we assert that according to the Buddhist scriptures, the personal, conscious life of the founder of that religion was extinguished in death. But this single fact points the contrast with Christianity. The teaching of Jesus differs in fact from the teaching of the Buddha not more in the ideal of salvation which he propounded than in the place held by the person who propounded the ideal. For Jesus Christ taught no method by which men might

---

[1] See app. note 4, p. 236.

attain the end of their being, whether He Himself, personally, existed or was annihilated : but as He offered Himself to men on earth as the satisfaction of their being—
their master, their example, their redeemer—so when He
left the earth He promised to sustain them from the unseen world by His continued personal presence and to
communicate to them His own life, and He assured
them that at the last they would find themselves face to
face with Him as their judge. The personal relation to
Himself is from first to last of the essence of the religion
which He inaugurated.

### III.

If we wish to account for the unique position which
Jesus Christ has held in religion it is only necessary
to examine the claim which He is represented to have
made for Himself in the earliest records which we
possess. History in fact gives a very distinct account
of the positions relatively to the faith of their disciples,
claimed by the three founders of religion whom we have
just been considering. For however busy legend has
been with the Buddha, there appears to be little difficulty
in obtaining a clear picture of what he claimed to be,
how he claimed to have become what he was, and
how he wished his disciples to follow his example.
Legend has not materially distorted the picture of his
own estimate of himself. No more than Mohammed does
he, on his own showing, enter into rivalry with the Jesus
of the Christian tradition. Whether history has or has
not left us the true image of the personal claim of Jesus
of Nazareth will be matter for consideration afterwards.
Here I am only concerned to make good the position

that the teaching and the claim of Jesus as it is represented generally in the Gospels, or (let me say) more
especially in the Synoptists, accounts for and justifies
the place assigned to Him in historical Christendom.

This will be most apparent if we confine our attention
chiefly to the education which He is represented as
giving to that little company who united themselves
to Him under various circumstances, and whom He
bound together into the body of Apostles. For, diverting attention from others, He concentrated it more and
more on these. We are admitted in the Gospels to observe how He trained these few men to understand His
person and commit themselves body and soul to Him.

Many passed to Christ from the school of John the
Baptist, and their initiation to discipleship consisted
in the experience of their former master laying down
his crown at the feet of Him, ' the latchet of whose
shoes ' he professed himself ' unworthy to stoop down
and unloose.' The personality of Jesus lays upon them
from the first its strong fascination. It is only gradually,
however, through the experience of His manhood that
they are led to any real conviction of His superhuman
nature. They listen to His words of power, as He
speaks like the embodied voice of conscience, 'as one
having authority,' convincingly yet without reason given,
setting aside, as inadequate, what the lawgiver of old
had spoken as God's own messenger, ' It was said to
them of old time ... But I say unto you[1].' They are
made to feel that it is no longer the servant who is
speaking, but the Son. Moreover in the midst of His
authoritative teaching, a claim makes itself heard, which

---

[1] St. Matt. v. 21, 22.

is of a piece with His general tone, and yet by itself is
of staggering import, the claim to pronounce at the last
the final divine judgment, not on the overt actions of
men only, but on their secret lives.  This claim is first
expressed in regard to His professed followers in the
Sermon on the Mount.  'Many will say to me in that
day, Lord, Lord, did we not prophesy by thy name, and
by thy name cast out devils, and by thy name do many
mighty works?  And then will I profess unto them, I
never knew you : depart from me, ye that work iniquity[1].'
It makes itself heard again and again, but it culminates
in the picture which our Lord draws of Himself before
His passion, when before Him shall be gathered, not
His own followers only, or the Jews, but 'all the
nations,' and He shall pass sentence on them individually, as one who knows them better than they know
themselves[2].  Conceive what it must have been to live
with one, who, however gently and carefully He re-
spected and dealt with human individuality and freewill,
yet declared Himself to be, and was believed to be, the
final judge of all human actions and human motives.
In such intercourse must not reverence inevitably have
tended to pass into worship, for is it not our great pre-
servative against idolizing any other human being that
we know that he and we alike are the simple subjects of
divine judgment?  The apostles had to do with one
who never spoke of Himself or seemed to conceive of
Himself, as liable to sin or failure under probation, and
who claimed to be the final enunciator and vindicator of
the law of right and wrong.  It was only the same claim
in other words which He made when He declared that

---

[1] St. Matt. vii. 22, 23.          [2] St. Matt. xxv. 31-46.

the Son of man had power on earth to forgive sins [1], for it
is the ultimate judge who is the proper absolver ; nor
could it seem strange to them that His moral power
should have its counterpart in His physical power to
impart life and to heal diseases.   There is—a pious Jew
at least would know—only one ultimate lordship in spirit
and in matter, and He who claimed and exercised it in
the one department would naturally claim and exercise
it in the other.   So it was that by teaching and miracle,
and still more by the subtle influence of long months of
companionship in work and in travel, He deliberately
trained the twelve men to trust Him utterly in His
presence and in His absence, as the unerring friend,
the all-powerful guide, the supreme and unfailing re-
source.   Such trust undoubtedly transcended the limits
of what is legitimate from man to man ; a mere man,
however exalted, must always point his fellow-men
away from himself up to God ; he must always exalt
his message above himself; he must always explain
that he is only one of the many messengers that God
in His wisdom can use.   But as in Jesus there was a
marked absence of all that sense of unworthiness, which
has clung to God's messengers before and after Him in
proportion to their goodness, so in Him also there was
the opposite of all that disparagement of merely personal
claims which made Moses cry, 'Oh Lord, send, I pray
thee, by the hand of him whom thou wilt send,' and St.
Paul, 'What then is Apollos? and what is Paul [2] ?'   What
Scripture calls the jealousy of God, that exclusive unique
claim which God alone can make on the souls of men,
because He alone can absorb without narrowing the

---

[1] St. Matt. ix. 6.          [2] Ex. iv. 13; I Cor. iii. 5.

allegiance of all spirits whom He has created,—that jealousy of God utters itself in the solemn words, 'No one knoweth the Son save the Father ; neither doth any know the Father save the Son, and he to whomsoever the Son willeth to reveal him. Come unto me, all ye that labour and are heavy laden, and I will give you rest [1].' Or again, 'If any man cometh unto me and hateth not his own father, and mother, and wife, and children, and brethren, and sisters, yea, and his own life also, he cannot be my disciple [2].'

Set yourselves to imagine what the effect of such language must have been, not on the crowd who came and went, who received the seed by the wayside, but on the good soil of the hearts of the apostles, kept under careful cultivation to receive the deliberately sown seed of the Master's word. Christ was systematically training them to trust Him with the sort of trust which can be legitimately given to God only. This becomes all the more conspicuous when we find Him repudiating from one who came with the vague language of casual respect, even the familiar title, 'Good Master [3].' Such ordinary and casual deference, the language of mere compliment commonly addressed to contemporary Rabbis. He would not accept ; but language far higher, devotion of far intenser meaning He was meanwhile deliberately encouraging in the disciples who did know Him, and had reasons for what they said and felt [4] : just as with the women, while He checked the vague enthusiasm of her who lifted up her voice out of the multitude to cry, 'Blessed is the womb that bare thee, and the paps which

---

[1] St. Matt. xi. 27, 28; cf. St. Luke x. 22.   [3] St. Luke xiv. 26.
[2] St. Mark x. 17.   [4] Cf. esp. St. Matt. xxii. 7 10.

thou didst suck,' He welcomed the more deliberate honours paid to Him by the woman who was a sinner, or Mary the sister of Lazarus[1].

The training of the apostles, which is always proceeding, has certain critical moments. Thus at Cæsarea Philippi, our Lord solemnly evoked, under conditions of trial and disappointment, the expression of the gradually clearing faith of His disciples in Himself, so far at least as the full acknowledgment of His Messiahship—that He was 'the Christ, the Son of the living God' or 'the Holy One of God[2].' Again, at the Mount of the Transfiguration, He revealed unmistakeably to the inner circle, to Peter, James, and John, something of His hidden glory, the glory of the only begotten of the Father[3]. More than once He gave more or less explicit utterance, so that the disciples might hear and take heed, to His inner consciousness of essential relation to the Father, as when He spoke of the mutual and exclusive knowledge of the Father and the Son[4], or distinguished Himself as the only son, in the parable of the vineyard and the husbandmen, from God's many servants and messengers[5], or confessed His divine sonship before the Sanhedrim on his trial in full view of the mortal penalty which that confession involved[6]. No doubt up to the time of the passion, the faith of the disciples in their Lord was dim and inchoate. It

---

[1] St. Luke xi. 27; vii. 36–50; St. Matt. xxvi. 6–13; St. John xi. 2.
[2] St. Matt. xvi. 16; cf. St. Mark viii. 29; St. Luke ix. 20; St. John vi. 69.
[3] St. Matt. xvii. 1–8; St. Mark ix. 2–8; St. Luke ix. 28–36; 2 Peter i. 16–18.
[4] St. Matt. xi. 27; St. Luke x. 22.
[5] St. Matt. xxi. 33–46; St. Mark xii. 1–12; St. Luke xx. 9–18.
[6] St. Matt. xxvi. 62–65; St. Mark xiv. 60–64; St. Luke xxii. 66–71.

was personal loyalty not yet theologically articulate
or self-conscious. The passion, the failure, the death,
were enough to crush it down for the moment, in spite of
all the intimations with which Jesus Christ had prepared
their minds for that foreseen catastrophe. The fact of
the resurrection was hardly and with difficulty believed.
But when it was believed, it lifted their faith to a new
level and planted it upon a solid rock whence it could
never be again dislodged. He was marked out for them,
and through them for the world, as the Son of God by
the resurrection from the dead[1]. The confession of
Thomas after the resurrection recorded in the fourth
Gospel, 'My Lord and my God,' is no less representative
than the earlier confession of Peter recorded in the three
earlier Gospels, 'Thou art the Christ of God,'—'the
Christ, the Son of the living God.' The last utterance
of Jesus, as St. Matthew records it, not only assured His
disciples of the universal authority assigned to Him as
the exalted Son of man, both in heaven and on earth,
and of His continual presence with them 'all the days
unto the end of the world,' but also gave permanence
and security to their highest thoughts of Him as Son of
God, by formulating the name, or revelation of God, for
all time, as the 'name of the Father and of the Son and
of the Holy Ghost.' After Pentecost, the apostles
had no doubt at all that Jesus Christ as Son of God was
the summary object of faith and worship, and that in
committing to Him their whole being, they were not
running the risk of idolatry, but were only attaining
union with God through His Son by the Spirit which
He had given them.

[1] Rom. i. 3, 4.

I have endeavoured briefly to traverse very familiar ground in thus recalling to your minds how the Christ of the Gospels does make a claim for Himself which warrants (to speak generally) the belief about Him to which we are accustomed in the Christian Church. That this is familiar ground, upon which it is not necessary long to dwell, is due in great measure to one, the tones of whose memorable voice the majority of us must have heard from this pulpit last Whitsunday, and heard for the last time. Among all Dr. Liddon's titles to our gratitude, none is more conspicuous than the service which he rendered when in his Bampton Lectures he put his faultless powers of analysis and expression at the disposal of his passionate faith in order to exhibit the nature and the significance of our Lord's assertion of Himself [1]. He is identified, as with hardly anything else, with the re-statement of the great dilemma based on the claim of Jesus Christ, that either He was what alone could morally justify that claim, the very Son of God, or He was indeed guilty of the supreme arrogance of putting Himself in the place of God,—'aut Deus aut homo non bonus [2].'

Thoughtful men generally view with distrust the dilemma as a form of argument. We in Oxford may remember how a very brilliant contemporary of Dr. Liddon gave expression to this distrust by saying that he had made it a rule when any one presented him with a dilemma to turn his back and refuse to have anything to say to it. But, after all, there are dilemmas, though they may not be many, the force of which grows upon us

---

[1] See Liddon, *Divinity of our Lord*, Lect. IV.
[2] See app. note 5, p. 238.

the more we consider them ; the dilemma based upon
the claim of Jesus Christ is one of these ; and it may be
asserted here at the beginning of our discussion, that to
represent our Lord only as a good man conscious of a
message from God, like one of the Prophets or John the
Baptist, is to do violence not to one Gospel only or to
single passages in various Gospels, but to the general
tenor of the Gospels as a whole.

## IV.

Among those who cannot accept cordially the propositions of the Christian creed, but at the same time
are anxious to maintain religion in society and in their
own lives, there is an unmistakeable unwillingness to
consider fairly what, historically and in experience,
Christianity has been, wherein its great strength lies
and has lain. They wish, for safety's sake, to fuse the
distinctive outlines of our religion in a vague atmosphere. But it is never wise to refuse to look steadily
at facts.

Whether Christianity can or can not be rationally
maintained is another question. But there is not much
doubt, so far, what Christianity is. I do not think it can
be reasonably gainsayed (1) that Christianity has meant
historically, faith in the person of Jesus Christ, considered
as very God incarnate, so much so that if this faith were
gone, Christianity in its characteristic features would
be gone also ; (2) that, thus considered, Christianity is
differentiated from other religions by the attitude of its
members towards its Founder ; (3) that this attitude of
Christianity towards its Founder is (speaking generally)

explained and justified by the witness of the earliest
records to His personality and claim.

Taking then these positions for granted, I am to ask
your attention in these Lectures to the Person of Jesus
Christ, with especial reference to His incarnation, that
is, to the truth that being the Son of God, He was made
very man ; and I am to endeavour to express and justify
the conviction that, however slowly and painfully, the old
faith in Him is being brought out in harmony not only
with our moral needs and social aspirations, but also
with that knowledge of nature and that historical criticism
which are the special growth of our time.

In presenting Jesus Christ to you, as Christians
believe on Him, I must necessarily present to you
one who, though human, is yet, what is called, miraculous and supernatural.   It will be my endeavour in the
next lecture, so to interpret these words 'supernatural'
and 'miraculous' as to make it apparent that the
supernatural in Jesus Christ is not unnatural, and the
miraculous not the 'reversal' or the 'suspension' of
nature ; rather, that Jesus Christ incarnate is the legitimate climax of natural development, so that the
study of nature—if only in that term moral nature is
included--is the true preparation for welcoming the
Christ.   In the third lecture it will be necessary to face
the objection made to the historical facts of the Incarnation, on the ground that, however credible in themselves, they lack adequate attesting evidence.   We shall
consider then the function of evidence, and the particular
character of the historical evidence, considered merely
as such, which the New Testament supplies, to the
facts of our Lord's birth of the Virgin Mary, life, death,

and resurrection ; and we shall ask ourselves whether
this evidence really allows us to suppose that in the
traditional Christ we have the result of His gradual
deification by the imagination of uncritical disciples.
Next, the question will present itself, whether it is
not possible to admit generally the historical character
of the New Testament records, and still to decline the
faith of the church, on the ground that the catholic
dogmas about the person of Christ do not in fact
simply represent or guard the faith of the first Christians
in Jesus Christ crucified and risen.  Thus in the fourth
lecture the view will be considered that elements
other than those supplied by the historical Christ must
enter in in order to link the faith of the New
Testament to the faith of the fathers of the councils.
We shall have to consider the nature of ecclesiastical
dogmas, their function and value, as well as the
dangers connected with them, and the limits to their
application.  Starting then from the assumption of the
Church's faith about Jesus Christ, we shall be in a
position to scrutinize reverently the revelation involved in
His person, and to ask ourselves what exactly it is in
our knowledge of the character and being of God, which
we owe to the fact that He has been manifested in manhood.  This will occupy the fifth lecture.  It will lead
on to the consideration in the sixth lecture of what
is taught us about human nature through the humanity
of the Son of man, and at this point it will be
necessary to examine what is the picture which the
Gospels present to us of our Lord's condition in the
days of His flesh ; what limitations upon the mode
of existence natural to the Son of God were accepted

in order that He might really enter into the experiences of manhood; what is the meaning of His 'self-
emptying.' In the seventh lecture our Lord will be
considered as the supreme authority and the fount of all
lower forms of authority in the moral and spiritual life
of man. It will be considered what was the method in
which He Himself exercised authority, and presumably,
therefore, meant that it should be exercised in His name;
what is the nature of religious authority, and what for
Christians its seat; what sort of authority Christ recognised in the Old Testament scriptures, what authority He
imparted to His apostles, what to the church. In the
last lecture, leaving aside for lack of space our Lord's
work of atonement, we will contemplate the moral
standard of human life which He erected by His teaching
and example, and we will consider Him in that part of
His redemptive work which He accomplishes from the
other world, as head of His body the church, redeeming
men by the infusion of His own life through the Spirit
and moulding them inwardly to the pattern of the
humanity which He set before them outwardly during
His life upon earth.

## V.

In these lectures it is obvious we shall be dealing constantly with such theological propositions as find their
statement in the Creed. Now it is impossible but that
in a congregation such as this, there should be some who,
more or less articulately, deprecate theology, and desire
the severance of practical Christianity from what they
would call ecclesiastical dogma, or perhaps in a more

recent phrase, Greek metaphysics.  Perhaps they would accept the phrase of recently-published Hibbert Lectures that the 'Sermon on the Mount is not an outlying portion of the Gospel, but its sum[1].'  If I am speaking to any of this mind, I would in the time that remains to me this morning, ask their attention to four brief considerations.

(1) Christianity became metaphysical simply and only because man is rational.  His rationality means that he must attempt 'to give account of things,' as Plato saw because he was a man, not only because he was a Greek. Man cannot go on acting without reason given and accepted for his actions.  Thus in morality, if he finds himself acting on a moral law, and regarding it as obligatory, he must give some account of its obligatoriness ; he must regard it as expressing the moral will of the Supreme Being, or as the law of reason, transcendental and prior to experience, making itself felt in his conscience as a 'categorical imperative'; or rejecting these metaphysical theories, he may explain morality as nothing else at the bottom than the desire for pleasure and shrinking from pain, disciplined and taught in the successive experiences of our race.  This last theory may be called unmetaphysical, but there can be no doubt that if it were commonly held, in a generation or two the old sense of absolute moral obligation would have yielded place to the more or less enlightened sense of self-interest.  For man, however inconsistent he may seem to be if you take a transverse section of humanity

---

[1] Dr. Hatch's *Hibbert Lectures*, 1888, p. 351 ; cf. p. 1.  See further, Lect. iv. app. note 25, p. 252.

at any point, presents a much more logical aspect if you
look down some long reach of his development; his
action at least settles down to his theory, if his theory
does not justify his higher action.    Just like morality,
then, Christianity must have become either metaphysical
or anti-metaphysical.    Christians found themselves
treating Jesus Christ, believing in Jesus Christ, as they
had never treated or believed in any other man, and that
because of His personality and claim, as moral master
and judge of mankind,—a claim, which, by the way,
appears nowhere more prominently than in the Sermon
on the Mount.    Because they were rational they must
have asked themselves, 'Why do we treat Jesus Christ
in this exceptional manner?    Who is He to be so
treated?    What is His relation to God whose functions
He exercises?    Why are we not idolaters if we yield
Him such worship?'    They must have asked these
questions because they were men endowed with reason,
and could not therefore go on acting without giving
some account of their action.    The questions once asked
must have been answered, and the answer must have
involved metaphysics, if Jesus Christ was to retain His
exceptional position.    He could only be treated in a
way in which no prophet or righteous man had ever been
treated, if in fact He was more than they were, in some
peculiar relation to God, in some transcendental sense
the Son of the Father.    Here is metaphysics.    Or if some
such explanation had been refused and Christians had
settled down to do without any fresh metaphysics, if they
had refused to give any account of Christ except that He
was a prophet, the special characteristics of Christianity
would have tended to vanish; as in fact, that class of

Ebionites [1], who most approximated to this refusal, were the least significant and progressive element of early Christianity.  Be it said, then, once for all, we cannot go on treating and believing in Jesus Christ in a way in which it would be wrong to treat and believe in another man, without a theory of His person, which explains that He is something more than man, which by the nature of the case must be metaphysical.  For metaphysics is nothing else than the attempt of rational man to take account of the rational, spiritual, eternal elements which enter into his experience.

(2) The glory of Christianity has been that it is a Gospel, a message of good tidings to mankind burdened with sin and pain, overwhelmed in despondency and dismay.  Jesus said, 'Come unto me all ye that are weary and heavy laden, and I will give you rest.'  Now what is it that has in fact made Christianity so real a Gospel?  It is the simplicity of its message.  It holds up the crucifix and says, 'Sic Deus dilexit mundum.' This is a simple message, and it is simple because it points to facts, to the old, old story of the life and death of Jesus.  But observe, the facts only constitute a Gospel, because a certain interpretation of them is implied.  It were no Gospel that the best of men, after a life of boundless self-sacrifice, should have been harried to death on Calvary.  It only becomes a Gospel if He who submits to this ignominious death really reveals the love, not of man only, but of God, if He really was the Son of God, who out of the love which is His own and His Father's, had come to give Himself in sacrifice for man. It only becomes a Gospel, again, if God's power is shewn

through the weakness of Christ's death, and He gave
assurance of this to all men in that He raised Him from
the dead. If He was the Son of God, if He was raised
from the dead, we have our Gospel for the world : ' God
sent his Son into the world not to condemn the world,
but that the world through him might be saved.' But
the power of this Gospel depends utterly on an interpretation of the facts which is necessarily theological, or
(considered intellectually) metaphysical, involving the
special doctrine of the pre-existent person of the Son
who was sent into the world.

(3) Many who are indifferent or hostile to the
theology of Christianity, have an even passionate enthusiasm for its morality. And indeed it is easy to see
why men should cling even beyond logical justification
to an objective moral standard such as Christianity
supplies. They may be impressed, like the author of
*Natural Religion*[1], with the lack in almost all classes of
English society of any clear moral ideal in the education
of children ; or they may be dismayed to feel how pre-
carious is the position held by some moral dogmas
which are yet intimately bound up with the well-being
of society, such as the indissolubleness of the marriage-
tie, or the obligation and possibility of purity, or the
absolute sinfulness of conscious suicide ; or again, in
prospect of the great social changes which seem to be
approaching, they may take note, not without the gravest
alarm, of the slight hold which the authority of the
moral law seems to have over men in masses. At all
costs, they feel, we must assert moral authority. Truly
we do need, beyond all question, the recognition over us

[1] See app. note 7, p. 239.

of an unbending moral law such as in fact is given, if
Jesus Christ is owned as our moral master. We may
be touched and not surprised then when we find men
doing homage beyond their logic to His moral lordship, treating Him as the ultimate authority who sets
the moral standard for all time, claiming of men, because
they are men, submission to the Son of man. And yet
such a position, if it is to be deliberate and reasoned,—
nay, if it is to be permanent at all,—requires for its basis
some belief, at least, in Christ's supernatural nature.
One man of a particular race and age cannot be the
standard for all men, the judge of all men of all ages
and races, the goal of human moral development, unless
He is something more than one man among many. Such
a universal manhood challenges enquiry : it demands an
explanation beyond itself : it quite transcends even the
position assigned to a Homer or a Shakespeare in the
realm of poetry.

(4) I have been asking you to consider how the
practical aspects of Christianity as a religion, a gospel,
a moral standard, are obviously enough bound up with
its theology. It has many other aspects which give it
affinities to art, to science, to history, but its spiritual
and moral functions are beyond all comparison the
most important ; and a great deal is gained if we see
that for the fulfilment of these, its primary functions,
Christianity depends upon its theological background.
There is only one other kindred consideration which I
will ask you to entertain.

On the doctrine of Christ's person the historical
Christian Church has committed itself beyond recall.
On many subjects, such as the doctrine of the atone-

ment or of the inspiration of Holy Scripture, the Church, while insisting upon the truths, offers no definite dogma, and binds us by none. Certainly the dogmas of the English Church are few and central, and consist mainly of those truths about God and the person of Christ which the Nicene creed contains. But on these points the Church's requirement is perfectly definite; so that, for example, she constantly requires her ministers to make public and unambiguous profession of their personal adhesion to the propositions of the creed, as the condition of their public ministry. On these central points, then, it is impossible for the Christian Church to exhibit any wavering or uncertainty, and still to retain credit as the teacher of a divine revelation. By these articles of our faith, Christianity certainly as a revealed religion, stands or falls.

It is well that these considerations should be present to our minds at the beginning of our enquiry into the truth about Christ's person. It may indeed be suggested that these are, in part, only considerations of 'consequences,' consequences which would follow if Christianity were not true, and that the consideration of consequences ought to be altogether excluded from any enquiry into matters of fact; but the suggestion is somewhat delusive. It is not only that the consideration of consequences gives us an adequate sense of the seriousness of our enquiry, it enters also into the actual argument. It forces us to remember that the rationality of any belief means more than its logical appeal to the intellect, for human life as a whole is rational, and a philosophy can hardly be true to reality which would leave our human nature, in some of its best and most universal faculties and aspirations, disconsolate and paralysed. To no one who in any sense believes in God, can it be an argument at any rate against Christianity that it is so satisfying, or in the common phrase, 'too good to be true.' Sounder surely is Abt Vogler's thought : how can we 'doubt that God's power can fill the heart that His power expands'?

On the other hand, the sense of the seriousness of what is at stake in our enquiry should make us more rigorous in demanding that the enquiry shall be real. The wish to believe, it has been truly pointed out, in the case of the best men of our day, sharpens their critical faculties instead of blunting them[1]. We do not want to be hoodwinked into believing, or to believe because it would be pleasant, or in defiance of the facts. Let us at any rate know the truth :

*ἐν δὲ φάει καὶ ὄλεσσον.*

Thus it is very right that we preachers should be jealously watched to see that we do not yield to what has been at all times the temptation of the pulpit, to substitute well-sounding phrases for real discussion. St. Jerome tells us that when once he asked his master Gregory of Nazianzus for the explanation of a difficult word in St. Luke, the saint, with no slight humour, replied that he would prefer to explain it in the pulpit; because when there is an applauding crowd around you, you are compelled to know what in fact you are ignorant of[2]. It has been the temptation of the pulpit at all times to explain without understanding,

[1] W. Ward, *The Wish to Believe* Kegan Paul, 1885 , pp. 7 10.

[2] S. Hieron. *ad Nepot. Ep.* 52. 8.

and to gloss over the weak points in the argument that
is being conducted.  Thus his audience can assist the
preacher by enabling him to feel that they will be severe
on any failure to face the point of an objection which he
professes to consider, or on any tendency to press an
argument further than it legitimately carries ; and we
may be sure that no refusal to examine, and no veiling
of disagreeable truth, can ever at the last resort be for
the good of human life, or to the honour of Him who is
not only the author of our redemption, but also the
light of our reason.

# LECTURE II.

## CHRIST SUPERNATURAL YET NATURAL.

*The Son .... the firstborn of all creation ; for in him were all things created, in the heavens and upon the earth ; .... all things have been created through him, and unto him ; and he is before all things, and in him all things consist. And he is the head of the body, the church : who is the beginning, the firstborn from the dead : that in all things he might have the pre-eminence.*— COLOSSIANS i. 14-18.

JESUS CHRIST, as the Christian Church presents Him for our acceptance, is a supernatural person. It is because He is this, that He has been ' believed on in the world '; it is because He is this, on the other hand, that many who have drunk more or less deeply of the spirit of our time withhold their belief from Him. For the supernatural, they say in effect, is the unnatural. Now the believer and the disbeliever in the supernatural Christ have this common ground, they believe in nature [1]. In whatever sense men believe in God, they believe that nature is God's ordinance, and nature's laws God's laws, and the knowledge of nature as far as it goes the knowledge of God. Here is a voice then which is on both sides admitted to be God's voice. That other voice which makes itself heard in Jesus Christ claims to be God's voice  His fuller and more articulate utterance. Now if there is an admittedly authentic work of an author, and a work of which the authenticity is disputed, the admitted work must obviously suggest important presumptions for or against the con-

[1] See app note *, p. 341

troverted work.   Thus we contemplate nature, God's admitted work, and we contemplate the Christ—so ardently
believed in, so vehemently rejected—and leaving aside
other considerations, we ask the question, whether nature
suggests presumptions against the Christ or for the Christ.
This is the controversy, and the chief law of its discussion
is that which has been laid down by minds characteris-
tically English as valid equally in the region of physical
and of theological enquiry.   Bacon and Butler alike warn
us, each in his own department, against putting too much
trust in abstract ideas, in the 'anticipatio mentis.'   We
are not then in this investigation of ours to suppose that
we can determine *à priori* how God's completer revelation of Himself ought to have been given, if given at all.
We must look as faithfully at the Christ of Christian
tradition who is declared to be the revelation of the
Father, as we do look at the phenomena of nature, and
when we have been equally faithful to both, we must
ask, what is the testimony of nature as a whole with
reference to Him.   And first let us clear the ground for
discussion.

## I.

There are some who see in nature no good evidence
of authorship at all, no good evidence, that is, of God.
Mind, as they view it, is simply a function of material life
in its highest developments, or a phenomenon of a distinctive kind, attached to it[1].   'He that made the eye,
shall He not see'; and He that planted the mind and
heart, shall He not think and feel?—is a question to
which, they allege, there is no answer.   Nature bears witness only to an inscrutable force, working by constant

---

[1] See app. note 9, p. 242.

laws, in the production of all structures and forms of life. It reveals no mind, no purpose, no being behind itself.

Now obviously to the atheist, if such a person exists, or to the convinced agnostic, the Christ is supernatural, and as supernatural, also unintelligible, because He falls outside the only nature which his eyes can see. But then his conception of nature has been formed by excluding from consideration important classes of facts which really exist in nature. For, first, the metaphysician, with his analysis of sensation and experience, discloses in mind, not merely one product of nature, but the necessary constituent of nature considered as an ordered, knowable system. Again, if Charles Darwin and the scientific world whom he represents have materially altered, yet they have not fundamentally impaired, the evidences in nature of divine purpose or design, nor have they touched the argument (to many minds the irresistible argument) from the beauty of nature to the spirituality of the Being which it reveals. Once more, ethical enquiry, where it is true to its subject-matter, postulates an absolute and superhuman law of righteousness, with which men are as truly brought into relation through conscience as they are, through the eye, brought into relation to the objective reality of light ;—postulates also a certainty of moral obligation, which has no meaning unless man has really a free will, however limited and conditioned its freedom. And the argument mounts one step higher. The universal mind and divine righteousness which are disclosed in nature, are inseparable from the idea of personality. for mind is only conceivable as a function. and righteousness only as an attribute, of a person ; and personality is the highest form in which life is known in the universe. God then, or the spiritual principle in nature, is, we believe, in some real sense, personal; transcending no doubt human personality in infinite degree, yet at least so truly personal as that man in virtue of his personality is liker to God than any lower form of life [1].

The arguments I have just summarized, I shall so far take for granted as to assume that none of those I am now reasoning with are, at any rate, convinced agnostics —men who positively disbelieve that God can be known to exist, or that nature's order can be ascertained to be more than mechanical. And from this point of view I again ask the question, What is the testimony of nature in regard to the supernatural Christ?

## II.

First, then, nature is a unity and an order. In nature there can be nothing detached, disconnected, arbitrary, as Aristotle said of old, like an episode in a bad tragedy. Secondly, nature, on the whole, represents a progress, an advance. There is a development from the inorganic to the organic, from the animal to the rational—a progressive evolution of life. Thirdly, this development, from any but the materialist point of view, is a progressive revelation of God. Something of God is manifest in the mechanical laws of inorganic structures : something more in the growth and flexibility of vital forms of plant and animal; something more still in the reason, conscience, love, personality of man. Now from the Christian point of view, this revelation of God, this unfolding of divine qualities, reaches a climax in Christ.

---

[1] See, however, further p. 117; and on all these arguments, app. note 10, p. 243.

God has expressed in inorganic nature, His immutability, immensity, power, wisdom : in organic nature He has shown also that He is alive : in human nature He has given glimpses of His mind and character. In Christ not one of these earlier revelations is abrogated : nay, they are reaffirmed : but they reach a completion in the fuller exposition of the divine character, the divine personality, the divine love.

Now if Jesus Christ had appeared as something in the universe of things apart from law, which could come into no order, which could not be rationally interpreted as part of the universal life and in correspondence with its fundamental laws, the reason of man would have been rightly staggered and rebellious. A Christ inconsistent with nature it could not have found a place for. But if He is supernatural, only in the sense of transcending, or advancing upon, what nature exhibits apart from Him, while at the same time He appears in fundamental harmony with the whole, and as incorporating its previous record, the reason should experience no such shock. Behind the veil of nature there has lain hid all along the divine power and righteousness and character, and there is no reason to believe that nature as it exists apart from Christ, exhausts the divine qualities, nay, there are manifold reasons to believe nature incomplete. The first volume of the divine author in fact postulates a second. God cannot be untrue to His own principles as nature exhibits Him, but He can advance upon the disclosure of them hitherto made in the moral and physical system of the world.

But you will say—in what real sense does the Christ present Himself to our imagination or mind as com-

pleting a world which is imperfect without Him? The
answer to this question will, I suppose, be most evident
to those who think most of the world as God's world,
and who are more particularly alive to the revelation
of His moral character. If God is righteous, if the
highest moral characteristics, such as goodness and love,
express God more adequately than the mechanical
motions of planets and suns, or than the life of plants
and animals, then we are driven to expect some fuller
revelation of God's being than is offered us, or seems
at all likely to be offered us, anywhere apart from
Jesus Christ : then the world without Christ, is nothing
else than an imperfect fragment. For certainly God's
righteousness and justice find in our present experience
very inadequate realization, His goodness very ambi-
guous expression ; and thus the contemplation of the
moral revelation of God in nature begets in the mind
what Bishop Butler calls, 'an implicit hope of somewhat further.' The earnest expectation of the creature
appears to be waiting for some manifestation not yet
given. And conversely, if personality, if character, is
the best image of God which nature affords, then we
are in a measure prepared for the occurrence of an Incarnation. There is a necessary kinship between God
and man, and if human qualities are not the measure
of the divine, yet they are cognate to them. It becomes
intelligible that God should take man's nature and
reveal Himself in it, without either annihilating our
manhood, or compromising His Godhead.

Christ then, I say, is the crown of nature : He is thus
profoundly natural, and to interpret the Christ we postulate only those spiritual realities, which (as every theist

must admit) do in part find expression and in part lie
hid behind the veil of nature.

But then is Christ supernatural? The term supernatural is purely relative to what at any particular stage
of thought we mean by nature. Nature is a progressive
development of life, and each new stage of life appears
supernatural from the point of view of what lies below
it. Moral life is thus certainly supernatural from the
point of view of physical life. The moral spirit in man
does indeed use the animal organism as its instrument,
and emerge out of the heart of physical development, but
it is supernatural, because, when it appears on the scene[1],
it is as a new kind of life, working by new laws of its
own, the laws of conscience and of choice, and exhibiting phenomena—such as the deliberate recognition of a
divine law of righteousness, self-judgment, penitence, conscious fellowship with God—which the merely physical
world cannot, considered by itself, explain or account
for. In the same sense Christ is supernatural from the
point of view of mere man, because in Him the divine
Being who had been always at work, in physical nature
as ' the persistent energy of all things,' and in human
nature as the rational light of man, here assumes
humanity, spirit and body, as the instrument through
which to exhibit with a new completeness and in a new
intensity His own personality and character. The same
force is at work all through the stages of life, for the
force of all things is God ; only God is progressively
revealed, and at the last with intensified reality in
Christ 'the life was manifested and we have seen it.'

[1] See app. note 11, p. 243.

## III.

This is the true account of the matter, but not yet the complete account, for to interpret Christ we have to recognise even from the beginning the reality of sin, as something which appears nowhere below in nature but first in man, the rebellion of free-wills. In other words, we have to recognise—what it is hard to see how any moralist can deny—that human nature, as we have had experience of it in history, presents in great measure a scene of moral ruin, so that Christ enters not merely to consummate an order but to restore it, not to accomplish only but to redeem. He is not only 'Christus consummator' but also 'Christus redemptor.' This idea of redemption will in its turn appear natural in proportion as it is believed, faintly or decisively, that God is good, and realized on the other hand that man is sinful. The more you contemplate from a moral point of view the condition of man, the more luminously certain it becomes that the Christian view of sin is the right one, so far as that sin as we know it now, in ourselves and in the world, is lawlessness—the violation of our true nature, not its expression, the taint in our development and not simply its necessary condition[1]. 'Our life is a false nature,' as Byron cried, ''tis not in the harmony of things.' Grant this, and you find it surely credible on evidence that the goodness of God should have moved Him to redemption. Thus it comes about that our readiness to believe in the Redeemer does in fact depend upon the

---

[1] See *Lux Mundi* (Murray, 1891), App. II. on *The Christian doctrine of sin.*

strength of the impression made upon our minds by
the sin of the world. Whatever impulse to belief may
come from intellectual or aesthetic considerations, the
primary force which stimulates to belief is the desire
for righteousness and the sense of sin.

And here we must not fail to remind ourselves how
possible it is to weaken or even to lose this desire for
holiness, and this sense of sin, through diverting our
faculties into other channels. It is very well known how
Darwin describes his own mind as having ' become a
kind of machine for grinding general laws out of large
collections of facts,' with the result of producing ' atrophy
of that part of the brain on which the higher tastes depend [1].' What is singular about this confession is probably its honesty. But we must not hesitate to recognise
that a mind thus exclusively organized for physical investigation is not a mind ' disposed,' as St. Luke expresses
it, for eternal life [2]. Christ would naturally seem to such
a mind an alien object. What Darwin is speaking of
in his own case is the atrophy of aesthetic, rather than
of moral, faculty. But a similar abnormal atrophy is
possible in the case of all disused faculties and in all
pursuits. For example, the pursuits of the priest and
pastor may tend of themselves to disqualify the mind
for physical or historical enquiry. At present, however,
we are concerned to notice this only: that the atrophy of
a man's *moral* faculty is a probable event in certain cases.
Thus literary or classical studies, intense concentration
on business, exaggerated athleticism, absorption in

---

[1] See app. note 12, p. 244.

[2] Acts xiii. 48, καὶ ἐπίστευσαν ὅσοι ἦσαν τεταγμένοι εἰς ζωὴν αἰώνιον. See
Alford *in loc.*

pleasures, higher or lower, each of these may preoccupy
the whole man, stunting and overgrowing the moral
faculties, making the Christ seem a remote figure, the
crucifix an unmeaning and disagreeable object, the vocabulary of Christianity unnecessary and unreal. But it
needs only to rekindle in a man the hunger and thirst
after righteousness, in himself or in the world, in order to
bring Christ near to him, and to teach him to look upon
His person with different eyes. Whatever in fact re-
awakens in him the sense of God and eternity gives him
faculties to acknowledge Christ. It may be any experience which stirs the depths of his being, possibly the
death of some one with whom his life was bound up,
and the sense which comes with it of the fragmentariness and incompleteness of the world. It may be
also something less personal to himself. For example,
suppose a man to devote himself to the bettering of
social conditions : suppose him so far Christian—and it
is a great way on the road—as to realize that he is his
brother's keeper and must go out to bear his share
of the world's burden. Such an one after a few years'
work will surely be impressed with the truth that,
much as can be done by improved laws, improved social
adjustment, improved organization, to remedy the evils
under which society groans, the heart of the matter lies
in character. The obstacles to progress in every class
are within rather than without ; they lie in jealousy, in
suspicion, in self-assertion, in lust, in dishonesty, in carelessness—in a word in sin. In sin, in the omnipresent
fact of sin, there is the evil. In redemption, redemption
from sin, there is the central and fundamental remedy and
the thing supremely needful. More and more, behind

legislator, instructor, economist, agitator, there dawns
upon the horizon of the true reformer, to refresh his
exhausted brain, to reinvigorate his desponding heart,
the true emancipator of man, his redeemer, Jesus of
Nazareth, whose remedies alone are adequate to human
ills, because He gauges so profoundly, so accurately the
nature and seat of man's disease, because He deals with
men as individual characters, and bases the regeneration
of society on the conversion and renewal of men. In a
word, brethren, the Son of man will seem in the highest
sense natural to you in proportion as you are human, in
proportion, that is, as what you are in contact with is not
merely things or laws or minds but persons, not problems
merely but characters.

Let me sum up briefly my positive contention : it
is that Christ is supernatural, if you mean by this that
He transcends all the manifested natures, and is not
explicable out of their elements. But if He is supernatural He is also natural. Nature as a whole, moral
and physical, demands Him to accomplish its yearn-
ings and to restore its order. Nor is this any other
position than that suggested long ago in the profound words of Bishop Butler : 'Persons' notions of
what is natural will be enlarged in proportion to their
greater knowledge of the works of God and the dis-
pensations of His providence. Nor is there any ab-
surdity in supposing, that there may be many beings in
the universe, whose capacities and knowledge and views
may be so extensive as that the whole Christian dispensation may to them appear natural [1].'

[1] *Analogy*, Pt. I. ch. 1 *ad fin*

## IV.

To the view of the relation of Christ to nature which I have been trying to express, there would be, I suppose, three main objections.

First, it would be asked, ' how is it then that in popular Christianity the Redeemer and His work have been so much isolated from nature, and indeed put into antagonism to it ? '   It is partly because in the mind of Christian preachers or their hearers there has been a confusion between 'nature,' that is, the ordered world, and 'nature' in the sense of our human nature as it exists in a state of sin : between the world as God's creation, and ' the world ' of human society considered as ' refusing to have God in its knowledge.'   But in theology worthy of the name, the sequence and fundamental unity of nature and grace, of creation and redemption, are always insisted upon [1].

Thus the doctrine of St. Paul and St. John will not allow us to separate the two parts of the self-manifestation of God.   I am not for the moment concerned to enquire how these first Christian teachers got at their conception of the Word or Son of God as the creator no less than the redeemer.   But certainly St. Paul and St. John do teach that the Son of God who redeems is also the creator, and that His mediation in grace is strictly on the lines of His earlier mediation in nature.

He is, according to those theologians of the New Testament, the author of the universe, and He abides in all His creation as its principle of cohesion.   He is the ground of its progress and the light of its rational

[1] See, in justification of the following paragraphs, app. note 13, p. 245.

members. Finally, He is the goal of all its movements.
When sin perverted His creation in part, He was not
baffled by its ravages, but came out again to redeem,
and in redeeming to consummate His creation, by the
same method as characterized His previous working. By
His Incarnation He inaugurated a kingdom of redemption
in the heart of the old kingdom of nature. Again He
abides in that new creation as the inner principle of its
life. Again He bears along this new work, and with it
the old work which it completes, to its final goal in Himself. In creation and in redemption He is author and
inherent life and final cause.

Thus the doctrine of St. Paul and St. John gives the
secure basis for a conception of order in nature. Indeed the idea of order in nature came to men's minds
at the first from a religious or philosophical rather than
a scientific point of view, in part among the Hebrews
and more emphatically among the Greeks. It had been
appropriated by Christianity in its cradle as part of its
heritage from the fusion of Greek and Jewish thought ;
it is developed in its full significance by the Greek
Fathers. Their teaching claims our notice at this point
in three particulars.

(1) They insist on the unity of God's work in nature
and in grace. The Incarnation is on the lines of God's
inherence in nature. No one, they argue, who believes
that God is living and manifesting Himself in the world,
can reasonably repudiate His intensified presence in
Christ. If the Word or Son reveals God through the
Incarnation, He has previously revealed Him in the body
of nature through its beauty, its order, its power. This
belief in fact gave many of the early Christians that fresh

delight in nature for its own sake, which Humboldt the naturalist rightly recognises as the distinctive merit of the Christian Fathers among ancient writers.

(2) They were very emphatic as to the necessary universality of order and law.   When, for instance, Gregory of Neo-Caesarea is describing Origen's method in training his pupils, he explains how after he had taken them through a course of 'logic' and 'dialectic,' by which he aimed at securing the accurate and truthful use of reason and language, he led them on to physiology or the study of nature.   And here he made it his object to substitute for the merely irrational wonder and terror at phenomena the rational delight in order and system.   It would be very easy to multiply quotations to illustrate the patristic appreciation of the divine principle of law ; but in fact, though modern science has an incomparably clearer view of the method of natural operations —though it thus gives to the idea of law a far more accurate content,—modern scientific men themselves cannot hold the conception of the necessary order of the world more strongly than some of the early Christian teachers.   Thus when they treat of miracles, they often teach us that even miracles must not be lawless, but in harmony with nature's fundamental law.

(3) In the moral and intellectual region, Greek theologians maintain the position that the Incarnation gathers into one and completes previous workings of God in the human mind and conscience.   Everywhere the same light had been lightening every man ; everywhere the same Son had been in a measure revealing the Father ; everywhere where men lived by right reason, they lived by Christ, and were the friends of Christ ;

philosophy was thus to the Greeks, as the Law to the Jews, a divine preparation for Him who was to come. The Bible is in one respect distinguished from other literature, because the noble truths which exist everywhere as scattered fragments, are there to be found purified and centralized, even as the silver which from the earth is tried and purified seven times in the fire.

We know now-a-days much more about comparative morality and religion, about the varieties and unities of religious beliefs among all nations. We are thus in a position to exhibit much more exactly how Christianity unifies the truths which appeal to Jew and to Greek, to Mohammedan and Buddhist and Brahman. But the idea of Christianity as superseding all other religions, not by excluding but by including the elements of truth which each contains, would be an idea thoroughly in accordance with the deeper thoughts of Greek Christian teachers in the first age. It militates in no way against the truth of the special vocation in religion assigned to Israel among ancient nations. In accordance with this view other masters would be regarded as hostile to Christ, only when they taught what was positively noxious, or when they began to enter into rivalry with Him ; as twilight is darkness, when it is once brought into comparison with light. If then we speak of the Incarnation as the crown of natural development in the universe, and in accordance with its law, we are not using a language new to Christianity. Indeed it could hardly have been otherwise than that the Church teachers should have expected to discover law throughout all creation ; because, in Hooker's language, 'the being of God is a kind of law to His working,' and the being of God as Christians believe, is an eternal process according to necessary law.

### V.

The second objection to our position would be on the score of miracles. 'Nature,' it would be said, 'does in fact bear witness against Christ on account of His miracles, for a miracle is a supposed event, which is described as inconsistent with nature, or a violation of natural laws, and as such it is contrary to order, and not its perfection.' This objection is constantly heard, and it cannot be denied that a good deal of language used on the Christian side has gone to justify it, but I cannot but hope, that the principles to which I have been endeavouring in this lecture to gain your assent will be seen to carry us most of the way—I do not say to the acceptance of miracles, for that is a matter of evidence in each particular case, but to a position from which miracle can be regarded as a rational and credible element in the revelation of the Christ[1]. For if we admit on the one hand that the force in nature is the will of a God, who through the whole process of the universe has been working up to a moral product in the character of man, and if we admit on the other hand that there is such a thing as sin in humanity which has disturbed the divine order of the world and made it necessary for God to come forth for the restoration of His own creation; if we admit these two positions we have already admitted by implication the reasonableness of miracle. For miracle depends on the one side on God's character, on the other side on the consequences of man's sin.

[1] See app. note 14, p. 245.

What is a miracle? It is an event in physical nature which makes unmistakably plain the presence and direct action of God working for a moral end. God is always present and working in nature, and men were meant to recognise Him in the ordinary course of events, and to praise Him as they recognised Him. But in fact man's sin has blinded his spiritual eye, he has lost the power of seeing behind the physical order : the very prevalence of law in nature, which is its perfection, has led to God being forgotten, His power depreciated, His presence denied. In a miracle then, or what Scripture calls a 'sign,' God so works, that man cannot but notice a presence which is not blind force, but personal will. Thus God violates the customary method of His action, He breaks into the common order of events, in order to manifest the real meaning of nature, and make men alive to the true character of the order, which their eyes behold. Miracles are God's protests against man's blindness to Himself, protests in which He violates a superficial uniformity in the interests of deeper law. An example will make this plain. The death of Jesus Christ occurred in the ordinary sequence of physical and social law. Granted social and moral conditions, such as in fact existed in Judaea when our Lord came into it, and it could not have been but that Christ should be rejected, and if rejected crucified. God did not cause the death of Christ by any intervention. He simply did not spare His only-begotten Son. He let circumstances operate, and they operated to slay Him. But such an event as the crucifixion of the Son of God, though it came in the physical order, did not represent the real divine order of the world, it was only possible

because of the monstrous anomaly of sin. The miracle
of the resurrection, on the other hand, does break into
the physical order : God bares His arm, and shows His
life-giving presence and will. But why? Only to vindicate, at the central crisis, the real order of the world, its
fundamental underlying law. There is a disturbance,
then, of the superficial order in the interests of the
deeper, the rational order. Now this (the ancient view
of miracles) can only be objected to, either on the ground
of defective evidence, with which we are not yet concerned ; or on the ground that the operator in nature
is a force and not a person. If God is personal, if His
being is better expressed in human will and character
than in mechanical motion and unconscious life, miracles
with adequate cause are neither impossible nor unnatural.
It is blind instinct which works on in monotonous uniformity where conditions are exceptional. It is rational
character which from time to time will violate uniformity
in the interest of rational consistency.

These considerations do not certainly leave us in the
attitude of welcoming all miracles indiscriminately. The
knowledge of God, which we gain from nature and
conscience, gives us certain criteria which we cannot
but apply. Thus we could not see the hand of God
in portents appealing simply to a barbaric love of lawless power—for God is a God of order : or in miracles
unworthy of God's character—for He is holy and just
and good : or in miracles calculated to subvert that
moral discipline which lies in ' enduring as seeing Him
who is invisible.' But the considerations we have been
entertaining do enable us to attach a rational meaning
to miracles, especially at great initiating moments in

God's revelation or vindication of Himself to man ; and in particular they lead us far towards the acceptance of miracles such as are presented to us in connexion with Jesus Christ.

What has just been said represents the ancient, perhaps the accepted, rationale of miracles ; as a general theory it seems to be valid and to hold its ground ; but so far as we are concerned simply with the miraculous works of Christ there is a prior, and to many minds a more satisfying, consideration which we must entertain, a consideration calculated to remove from miracles *in His case* the appearance of being abnormal or exceptional events.

The incarnate Son of God could not have been otherwise than, to our view, miraculous. Formerly men spoke of the uniformity of nature as ' our intuitive conviction that the future will resemble the past.' Now we have learnt to view nature as a progressive order, and we know that it admits of new departures, of moments when a fresh level seems to be won, and a fresh sort of product begins to exhibit new phenomena. Thus when in the midst of the inorganic world, the germ of organic life first appeared, however you account for it, the future did not resemble the past. Organic growth, unknown before, became a fact. Once again, when rational life appeared, when men first talked and planned, and learnt by experience, and developed civilization, it was a new thing, and the future in consequence did not resemble the past : a new nature or kind of life had begun to exhibit new phenomena in accordance with new law. Now on the Christian hypothesis Christ is a new nature. He is the creative ' Word made flesh.' If so, it is to be expected that, as a new kind of nature,

He will exhibit new phenomena. A new vital energy will radiate from Him, for the very springs of the universal life are in Him. As in human nature the material body is seen for the first time more or less adapting itself to spiritual ends, as the organ of a spiritual being, so in Christ we should expect the material body to exhibit a far higher degree of this subserviency to spirit. And this, in fact, is what appears to be the case; a new energy of spirit is seen in Him controlling the material forces. It is not that the old laws are either violated or suspended. All natural processes go on, but they are counteracted or interacted by a new kind of nature working by a new law with a new power. Thus Christ's miracles in fact appear as laws of His nature: there is a healing power or 'virtue' which goes out from Him, occasionally even without any special action of His will, as when He perceived that some one had touched Him, for virtue had gone out of Him[1]. Miracles are described as 'his works[2],' they are the proper phenomena of His person. In fact, the more we consider the character of the personality of Jesus, the more natural do miracles appear *in His case*; they are not arbitrary portents, but appropriate phenomena. Matthew Arnold once suggested, as against the evidential power supposed to belong to miracles, that 'if he could change the pen with which he wrote into a pen-wiper, he would not make what he wrote any the truer, or more convincing[3].' But such a sugges-

---

[1] St. Luke viii. 46; St. Mark v. 30; cf. St. Luke iv. 14, vi. 19.
[2] St. John vii. 3, x. 38, xiv. 11.
[3] *Literature and Dogma* (Smith, Elder and Co. 1873), p. 128; cf. Bruce, *Chief Aim of Revelation* (Hodder and Stoughton, 1881), ch. iv.

tion, as directed against the miracles of Christ, wholly
misses the point. For certainly Christ's miracles are
not meaningless and detached portents, they are 'redemptive acts'; they are evidential because they give
to the eye, as object-lessons, exactly that same instruction in mercy and judgment which the words of our
Lord teach to the ear. The moral miracle of forgiveness is interpreted by the physical miracle of the
renewal of vital power. 'That ye may know that the
Son of man hath power on earth to forgive sins (then
saith he to the sick of the palsy), Arise, and take up
thy bed, and go unto thy house.' And we may still
ask, 'Whether is easier, to say, Thy sins are forgiven;
or to say, Arise, and walk.' Depend upon it, the more
you contemplate the personality of Jesus Christ and
His moral authority and purpose, the more you will
find that His miracles are according to the law of His
being, 'in rational sequence,' to use an expression of
St. Athanasius[1], with the character of His person and
mission. It is not that the miracles prove the doctrine
or that the doctrine makes credible the miracles. It
is rather that as parts of one whole they cohere as soul
and body. True, Christ depreciated miracles in comparison to teaching. 'Believe me,' He said, that is, My
person, Myself, 'or else believe me for the very works'
sake[2].' He puts the miracles below the person. Still
it is hardly conceivable how without miracles His revelation of Himself could have been made. Without the
resurrection His death, instead of being an encouragement to faith, would have been the supreme obstacle
to it. With the resurrection it gives us the final and

[1] *De Incarn.* 31.          [2] St. John xiv. 11.

E

adequate evidence of what faith demands—namely, that there is only one ultimate lordship in matter and spirit, and that the whole universe at the last resort subserves a divine and moral purpose.

## VI.

The last objection which I must very briefly consider may be expressed thus : ' If at a certain moment in the world's development, a new type of being had appeared, such as you describe, an incarnation of God in humanity, and had propagated itself by methods corresponding to its nature—so that the Christ-life was at the present moment a fact among us, like plant, or animal, or man, concordant with the rest, and yet distinct, as an advance upon them—all would be plain, and we should no more urge objections against the naturalness of Christ than against that of the plant or man. It is the isolation of the Christ which constitutes His inconsistency with nature. If, as you would urge, His appearance is in continuity with what preceded it, yet it has no persistence; the Christ-nature does not become part of permanent experience. It is the isolated Christ which is to us so incredible.'

Now, so far as this objection rests on the fact that Christ is out of the order of gradual development, and leaves us looking backwards for the highest point of attainment, it is met by the consideration that development on the moral and intellectual level is not generally a gradual progress. Personality has something in it always incommunicable. The great geniuses who inaugurate epochs in human history vanish and leave no suc-

cessors worthy of them ; we are in fact often in the position of men looking backwards for our ideals. The poetry
of Homer, the statues of Phidias and Praxiteles, the painting of the Italian Renaissance, the dramas of Shakespeare, represent levels once attained and not again. In
religion St. Francis is greater than the Franciscans,
Gautama than the Buddhists. Jesus Christ even on the
humanitarian estimate remains unique. The history of
religious movements is, in fact, very generally the history of a continuous decline, through a long period of
years, from the level attained by a founder or a reformer.
Thus we are not to look for steady advance or persistent
realization in moral and spiritual matters. Moreover
in regard to Jesus Christ, His unique greatness is inseparable from the facts of the case. If it is in accordance with the true nature of things that God should
manifest at last, not His attributes only, but His personality,—if this is the crown of universal development—
then that personality whenever manifested must remain
supreme. ' The Word made flesh ' must be the highest
thing possible in all creation. There can be no second.
No relation of God to the creatures, or of the creatures
to God, can be even conceived of equal to that which is
realized in Him. The most that He can do is to impart
to other men for their perfecting and redeeming a share
in His divine Sonship ; and this He has done. Thus, it
Christ is truly unique, if by the necessities of the case
there cannot be more than one incarnate Son, yet He is
not isolated, He has set at work a new development, which
is the movement of the redeemed humanity. He has
left this world, indeed, for manhood in the process of its
perfecting breaks through the boundaries of this world

into the wider sphere of eternity, and the heavens must receive Him 'until the times of restoration of all things': but He is still spiritually present and operative in the world.

I must leave this thought for development until the last lecture, only let me say that we believe that when the slow-working forces of the Incarnation have borne their perfect fruit, it is not Christ the Head alone, who will be seen to crown and justify the whole development of the universe, but Christ as the centre of the redeemed humanity, the Head with the body, the Bridegroom with the bride ; and things in heaven and things in earth and things under the earth shall acknowledge in that triumphant society the consummation of the whole world's destiny.

It may have been irksome to some to be asked to deal, as we have been dealing more or less in this lecture, with abstract ideas and *à priori* credibilities. Opponents of Christianity from the side of science may make Professor Huxley their mouth-piece [1], to protest that they take exception to miracles solely on the ground of evidence, not at all on the ground that they are antecedently incredible. But it cannot be denied that objections to miracles do still in a majority of cases rest largely upon negative presumptions, the serious consideration of which it would not have been possible to omit. On the basis of such consideration we can approach more freely the examination of the evidence.

Meanwhile let me summarize my preliminary contention. Read, then, I would say, the book of

[1] See app. note 15, p. 246.

nature which is God's book, read especially its later chapters, when moral beings appear upon the scene ; you find it a plot without a *dénoûment*, a complication without a solution, a first volume which demands a second. Study the Christ. He appears as the second volume of the divine word, in which the threads are being disentangled. The justifying principle emerges, the lines of incident are seen working towards a solution, the whole becomes intelligible and full of hope. But the eye is still carried forward, there is a third volume yet expected. It is to contain 'the revelation of the glory,' the 'far-off divine event to which the whole creation moves.'

# LECTURE III.

## THE SUPERNATURAL CHRIST HISTORICAL.

*Of the men therefore which have companied with us all the time that the Lord Jesus went in and went out among us, beginning from the baptism of John, unto the day that he was received up from us, of these must one become a witness with us of his resurrection.*—ACTS i. 21, 22.

THERE is an admirable scene in Mrs. Gaskell's *Mary Barton*, which probably holds a permanent place in the memory of many of us. It is where the sailor Will Wilson is telling tales of his experiences at sea to Job Legh, the self-taught naturalist, in the Manchester cottage. He tells him with the same simplicity of assurance how his party saw a mermaid, and how he saw a flying-fish, and he is angry because the old man, who knows what belongs to nature and what does not, treats his first story with contempt, and welcomes his second with enthusiastic acceptance. 'You will credit me,' he complains, 'when I say I have seen a creature half-fish, half-bird, and you won't credit me when I say there are such beasts as mermaids, half-man and half-fish ; to me one is just as strange as the other.'

## I.

We are to consider to-day the witness of history to our Christian faith, and this conversation may serve to illustrate at starting the limits, which ordinarily exist, to the power of external testimony in carrying conviction. The witness which suffices to prove the flying-fish does not suffice to prove the mermaid. To make even excellent testimony convincing it must be able to appeal to an antecedent sense of probability in the mind of the recipient. Where a supposed event, for which witness is offered, can find no point of cohesion with our general sense of what is credible, we tend all of us to act upon Hume's canon, and to suppose that it is more probable that the witness was mistaken than that the event happened[1]. Testimony is not like mathematical demonstration. Thus, in the case of Christianity, the mere external testimony of history will not produce conviction that Jesus Christ was really raised from the dead the third day, unless the man who is to be convinced is responsive to the idea of redemption, and alive to the place which the resurrection holds in it. He will not believe the Christian witness, unless he is at home with the Christian spirit. On the other hand, Christian faith is meant to depend upon testimony, and a large part of our intellectual duty, in the case of Christianity, as also in enquiries which have nothing to do with religion, lies in submitting ourselves to evidence.

Real submission of mind to good evidence, contemporary or historical, is not so common a quality as is sometimes supposed. Very many men are mentally preoccupied with their own ideas ; they are full of prejudices ; they see in experience and welcome in evidence, only what they want to believe. It is the few who are real observers, who know the difference between a fact and a

[1] See app. note 16, p. 247.

fancy, and when they are face to face with a fact allow it to mould and control their ideas.  Undoubtedly the tendency to be too subjective in the estimate of evidence needs to be jealously watched and kept in check.   It is very apparent in the intellects of many of the great Germans, and their followers in their own country and in England— witness Dr. Martineau's recent treatment of the Gospel story.   It is equally apparent on the other hand in so un-German a mind as that of the late Cardinal Newman. In his essay on Ecclesiastical Miracles, for instance, the *à priori* faculty, the 'illative sense,' is allowed almost to run riot, and destroy the distinction between a fact and an idea, between what is historical and what is supposed to be appropriate [1].   Passing behind the work of our own time, we may enter the Bodleian Library and scan long rows of tomes—shall we say in ecclesiastical history ?—to find them suggest nothing so much as the melancholy reflection how easily boundless industry and rich capacity can be rendered fruitless by the wilfulness which will not be true to the evidence.   The fact is that in order to estimate rightly the function of external evidence in producing conviction, it is necessary to pay impartial regard to two opposite elements of truth.   On the one hand it is absurd to deny the necessity for presuppositions in accepting evidence—absurd to pretend that, in matters affecting us nearly, we can possibly annihilate the wish to believe or to disbelieve ; indeed this sort of wish has been actually the great stimulus to enquiry of all sorts.   On the other hand we must recognise the obligation, and courageously encourage in ourselves the tendency, to submit simply to evidence.

[1] See app. note 17, p. 248.

Nor are we in this respect without great hopes for the future. There is, not least among Christians of our own country and our own communion, an increasing spirit of candour, an increasing desire to know the truth, an increasing reverence for fair enquiry, which is of good augury for the time which lies before us.

Jesus Christ undoubtedly intended religious belief to rest upon a double basis. If we watch the method by which, in the Gospels, conviction is represented as being generated in the minds of the apostles, we find that it includes both inward faith and outward evidence. On the one hand our Lord, more perhaps than any other master, caused His disciples to be educated by external events, ordering circumstances, and letting them teach ; and He chose for His apostles men of such sort, as are most simply receptive and least possessed by *à priori* ideas.    Christianity in a unique sense is a religion produced by outward facts, and promoted by the witness of those who saw.    On the other hand, Jesus Christ deliberately made His appeal to faith, properly so called, and educated in His disciples the faculty of faith, and challenged and welcomed its spontaneous activity, and refused to demonstrate mathematically what He wished men to believe, nay rather He appears as giving men loop-holes for escape, and not pressing conviction too forcibly upon them.    He did not, for example, appear after His resurrection to unbelievers but to believers ; which means that this crowning miracle was to be used to confirm an existing faith, not to create it where it did not exist.    Again He deliberately refused to respond by demonstration to the complaining request of the Jews.   ' How long dost thou keep our souls in suspense? if thou art the Christ, tell us plainly':—pointing out that disposition is always necessary for belief; that 'his sheep hear his voice;' that He spoke and acted clearly enough for them [1]. So on another occasion He asserted the limits of external evidence in moral matters: 'If they hear not Moses and the prophets, neither will they be persuaded if one rise from the dead [2].'

Jesus Christ then taught by events, He made His apostles not so much prophets as witnesses; but He also postulated a will to believe. It is faith based on evidence that He wishes to generate, but still faith. We then will approach the consideration of the evidence for our religion on the one hand with the disposition of faith, that is, in the intellect a perception of the need and reasonableness of redemption, in the heart the desire for the word of God, and the will to surrender ourselves to Him; on the other hand with a simple and open-minded determination to submit ourselves to the results of real enquiry at its last issue.

## II.

The enquirer into the historical grounds of our Christian faith will be wise to make a beginning with St. Paul's epistles, and he had better go back at once to that specially characteristic group, which bears the most unmistakable evidence of authenticity, that is to say, the epistles to the Galatians, to the Romans, and to the Corinthians [3]. Now what is the conception of Christ's person which he finds there expressed or implied? He

---

[1] St. John x. 22-28.    [2] St. Luke xvi. 31.    [3] See app. note 18, p. 248.

finds Jesus Christ co-ordinated with God in the necessarily divine functions and offices, both in nature and in
grace, in a manner impossible to the mind of a Jewish
monotheist like St. Paul, unless the co-ordinated person
is really believed to belong to the properly divine being.
So complete is this co-ordination that (to quote the
language of Professor Pfleiderer) 'we need feel no surprise when Paul at length calls Him without reserve
"God who is over all blessed for evermore."' And St.
Paul can thus pay divine honour to Jesus Christ in the
present, only because of what He was antecedently to
His appearance in our flesh. Thus there is no disputing
that these epistles teach—or, more truly, assume as believed—the doctrine of the Incarnation. Jesus Christ
was the mediator in creation, 'through whom are all
things,' before He was manifest to human eyes. He was
with the Jews in the wilderness supplying their wants,
'for they drank of a spiritual rock that followed them :
and the rock was Christ.' Before the days of His flesh He
existed as the 'Son of God,' 'God's own Son,' before He
was 'sent forth born of a woman.' Thus the 'second man'
is 'from heaven,' but that not without a change. His Incarnation was a voluntary act of self-beggary, an act by ✓
which the divine Son for our sakes 'became poor,'
depriving Himself of the riches of His previous state, in
order for our redemption to become true man, in the
reality of our nature 'according to the flesh,' and, though
He 'knew no sin' Himself, 'in the likeness of the flesh
of sin.' Thus in order of time, He is first divine, afterwards human. But in the order of His self-disclosure
He is first human, then divine. He showed His Divinity
through His humanity. He appeared as man, after-

wards through the evidences of His manhood men came
to believe in His Godhead.   In part this belief was due
to His miracles or power, in part to the spirit of holiness which gave His miracles a moral character and
impressiveness, at the last resort it was to His resurrection.    So St. Paul summarizes the matter, ' He
was born of the seed of David according to the flesh,
and marked out as the Son of God in power (that is,
according to a recognised use of St. Paul's, by miraculous working) according to the spirit of holiness, by
the resurrection of the dead.'

Of detail of our Lord's life St. Paul gives us very little.
He was not, we remember, like the other apostles, an eye-
witness of its incidents.   But he does in the epistle to
the Corinthians lead us to recognise an important fact,
viz. that his first preaching to his converts contained
more of narrative than his subsequent letters.   On two
occasions he recalls the memory of the Corinthians to his
original teaching in the form of a narrative of events, ' I
delivered unto you first of all that which I also received ; '
' I received . . . that which also I delivered unto you,'—
that is, the account of the institution of the holy eucharist at
the last supper, and of the appearances after the resurrection.   In the former case the narrative is in obvious
correspondence with that of the Synoptic Gospels ; in
the latter case, it is a summary narrative, which, omitting
for whatever reason, all appearances to women, is our
best help in combining the statements and implications
of St. Matthew and St. Luke in the Gospels and the
Acts taken together.

In a word, we get in St. Paul's undisputed epistles,
first a clear doctrine of the incarnation and person of

Christ not developed into a theology, but unmistakable in character ; secondly, an account of the method of Christ's manifestation, the manifestation of the divinity through the humanity, which corresponds with the evangelic record ; thirdly, an appeal back behind his present teaching to primary instruction in the events of Christ's passion and resurrection, which presupposes an evangelic narrative already existing in the memory of the Church.

These epistles of St. Paul were written in the year 57 or 58, but the teaching they contain is no new thing at that moment, it goes back in its main features to the time of his conversion twenty years before, not more than ten years after the death and resurrection of Jesus. At that time he 'learnt Christ,' and began his career as an apostle, and after that time he preached no other gospel than that which his converts first received [1]. Moreover, whereas these epistles are epistles of controversy with the Judaistic party, we are enabled to perceive that among the points of dispute between St. Paul and the false conservatives, the doctrine of Christ's person was not one. St. Paul does, indeed, imply that unless the Judaizers are prepared to advance in practice to a fuller recognition of the newness and largeness of Christ's work, they will evacuate the Gospel of meaning and play false to Him—and in fact the Pharisaic Ebionites of Church history are a fulfilment of St. Paul's prophetic warning :—but he never allows us to suppose that the doctrine of Christ's person or the reality of the resurrection were at all in controversy either among the apostles or in the body of

---

[1] Gal. i. 8, 9.

the Church, at a date when the greater part of those who had seen the risen Christ were still alive.

We can be sure then that, if we could be carried back across the centuries and planted of a sudden in these earliest Christian churches, our traditional faith would not receive a shock, at least in fundamentals ; we should find them believing in the Incarnation, instructed as to the manner in which Jesus Christ manifested Himself in miraculous working, and recognising that the most significant of the miracles accompanying His manifest-ation was the resurrection on the third day from the dead. Certainly, then, neither the belief in the divinity and incarnation of Jesus Christ, nor the belief in His miraculous manifestation, can, consistently with St. Paul's epistles, be regarded as an accretion upon the original belief of the apostles and their first disciples.

### III.

The question next arises, have we in our present Gospels something which represents faithfully the original narrative of the apostolic witnesses ? In answer to this question an enquirer who aims rather at satisfying his faith than at solving the complicated literary problems of the first three, the Synoptic, Gospels, will do well to give his attention first of all to the Gospel according to St. Mark. Can we with reasonable cer-tainty assign a date to this Gospel? A recent critic, Mr. Estlin Carpenter, who writes in a sense strongly adverse to Christian theology, dates St. Mark's Gospel about A. D. 70 [1]. We may depend upon it that that is

[1] *Synoptic Gospels* (Unit. S. School Assoc., 1890 , p. 381.

at least not too early a date, and it commends itself
more or less exactly to a great many independent
critics.   What is of more importance is to notice that
this Gospel, or what was in substance this Gospel, has
formed the basis both of St. Matthew's and St. Luke's
narrative.   Here, then, in the matter common to St.
Mark with both the other evangelists—or we may say,
though for our present purpose it makes little difference,
with either of the other evangelists—we get as near as
we can to the roots of the evangelical tradition.   Let
us consider this (as it is called) 'first cycle' of teaching
about Jesus Christ, and learn its main lessons :—

(1) First I would rank the impression made upon the
mind of reality and historical truthfulness.   Let a man
read St. Mark afresh, in some accurate text which
divides the narrative into sections, rather than into the
customary chapters and verses, let him read the Gospel
as a connected whole, and he will receive a fresh and
vivid impression that the picture brought under his eyes
represents no effort of imagination or invention, but is
the transcript of reality on faithful and simple memories.
There is nothing in the literary situation out of which
this Gospel, or the Gospels generally, sprang, which
justifies us in believing that it could produce a supreme
effort, or rather several supreme efforts, of the creative
imagination.   Considering the supernatural character of
the central figure in the Gospels, and the unity which
underlies their varieties, it is not an exaggeration to
say that the Christ of the Gospels, if He be not true
to history, represents a combined effort of the creative
imagination without parallel in literary history.   But the
literary characteristics of Palestine in the first century

make the hypothesis of such an effort morally impossible. Moreover, the existing legends about our Lord's childhood in the apocryphal Gospels show us what the imagination of early Christians or half-Christians could in fact produce—something which is as different from the canonical Gospels as the real light of the sun is from the imitation of it on the stage.

(2) Secondly, as we look more closely at the matter of St. Mark's Gospel, we shall see great reason to believe the tradition which Papias first records, who himself lived under the shadow of the apostolic age. 'This (he writes) the elder used to say: "Mark, having become the interpreter of Peter, wrote down accurately everything that he remembered, without however recording in order what was either said or done by Christ. For neither did he hear the Lord, nor did he follow Him; but afterwards, as I said, [attended] Peter, who adapted his instruction to the needs [of his hearers] and had no design of giving a connected account of the Lord's oracles. So then Mark made no mistake while he thus wrote down some things as he remembered them; for he made it his one care not to omit anything that he heard or to set down any false statement therein."' Internal evidence makes it very difficult to doubt that this 'teaching of Peter' is the bulk of our second Gospel. It would have constituted the material of the catechetical instruction which, as St. Luke's preface assures us, formed the basis of the written Gospels. Here is a narrative simple and brief enough to have easily been the subject of oral instruction in the different churches of St. Peter's foundation. St. Peter was never a theologian, like St. Paul or St. John, and his Gospel was

probably a narrative of incidents which impressed themselves most vividly on his memory, and which he judged
especially suitable for primary instruction, with but small
accompaniment of discourse.

We scan then this first cycle of evangelic teaching,
and what do we find in it? A record which impresses us with its fidelity, but which is pre-eminently
miraculous. Miracle is here at its height, its proportion to the whole narrative is greater than in any
other Gospel, because of the comparative absence of
discourses, and the miracles are exhibitions of supreme
power such as do not admit of any naturalistic interpretation. There is the feeding of the five thousand,
and the raising of Jairus' daughter, and the healing
of the paralytic, and of the man with the withered
hand, and of the leper, and the stilling of the tempest,
and the walking upon the water. Moreover, the impression which Christ's person makes on us, in spite
of the comparative absence of discourses, is exactly the
same as that which we receive from St. Matthew and
St. Luke. The absolute authoritativeness of the Christ
is the impressive fact, 'He taught as one having
authority.' With authority He announces beforehand
His passion and resurrection after three days, and the
world-wide spread of His gospel, and the glory of the
saints with Himself when He shall come at the last day
to exercise divine judgment. With authority He controls
the devils. With authority He governs physical nature.
He heals men's bodies even in His absence, and absolves
their sins, and commands their allegiance. And this
because of what He was; because though Son of man,
He was not mere man, there was something behind what

F

appeared, which He would not freely disclose, which He
left men mostly to find out, but which the devils recognised; 'Jesus, the Son of the most high God.' This
He was declared to be at His baptism and His transfiguration by the voice of the Father. So He described
Himself in the parable where He distinguishes Himself
as the only Son from the servants who were God's
previous messengers. Because He is this, He would
have the Jews think of the Messiah as David's Lord
rather than as David's son. It is when He confesses
Himself 'the Son of the Blessed,' in response to the
demand of the High Priest, that He announces also
that He shall be manifested at the last, 'sitting at the
right hand of power and coming with the clouds of
heaven.' As Son once more He speaks of Himself as
superior to the angels, even when He is declaring Himself ignorant of the day and hour of the end. In a
word, the brief statement of St. Paul, already referred
to, is a sufficiently accurate analysis of this Gospel.
It is the Gospel of 'one born of the seed of David
according to the flesh, and marked out as the Son
of God in miraculous power according to the spirit of
holiness by the resurrection of the dead.'

Once again, then, a sifting of the evidence discloses in
the earliest Gospel the Christ of the Apostles' Creed.
It affords us no justification for supposing a process of
accretion by which a naturalistic Christ was gradually
deified, or became the subject of miracles. The Christ
of the original apostolic testimony appears unyieldingly
the miraculous Son of God as the most human Son of
man [1].

[1] See app. note 19, p. 249.

## IV.

At this stage of our enquiry we shall do well to exercise a strict self-denial. Tempting problems lie before us in the relations of the Gospels to one another, but we will deliberately refrain from touching these problems at all. Again, we hear it suggested that there are indications in St. Matthew and St. Luke of deteriorations in the common tradition; again that there are discrepancies between the three Evangelists. For the moment we will let the case go by default in favour of these suggestions, but at least, as we read each of the three Gospels in turn, we shall find the Christ presented to us the same figure, only with such characteristic features as would be derived in part from independent testimony, in part from fresh treatment of the same material. Discrepancies, if they are made the most of, do not approach the point at which, according to the rules of ordinary historical enquiry, they would be supposed to invalidate the record as a whole.

But even at the first stage of our enquiry we must pause over St. Luke's preface. We shall feel that these few verses[1] give us an account, as true as it is simple, of the origin of the written Gospels.

They tell us how the evangelical narrative was at first delivered by eye-witnesses and authorized expositors of what they related, 'eye-witnesses and ministers of the word'; how it became familiar to Christians orally in the catechetical system of the churches; how after a time many began to write down the familiar record, according to their ability; how St. Luke had special

---

[1] St. Luke i. 1-4.

F 2

opportunities of accurate information extending over
the whole period of our Lord's life from the beginning,
and therefore thought it right to be at pains to construct an orderly narrative, which he offers to Theo-
philus as something which may be depended upon for
a trustworthy account of the subject-matter of his faith.
What a fund of re-assurance lies in those simple verses
with which St. Luke opens his Gospel! How vividly
they enable us to realize that, behind the written
Gospels, reducing them, at the moment of their composition, even to comparative insignificance, lay the
authoritative apostolic message, enshrined in the memories of churches.

## V.

I must here be allowed to assume the results of my
predecessor's labours in this lectureship[1], and state
simply, though with sincere conviction, based on the
best enquiry I can give, that it is those who deny, and
not those who affirm, St. John's authorship of the fourth
Gospel who do violence to the evidence. The evidence,
external and internal, combines to press it home upon
'the disciple whom Jesus loved.' Here, then, we have,
to piece in with the testimony of St. Paul and the
Synoptists, the witness of the old apostle.

Fifty years of brooding meditation, and many years
of constant teaching, since Jesus left this world, have
crystallized the record of his memory into clear-cut and
distinct images of the person, the words, the deeds of
his friend, his master, his God. He has passed into a
wholly new world at Ephesus, half-Greek, half-Asiatic,

[1] See app. note 20, p. 250.

where Gnostic questions are beginning to be agitated, and men are seeking to locate the person of Jesus Christ in some universal cosmogony or system of aeons. The central problem is, 'Who Jesus was?' 'He was,' answered the old apostle, 'the Word made flesh.' The phraseology of the famous prologue is obviously familiar phraseology, which requires no explanation in St. John's new home; and it is apparently deliberately applied to suggest answers to the new questionings. But the characteristic force of its central term, 'the Word' or 'Logos,' appears to be derived from Hebrew, not Greek, sources and from the atmosphere of Palestine rather than of Alexandria.

In the philosophical language of Alexandria, as it appears in the writings of the Jewish Philo, the term 'Logos' is used to express the divine reason or thought, which is the archetypal idea or moulding principle of the material world. 'Logos' in Philo must be translated 'reason.' But in the Targums, or early Jewish paraphrases on the Old Testament, the 'word' of Jehovah ('Memra,' 'Debura') is constantly spoken of as the efficient instrument of divine action, in cases where the Old Testament speaks of Jehovah Himself. 'The word of God' had come to be used personally, as almost equivalent to God manifesting Himself, or God in action. Now in the Apocalypse[1], it is plain that the person whose name is the 'Logos' of God expresses not the divine reason, but the divine word or power: and the same is true of the fourth Gospel. Here also 'Logos' must be translated not 'reason' but 'word': and this means that the phraseology of St. John has its roots

[1] Rev. xix. 13.

not in Platonic or Stoic idealism, but in the Jewish belief in the word of God, the manifestation of His will in creation or in revelation [1].

In effect St. John's theology of the Incarnation is the same as St. Paul's; but in St. John it has a peculiar interest, because in a unique sense it is the outcome of his own experience. He could never forget how he had passed from John the Baptist to Jesus, and had even at the first, according to the Baptist's own witness, perceived the vital difference between the old master and the new. This perception of difference had deepened into a conviction in which faith was indistinguishable from experience, in which it became certain knowledge. 'The Word, who in the beginning was in fellowship with God, who was God, by whom all things were made, whose life was the light of men, who was all along coming into the world,' now at the last 'had been made flesh and had tabernacled among them, and they had beheld His glory, the glory as of the only-begotten of the Father.' This is St. John's summary and emphatic witness, and he passes on to give those vivid memories of the life of Jesus on which that witness is based. For whatever intention St. John may have had of supplementing existing records, the impulse which mainly determined his selection of incidents seems to have been his own special memory and the fruit of his long meditation. Thus he depicts for us scenes in that early, especially Judaean, ministry of our Lord, which, though not recorded by the Synoptists, is yet—as critics of all schools are increasingly inclined to recognise, —postulated by the relations in which our Lord is seen

[1] See app. note 21, p. 250.

to stand to the Jews at Jerusalem in the closing days of His life. Again he gives us memorable pictures of our Lord's dealing with single souls, with Nicodemus, with the woman at the well, with the man who was born blind, with individual disciples before and after the resurrection. Again he unfolds before our eyes our Lord's relations to men, as a great drama of belief and unbelief. Once more he fills in the Synoptic history of the trial and passion of Jesus with scenes and touches of living power, producing a whole of wonderful harmony, even though his narrative introduce one, perhaps insoluble, difficulty, as to the relation of the Last Supper to the paschal meal. But the pre-eminent interest of St. John's Gospel lies in his representation of our Lord's discourses, and in the witness which these bear to His eternal pre-existence. Our Lord's general method was to let men come to believe His Godhead gradually through their experience of His manhood. In His discourses in St. John there is a distinct note audible. He is heard to assert plainly His own pre-existence and His own essential relation to the Father. Now did this assertion of His own eternal being historically form part of the teaching of Jesus?

We shall not lay stress on the exact form of the discourses as they appear in St. John. The literary habit of the age (as Cardinal Newman well pointed out[1]) allowed great freedom in the use of 'oratio directa.' We have every reason to believe that that freedom was used in those summaries and combinations of our Lord's discourses which are given in St. Matthew. Accordingly we shall not hesitate to recognise that

[1] See app. note 22. p. 250.

the discourses in the fourth Gospel as well, have taken their verbal tone and form in St. John's own mind. But if the author of the Gospel was St. John; if he was the special friend of Jesus; if he was the most spiritually apprehensive of all the disciples; if (as he tells us) he believed that he, with the rest of the apostles, had been endowed with a special gift of the Holy Ghost 'to bring all things to his remembrance that Jesus said to them';—we cannot but admit that these discourses do in substance come from Jesus Christ; Jesus did Himself bear witness to His own eternal relation to the Father. In support of this conclusion we shall remember :—

(1) that it would be otherwise very difficult to explain the thoroughly accepted position of this doctrine in the earliest churches as St. Paul bears witness to it ;

(2) that there are utterances in the Synoptists parallel to those in St. John. 'All things have been delivered unto me of my Father, and no man knoweth the Son save the Father, neither doth any know the Father save the Son.' Or again, 'Of that day and that hour knoweth no one, not even the angels in heaven, neither the Son, but the Father.' Or again, 'Go ye . . . and make disciples of all the nations, baptizing them into the name of the Father and of the Son and of the Holy Ghost,' a formula which certainly implies the Son's eternal existence with the Father and the Spirit. If Jesus Christ was in this transcendental sense 'Son of the Father,' He could only be a visitant from the higher, the eternal world.

(3) We shall remember that the absolute moral authority of the Son of man and His coming as divine judge of the whole world in glory at the last—this

authority which appears so emphatically in the discourses of the Synoptists—is not really dissociable from
divine, that is, eternal being.   We need only to suppose
that St. John's theological mind seized and retained,
more than that of the other apostles, the particular class
of sayings which characterizes his Gospel: that while the
words and works of authority and the claims of judgment made most impression upon the minds of St. Peter
and St. Matthew, the more mysterious utterances were
(in the ways of Providence, which works under the guise
of accident) retained and recorded by St. John.

We have traced up the evidence of our faith along
three chief lines : we have examined the testimony of St.
John, we have scrutinized the earliest evangelical narratives, which certainly reproduce for us the apostolic teaching, and we have investigated the belief of the earliest
churches under the guidance of St. Paul.   The result of
our enquiry is that we are able to repudiate as un-his-
torical the notion of a naturalistic Christ hidden behind
the miraculous Christ, the incarnate Son of God, of the
Church's belief.   Historical evidence, let me repeat, cannot create faith, but it can, and it does, satisfy it where it
exists, and rationally justify the venture that it makes.
In a word, it is those who deny and not those who
affirm the traditional belief, who do violence to the
evidence.

VI.

The force of such positive historical evidence as I have
been trying to present, is sometimes met in our day
by depreciating not, as of old, the moral honesty, but
the intellectual or critical capacity, of the apostles and

first disciples. ' If first-hand evidence is always good
evidence,' it is said, ' we have very good evidence for
multitudes of mediaeval miracles. If we are not prepared
to interpolate accepted history with miracles *passim*, we
cannot place exceptional reliance on the testimony of the
disciples of one particular man.'

Now it is undoubtedly true that there are certain ages
when belief is so utterly uncritical that it does seem as
if they could not under any circumstances afford us satisfactory evidence of miraculous occurrences ; and in every
age, including our own, there are a great number of people
whose superstition, or prejudice, or careless untruthful-
ness, is so great that we could never rely on their evidence
for any exceptional event, where their interests were en-
listed or their passions excited. But I feel sure that if
ever such a book as the ' History of testimony' is worthily
and fairly written, the apostles will take very high rank
among the world's witnesses. As represented in the
Gospels they were men not of the poorest, but of the
more independent trading class ; simple, literal-minded
men ; not superstitious and still less romantic ; free from
all traces of morbidness ; slow of belief through lack of
imagination ; as individuals strikingly different in character, so as not easily to be led the same way; with the exception of St. John not well adapted to be theologians and
none of them (like St. Paul) controversial theologians; but
singularly well qualified as witnesses. They were qualified as witnesses because, free from all preoccupation with
ideas and systems, they were plain men who could receive
the impress of facts ; who could tell a simple plain tale
and show by their lives how much they believed it. And
they were trained to be witnesses. Jesus Christ intended

His Gospel to rest on facts; and in correspondence with this intention, the whole stress in the apostolic Church was laid on witness. The first thing the Church had to do, before it developed its theology, was to tell its tale of fact. 'We are witnesses of these things[1].'

And in what atmosphere, we ask, did the apostles bear their testimony? It was in face of the Sadducees who were their chief opponents and who sat in the seat of authority. And the Sadducees were sceptics, with the scepticism of worldly men who have a political cause to maintain, and would fain keep the supernatural at arm's length; men who were regarded as denying resurrection and angels and spirits.

And of what sort was the testimony of the apostles? Consider its originality. When once a type of appropriate miracles has been set, it is very easy, so to speak, to go on taking off impressions as in mediaeval hagiology. Again, miracles of mere healing or portents of power any one can invent. But for the sort of miracles which Jesus is mostly described as working, so spiritual and original, so characteristic, there was no type. For a resurrection body there was no pattern. If Jews full of Messianic hopes, as is supposed, had pictured a Christ coming again from death, it would have been, like the 'Son of man' of the Book of Enoch, a Christ in glory, or 'one like unto a Son of man' of the Apocalypse. What was there in the imagination of this group of Jews which could project into the outward world the strong vivid image of the risen body of Jesus, spiritual, superior to the limitations of the grosser material life, yet so real; the pierced body of the same Christ, yet so

---

[1] See app. note 23, p. 251.

changed ?  For observe : visions which are subjective can
be explained out of the images and presuppositions which
already exist in the visionary's mind.  For St. Theresa's
visions, or Joan of Arc's vision, the pattern existed within.
It needed but an imagination to project it.  Disbelieve
their visions—their lives are still intelligible wholes, with
adequate causes to interpret, and to account for them.
But the apostles were men whose later lives can only be
accounted for by a certain fact, the fact of the resurrection.  This fact transferred them from one level of character to another ; it transferred men first confounded
and desperate after their Lord's death, then slow of heart
to believe what seemed too good to be true, into men
confident, quiet, strong, invincible in the might of a fact
experienced on certain definite occasions, and not again.
Depend upon it, merely subjective visions do not trans-
form human lives.  If mediaeval visions of Jesus exercised
power, they were only recurrences of a known image,
fresh impressions of a known truth.  The apostles' lives
were rapidly driven round a sharp turning with a force
which only objective facts can exercise.  The resurrection moulded them, they did not create the resurrection.
The more closely you consider the originality of such an
event as the resurrection, of such a figure as the risen
Jesus, the less ready you will be to attribute it to
imagination.  The more you consider the intellectual
and moral character of the apostles—not imaginative
men, even in the sense in which St. Paul was—the more
you will trust them as witnesses.

This consideration also you will not neglect—their
fairness to their opponents.  The mediaeval disciples of
a persecuted master would indulge in diatribes, would

grossly caricature their opponents, like partisans in even later ecclesiastical conflicts. But while the evangelists record our Lord's denunciations of certain classes, how wonderfully they (or the apostles whose teaching they reproduce) abstain from imprecations of their own. How free from abuse are the Gospels; how simply drawn, how justly, are the characters of even a Pilate, a Caiaphas, a Herod, a Judas. They are not abused, they are photographed. The sin of a Judas and of a Peter is told with the like simplicity. Such fairness, wherever you find it, belongs to a trustworthy witness.

## VII.

There is one event commemorated in our Creed which does not rest primarily on apostolic testimony. It is the virgin-birth of Jesus. And a few men—very few perhaps, but still a few—who believe in His resurrection, deny or doubt the miracle that accompanied His birth. Now there is no doubt that this event was not part of the primary apostolic preaching. as it is given us in St. Mark's Gospel, simply because that preaching was limited by what the apostles had actually witnessed during 'the time that the Lord Jesus went in and went out among them, beginning from the baptism of John unto the day that he was received up from them.' The first preaching was simple personal testimony. There is also no doubt that the apostles themselves were to be taught by their own experience of Jesus, and had no knowledge given them to start with of His miraculous origin. But when once they had believed, they must have been interested to know the circumstances of the Incarnation.

There were two sources of original evidence, Joseph and
Mary. Have we reason to believe that we have their
testimony in the opening chapters of St. Matthew and
St. Luke? Having asked this question, read St. Matthew's account of the birth, and you will see how unmistakably everything is told from the side of Joseph,
his perplexities, the intimations which he received, his
resolutions and his actions. The narrative has been
worked up by the Evangelist in his dominant interest
in the fulfilment of prophecy, but it has all the marks
of being Joseph's story at the bottom, though we cannot tell by what steps it comes to us.

On the other hand, St. Luke's narrative, an intensely
Jewish document following on his markedly Greek preface, has all the appearance of containing directly or
indirectly Mary's story. It is so intensely coloured by
Jewish national hopes that it is hardly possible to think
of it as embodying feelings subsequent to the rejection
of the Christ. It appears to be in special view of this
opening narrative that St. Luke in his preface emphasizes
the fact that his accurate information reaches back to the
beginning. Once again, whatever the independence of the
two narratives of St. Matthew and St. Luke, at least they
agree on that which alone concerns us at present, the
virgin-birth at Bethlehem. Further, that event holds a
firm place in the earliest traditions of East and West.
'The virginity of Mary, her child-bearing, and the death
of the Lord,' constitute to Ignatius at the beginning of
the second century 'three mysteries of shouting (that is,
of loud proclamation) which God wrought in silence[1].'
If we turn from the question of evidence to *à priori* con-

---

[1] Ign. *ad Eph.* 19.

siderations, we find that the virgin-birth, so far from being an incongruous portent, has appeared to Christians at large as hardly dissociable in thought from the occurrence of the Incarnation. I would affirm, then, that though it is a perversion of evidential order to begin with the miracle of the virgin-birth, yet when we approach it on the basis of the apostolic testimony already accepted, with confidence in the evangelical narrative already secured, we find good reason for believing, and no good reason for doubting, this element of the Christian creed, constantly emphasized from the beginning [1].

We Christians then may say our Creed in the confidence that we can face the facts. The primary *motive* to belief is the appeal which Jesus makes to our heart, and conscience, and mind. The *power* to believe, or to maintain belief, is the gift of God which we must earnestly solicit in prayer; it is the movement of the Spirit. ' No man can say, Jesus is Lord, but in the Holy Ghost.' But belief, Christian belief, is justified and supported by the evidence. We will be a little afraid of *à priori* conceptions and abstract anticipations, but we will not be afraid of evidence, of facts, for the witness standeth sure.

---

[1] See app. note 24, p. 251.

# LECTURE IV.

*Have this mind in you, which was also in Christ Jesus: who, being in the form of God, counted it not a prize to be on an equality with God, but emptied himself, taking the form of a servant, being made in the likeness of man.*—PHILIPPIANS ii. 5.

IN the lectures which have preceded we have been occupied with justifying at the bar of nature and of history the faith of the Christian in the incarnate Son of God. We are to pass now to a more exact examination of what that faith means, of what the Incarnation of the Son of God teaches us about the God who is incarnate and about the manhood which He assumes. But in doing this, we shall constantly find the need of some definitions of the terms we use, and there are definitions which of course suggest themselves for our guidance, ancient, famous, venerable, contained in the catholic creeds, and dogmatic decisions of the general councils about the person of Jesus Christ.

## I.

These definitions consist in substance of four propositions;

(1) that as Son of God, Jesus Christ is very God, of one substance with the Father;

(2) that as Son of man, He is perfectly Man, in the completeness of human faculties and sympathies;

(3) that though both God and Man, He is yet one person, namely the Son of God who has taken manhood into Himself;

(4) that in this incarnation the manhood, though it is truly assumed into the divine person, still remains none the less truly human, so that Jesus Christ is of one substance with us men in respect of His manhood, as He is with the Father in respect of His godhead.

Now of these dogmatic formulas different views are taken[1].

In the view of ancient and Anglican orthodoxy, the creeds are simply summaries of the original Christian faith as it is represented in Scripture. They are summaries such as are necessary for the purposes of a teaching church, to serve as introductions to the study of Scripture and guides to its scattered, but consistent, statements and implications: summaries which always refer us back to Scripture for their justification or proof, it being the function of 'the church to teach,' as the phrase goes, 'the Bible to prove.' And, according to the same view, the dogmatic decision of councils are formulas rendered necessary for no other purpose than to guard the faith of Scripture from what was calculated to undermine it. They do not make any addition to its substance, but bring out into light and emphasis some of its most important principles.

This, the ancient view of ecclesiastical dogmas, has never been abandoned in the authoritative documents

---

[1] See app. note 25, p. 252.

of the Roman church, but some Roman controversialists, when confronted by the fact that ancient Christianity certainly did not recognise their more recent dogmas, have made a reply of this sort: 'It is true that our modern theology represents an advance of the religious consciousness of Christendom upon ancient catholicity, but the catholic theology of the fifth century represents the same sort of advance upon primitive Christianity.' Thus, on this view the ancient decisions of councils represent simply one stage in a gradual process, by which the rudimentary consciousness of primitive Christianity was gradually expanded into a great dogmatic system, covering a much wider area of positive teaching than the original Christian faith, and supplying a good deal of additional information.

With a not dissimilar conception of the facts, but from a widely-opposed point of view, the theology of the councils has been viewed as a needless metaphysical accretion upon genuine Christianity which it would do well to get rid of.   Christianity began as a moral and spiritual 'way of life.'   It was under Hellenic influences, and by incorporating the terms and ideas of late Hellenic philosophy, that it developed its theology. It can throw this off and be only the freer for the loss, for 'what was absent from the early form cannot be essential.'   Christianity can end as it began, with the Sermon on the Mount and the spirit of brotherhood for its substance and its sum.

These are the current views about Church dogma : we are concerned with them here only so far as is necessary for answering the question which forms our subject for to-day—'what is the relation of the theology of the

creeds and dogmatic decrees to the faith of the New
Testament in Jesus Christ?'

## II.

Can we then describe in general outline the process
connecting the church of the New Testament with the
church of the General Councils?

The apostolic churches must be recognised on any
view which can make a reasonable claim to being
historical, as a confederation of spiritual societies, united
by a common faith as well as by a common rule of life.
Their relation to Christ's person, that is, their belief in
Him as the Son of God, who had taken their nature in
order to redeem it, and had sent His Spirit to dwell in their
hearts, did, as has been already pointed out [1], involve a theology of Father, Son, and Spirit, and of the Incarnation
of the Son. This theology is implied from the first [2], not
in the epistles only, but in the utterances of our Lord
about Himself as recorded in the Gospel of St. John and
also in the Synoptists. Even the least theological of the
epistles, that of St. James, implies a theology of Christ's
person, by identifying Him as Lord with the Lord
Jehovah of the Old Testament. A theology is conspicuous again in the formula of baptism, 'into the name
of the Father and of the Son and of the Holy Ghost.'

It has, of course, often been made an objection against
the originality of this formula that it is only once
mentioned in the New Testament, while, on the other

[1] See above, pp. 21–23, 58 ff.
[2] See on following paragraph app. note 26, p. 254.

hand, the phrase ' to be baptized in (or into) the name of
the Lord Jesus ' occurs more than once in the Acts of
the Apostles [1].    But whatever force such an objection
may have been supposed to have, has been greatly
weakened since the discovery of the *Teaching of the
Twelve Apostles.*    For that early document, which is
sometimes referred to as if it represented a Christianity
more original than that of the New Testament, mentions
twice over the formula of baptism into the three-fold
name, and thus interprets the expression which it also uses
in common with St. Luke, that of being ' baptized into the
name of the Lord [2].'    There is, in fact, no difficulty in
seeing how the two phrases could be used indifferently ;
for he that hath the Son hath the Father and the Spirit
also, and to be baptized into the ' name,' or revelation,
of the Son is to be baptized with the formula of the
three-fold name, which the Son reveals.

That this ' one faith,' in the three-fold name of God, the
Father, the Son, and the Holy Ghost, and in the incarnation of the Son, was a main connecting link, or basis
of union, among the apostolic churches is unmistakably
witnessed in the documents of the New Testament and
the subapostolic epistles of St. Ignatius and St. Clement.
This has become a still more certain proposition, since
the missing portions of St. Clement's letter have been
discovered, and the genuineness of the Ignatian letters
finally vindicated.    Thus to represent the original
Christianity as a way of life without a theology, as the
Sermon on the Mount and nothing more, even if the
Sermon on the Mount did not involve a theology, would
be an arbitrary act which could only be paralleled for

---

[1] Acts viii. 16, x. 48, xix. 5.        [2] *Didachè*, vii. 1, 3, ix. 5.

unhistorical boldness by (shall we say?) the identification of early Christianity with the mediaeval Papacy.

There was then from the first a common faith which is often alluded to in the New Testament as 'the tradition' to be 'held' by Christians, or the 'pattern of teaching to which they were delivered,' or 'the apostolic teaching,' or 'the pattern of sound words,' or 'the faith once for all delivered to the saints [1].' Thus the churches, as left by the apostles, believed themselves to possess, in the person of Jesus Christ, God's full and, for this world, final revelation of Himself to man. Their duty was to hold this word or message of God fast till the end. But the revelation, as they knew it, was not in the form of ordered knowledge ; its meaning, its coherence, its limits, were very imperfectly recognised, its terminology was not exact. The faith of the Church as it expressed itself in life, in worship, in fervent statement, in martyrdom, was vigorous and unmistakable in meaning ; it referred back for its authorization to apostolic teaching and apostolic writings ; but it was a faith, not a science ; a faith which in some sub-apostolic documents finds such inexact or even careless expression as impresses upon us the difference between the writers within, and those without, the canon [2].

Then the Church—whom we cannot help, as we watch the process, speaking of as a person—is seen subjected to a series of interrogations from various quarters. The most important of her questioners were the Gnostics. Would she admit these half-orientalist, or theosophist, speculators, with their denial of the unity

---

[1] 1 Cor. xi. 2, 23, etc.; Rom. vi. 17 ; Acts ii 42 ; 2 Tim. i. 13 ; Jude 3.
[2] See app. note 27, p. 257.

of all things, their belief in rival gods, good and bad, or
higher and lower deities, their denunciation or depre-
ciation of the material world, their rejection of the Old
Testament and mutilation of the New, their denials of
a real incarnation, their depreciations of simple faith and
exaltations of Gnosis or abstract speculation, their shifty
idealism—would she admit these bold theorizers into
fellowship, on the ground of a good deal in Gnostic asceti-
cism and mysticism which sounded lofty and Christian
enough ?   Would she admit Gnostics to brotherhood and
let them mould her creed ?   Or, on the other hand, would
she put up with the Ebionite's lower view of Christ as a
prophet like Moses or Jonah, or a restorer of primitive
religion?   Might the Sabellian regard her Trinity as
only three manifestations of a unitarian God?   Might
the Adoptionists regard Christ as a deified man?   So
she was cross-questioned, and with more or less of
difficulty and hesitation—like a person, as I say, subjected to cross-questioning about his convictions—she
elaborated her negative answers and so interpreted her
creed.   Finally, in response to the defined positions of
Arius and Apollinarius, of Nestorius and Eutyches, she
laid down clear and formal replies.   The result of
this process is that the Church passes from holding her
faith simply as a faith, to holding it with a clear consciousness of its intellectual meaning and limits, with
ready formulas and clearly worked-out terminology.
Great theologians have done good service at different
stages of this process.   Ignatius, Justin, Irenaeus, Tertullian, Origen, Athanasius, Gregory of Nyssa, Cyril of
Alexandria, Augustine, Leo, leave their stamp on the
Church's terminology and thought, but no one of them

enslaved her : she corrects their one-sided bias, when such becomes apparent, and in spite of strong pressure on this side and on that, she keeps her middle way, holding together the terms of the great synthesis, which is involved in her faith in God, three in one,—in Christ, God and man, the highest and the lowest made one.

Now intellectually, the special interest of this process, which connects the New Testament with the Creeds, lies in two points :—

First we observe here, as perhaps nowhere else in history, a corporate consciousness, the mind of a society, gradually taking explicit and formal shape. Underneath the superficial disturbances of the church's life, one steady current has been moving. Beneath general confusions of thought, violent partisanships, imperial influences—stronger than all in the result, stronger to the point of obliterating the traces of their action from the final product—one continuous faith or consciousness has been holding its own and gaining clearer expression. We have other instances in history of the genius of a nation or a society finding expression. It is the Roman genius, and not the thought of any individual merely, which is expressed in Roman law. The social theory of Plato and Aristotle has behind it the social experiences of the Greek city. But there is not, I believe, any case where a product which appears so purely intellectual as the formula of the Council of Chalcedon[1], a product so exact and definite, can be ascribed so little to any individual or individuals, can be regarded with the same truth as the expression of the consciousness of a historical society, gradually through

[1] See app. note 2s, p. 258.

many efforts of many individuals, elaborated into explicit and formulated utterance.

Secondly, the intellect is attracted by the balanced, antithetic, form of the dogmatic product. The period of the ecumenical councils, like the period of Gnosticism, seemed to Christian theologians, who lived in it, a scene of wild confusion[1]. The student of its ecclesiastical history to-day, appears to himself to be fighting his way through a wild sea of conflicting determinations and shifting views. Yet out of it, by some process, which at lowest must have been the survival of the fittest, emerged a frame-work of dogmatic statement, which is a very synonym for unshaken consistency and balanced strength. In fact, the thoughtful man cannot look back upon the result of that period without being struck with the sense that something was going on, greater than can be accounted for by what appears on the surface of events. For on the surface imperial influences or the tyranny of chance majorities are apparently all-powerful. In spite of the venerable dignity of an Athanasius, a Basil, a Gregory, a Flavian, a Leo, there is violence and partisanship, not only in little men, but in great theologians, like Cyril of Alexandria. Yet the results are just what these sorts of causes cannot produce. For the decree of the Council of Chalcedon, which practically sums up the results of the epoch, is not merely a solid and substantial framework ; it has another quality which accidental party majorities could never have produced ; it has balance, moderation, reserve, antithetic exactness, equal respect for both elements in a double truth. It is, as it was called from the first, the *via media*[2],

---

[1] See app. note 29, p. 259.    [2] See app. note 30, p. 259.

which means not the way of compromise, but the way of combination and impartiality. There has been some influence at work here besides what has appeared on the surface of history; 'this is the Lord's doing, and it is marvellous in our eyes.'

### III.

But the dogmatic product is something more than the survival of the fittest formulas. It represents simply and faithfully, in language supplied by the Greek philosophical schools, the original apostolic creed in Christ the incarnate Son of God. To justify this position I must recall to your minds, with greater exactness, what are the four main determinations about the person of Jesus Christ, which form the material of the Chalcedonian formula.

The first decision, as against Arius, assigned to Christ as Son of God the epithet ὁμοούσιος, 'of one substance with the Father.' Arius' conception of Christ, whatever the intellectual motives which produced it, assigned to Him in effect the position of a demi-god. Current, non-christian religious beliefs, popular and philosophical, had made men familiar with the notion of intermediate beings, the objects of religious worship, who represented on a lower plane, something greater and more eternal behind themselves. In particular, philosophical paganism had given currency to the notion of a mediating Mind, which stood half-way between the material world and the absolute and unknowable God. On this model Arius moulded his conception of Christ: a Christ whom men were to worship and treat as God, while all the time He only represented God, and was not God, but was in fact a creature, though the supreme creature, and if older than all others, yet not eternal nor really belonging to the being of God. Observe then that in repudiating this conception of Christ, and in declaring it to be un-christian, the Church was not only for her Lord's honour vindicating His real Godhead, was not only, as she believed, defending Scripture and tradition, but was also reasserting the first principle of theism as distinct from pantheism and idolatry. For the very principle of theism is, that there is no gradual descent from Creator to creature, no intermediate half-gods, no legitimate multiplication of the objects of worship. Thus if Christ was to be worshipped, it could only be because He was God, very God ; belonging to the one eternal nature. I shall have occasion in the next lecture to develope the position that the Christian doctrine of the Trinity is the true safeguard of theism. Here I am only concerned to point out, how Christianity in asserting the doctrine of the ὁμοούσιον was doing nothing more metaphysical than is involved in asserting the first principle of the theist's creed, that there is only one God, one supreme object of worship, that Christ is, if God at all, then the very God of the Father's substance and essential nature. That the aim of the Church was practical, rather than metaphysical, is in fact shown by her being content to use the same word to express Christ's relation to God and His relation to man—'of one substance' with God, 'of one substance' with us men. It was enough for her, that as He was really man, so also He was really God.

It is worth noticing that we have independent witnesses, such as Thomas Carlyle and our own

Thomas Hill Green, to the necessity of the Church's
action in the condemnation of Arius. 'The tendency of Arianism,' said Professor Green [1], 'was in one
respect just the reverse of Gnosticism. It was not
the moral, but the metaphysical side of Christian
thought which it lowered, and we owe it to the firm
front opposed by orthodox dogma, that Christian dogma
is still a thing of the present: one need not be an orthodox trinitarian to see that if Arianism had had its
way, the theology of Christianity would have become
of a kind, in which no philosopher, who had outgrown
the demonism of ancient systems, could for a moment
acquiesce.' Again, Mr. Froude writes of Thomas Carlyle [2]: 'He made one remark which is worth recording.
In earlier years he had spoken contemptuously of the
Athanasian controversy,—of the Christian world torn
in pieces over a diphthong: and he would ring the
changes in broad Annandale on the Homoousion and
the Homoiousion. He now told me that he perceived
Christianity itself to have been at stake. If the Arians
had won, it would have dwindled away to a legend.' Nor,
in fact, is this mere theory. The Goths were converted
to Christianity in its Arian form ; they accepted Christ
as a hero-God, like those to which they were accustomed.
Provided thus with a platform which lay between
heathenism and Christianity, they came to a premature
halt. The Christianity of the later Goths in Spain
appears to have admitted of a certain impartial veneration
for the Christian God and heathen idols. 'We do not.'
says Agila, the envoy from the Arian Leovigild to

---

[1] On *Christian Dogma*, see his 'Works,' iii. p. 172.
[2] See *Life in London*, ii. p. 462.

Chilperic at Tours —'We do not reckon it a crime to worship this and that : for we say in our common speech, it is no harm if a man passing between heathen altars and a church of God makes his reverence in both directions [1].'

Thus by its first dogmatic decision the Church at Nicæa refused to admit into Christianity the conception of the demi-god, just before the period when the rough German tribes, to whom this conception was dangerously familiar, were turned over to her for schooling.   That Christ was very God of very God, fixed itself in the mind of an able and interesting man, Apollinarius of Laodicea.   As being God, Christ, he went on to argue, must be morally unalterable ; yet He is in some sort human, and the human mind and will is alterable, liable to sin—nay, he seems to have thought, necessarily sinful.   How then can Jesus be human ?   To solve this problem, Apollinarius endeavoured to develope a systematic theory of the person of Christ on the basis of a more or less philosophical psychology.   He drew a distinction between the body, the soul or animal life, and the reason or spirit, in man's nature,—a distinction to some extent sanctioned by St. Paul ; and he conceived that in Christ the eternal and immutable mind or spirit, the Word of God, took the place of the human mind, and united itself to the soul and body, that is the animated body, so that Christ was made up of the Godhead, manifesting Himself in the living body of man.   That Christ was, as thus conceived, if like man, yet not really man, because without that human mind

---

[1] Greg. Tur. *Hist. Franc.*, v. 44.  Cf. Mr. Scott's *Ulfilas* (Macmillan, 1885), cap. v.

or spirit, in virtue of which alone the body in man becomes human and not merely animal,—Apollinarius frankly recognised. Yet he seems to have suggested, that the archetype of manhood exists in God, who made man after His own image, so that man's nature in some sense pre-existed in God. The Son of God was eternally human, and He could fill the place of the human mind in Christ without His thereby ceasing to be in some sense human. Such refinements, when their point was plain, the Church again met with a very emphatic negative: if man is made in God's image, yet man is not God, nor God man. It is, again, a first principle of theism, as distinct from pantheism, that manhood at the bottom is not the same thing as God-head. This is a principle intimately bound up with man's moral responsibility and the reality of sin. Thus the interests of theism were at stake in this controversy no less really, though less obviously, than the reality of Christ's human sympathies. At any rate, the Church could not have Christ's real humanity explained away. He had a really human will, human mind, human reflectiveness, human sympathies: He was completely man in all human faculties, to be tempted, to pray, to suffer, to learn, as truly as He was very God. That was the second determination—reasserted in the sixth century against the Monothelites, in connection with the truth of Christ's human will.

But if Christ was God and man, how was the union to be conceived of the Godhead and the manhood? The man-hood—so insisted a school of theologians from Antioch—if it be truly manhood, must have free-will and self-deter-mination. Christ then must be really a free human person.

how then is He God? Because, they replied, God unites
Himself to man; to all men in proportion to their merit,
to Christ in a unique and exceptional manner on account
of His unique and exceptional merit. As this merit was
foreseen, so the man Christ Jesus was from the first
united in a special degree with God. But that which was
born of Mary was not, properly speaking, God the Son :
it was a human child Jesus, who, when He had grown
to manhood, became Son of God by adoption at His
baptism, and at last was made one with God in glory.
This was the theory which, as originated or suggested
by the famous commentator Theodore of Mopsuestia,
was adopted and popularized by Nestorius. But the
Church saw clearly enough that it is not what the Bible
teaches, or what our redemption requires. The Christ
of Nestorius was, after all, simply a deified man, not
God incarnate : He was from below, not from above. If
He was exalted to union with the Divine essence, His
exaltation was only that of one individual man. This is
not the Gospel, that 'the Son of God for us men and for
our salvation was incarnate and was made man.' According to the Gospel, the person who was born of Mary,
who lived and taught and died upon the cross, who was
raised again the third day from the dead, was no other
person than the eternal Son in the human nature which
He had taken. The Nestorian theory, then, was met
with a negative as emphatic as possible in the decree
of Ephesus. Jesus Christ, as born of Mary, was truly
God incarnate, albeit it was only in respect of His manhood that Mary was His mother. This was the third
determination.

Christ then is God incarnate. In Him the human

nature is assumed by the divine Person. But, in that case, can the human nature be said to remain? No, persisted an abbot of Constantinople, named Eutyches; distinct as manhood and Godhead are before the incarnation, by the incarnation the manhood loses its own proper and distinct nature. It is transubstantiated into that which assumed it: it is no longer of our substance. Once more, this position was met by the Church with an emphatic negative in the Council of Chalcedon. The humanity in Christ remains distinctively what it was: it is not transmuted out of its own proper character; the eternal person assumes the human nature, and acts through it, without its ceasing to be human. Christ, who is of one substance with the Father in respect of His Godhead, is of one substance with us in respect of our manhood, and that for ever. In Him the two natures, divine and human, subsist in the unity of the one person.

This is the last determination that we need consider, for later ones only reassert principles already determined. Thus the dogmatic matter is summarized in the decree of the Council of Chalcedon, or in the more familiar language of that exposition of the faith, converted into a psalm of praise, which we call the Athanasian Creed: 'for the right Faith is, that we believe and confess that our Lord Jesus Christ, the Son of God, is God and Man: God, of the Substance of the Father, begotten before the worlds: and Man, of the Substance of His Mother, born in the world: perfect God, and perfect Man: of a reasonable soul and human flesh subsisting. . . . Who although He be God and Man, yet He is not two, but one Christ: One; not by conversion

of the Godhead into flesh : but by taking of the Manhood into God ; One altogether; not by confusion of
Substance : but by unity of Person.'

## IV.

Now these decisions do, it is contended, simply express
in a new form, without substantial addition, the apostolic
teaching as it is represented in the New Testament.
They express it in a new form for protective purposes,
as a legal enactment protects a moral principle. They
are developments only in the sense that they represent
the apostolic teaching worked out into formulas by the
aid of a terminology which was supplied by Greek
dialectics.

In justifying this position, it is obvious to admit,
first of all, that the earliest language of the apostolic
teachers has not the explicitness of the later language
of the Church. But there is a development inside the
New Testament, and the reason of this gradual unfolding of teaching, in part at least intentional, is sufficiently plain. The apostles themselves had been led
gradually on in correspondence with their consciences
to explicit belief in Jesus Christ. They led their first
disciples by a similar process. To have preached
'Jesus Christ is God,' nakedly and simply, would have
shocked every right-minded Jew, who would have seen
in the assertion the proclamation of a second God, and
would have been welcomed by every pagan, only too
easily, because he believed in 'Gods many.' Thus,
according to the account given in the Acts of the
Apostles, the early preaching of St. Paul to the heathen
goes to lay a basis of belief in the one true God as a

background for Christianity, and the early preaching to Jews, or those under Jewish influence, goes to make good that Jesus was the Christ. Both Jews and Greeks are to be brought to their belief in Christ's true nature, through acceptance, along different lines of argument, of His moral authority and divine mission. They are to obey and trust Him first of all, that is, to believe in Him practically; and so afterwards to know the true doctrine about Him. Thus if you take St. Paul's early epistles, those of the first two groups, or the first epistle of St. Peter, or the epistle of St. James, you find the Godhead of Jesus Christ more often implied than asserted; but when you advance a step further, you find it dwelt upon, and made explicit and unmistakable, though in language still carefully calculated to guard the unity of God and the truth that in the Father only is the fount of Godhead—as in the great dogmatic passages of St. Paul's epistles to the Philippians and to the Colossians, or in the epistle to the Hebrews, or in St. John's epistles and his Gospel [1].

The language of these writings is such that I say, not only that is there nothing in the decrees of the councils that is not adequately, if untechnically, represented there; but that also, whereas the decrees of the council are of the nature of safeguards, and are rather repudiations of error than sources of positive teaching, the apostolic language is a mine from which, first taught and guided by the creed of the Church, we can draw a continual and inexhaustible wealth of positive teaching. The decrees are but the hedge, the New Testament is the pasture-ground.

[1] See app. note 31, p. 259.

II

Thus to come to details. St. John calls the Word who is Christ Jesus, God with God, God only-begotten. He is represented in the Revelation as the Lamb receiving the adoration given to God : ' Unto him that sitteth on the throne, and unto the Lamb, be the blessing, and the honour, and the glory, and the dominion, for ever and ever.' St. Paul speaks of Him as 'pre-existing in the form, or characteristics, of God,' and as 'God over all.' The author of the epistle to the Hebrews calls Him the ' very image, or counterpart, of God's substance.' The apostolic writers generally identify Him, as Lord, with the Jehovah of the Old Testament. Now if these apostles being all of them monotheist Jews, who knew that God would not give His glory to another, do thus speak of Christ, it is not reasonable to doubt that they would have been with Athanasius against Arius, in affirming the position that Christ, as Son of God, if subordinate to the Father, yet really belongs to God's eternal being [1].

Again, the Evangelists, including St. John, and the author of the epistle to the Hebrews, dwell much on the complete humanity of the Son of man : on the action of the human will in obedience, of the human spirit in prayer, of the human mind even in limitation of knowledge. St. Paul describes Him as taking the characteristics, or form, of man's servile nature. St. Peter speaks of His human spirit, side by side with His human body [2]. Can we doubt, then, that they would have repudiated Apollinarius as warmly as Gregory of Nyssa, and (let me add) more accurately?

---

[1] St. John i. 1, 18 ; Rev. v. 13 ; Phil. ii. 6 ; Rom. ix. 5 ; Heb. i. 3.

[2] 1 St. Peter iii. 18 : on the previous reff. see further, Lecture VI.

Once again, if St. Paul speaks of the Son of God as emptying Himself, beggaring Himself, to become man: if he speaks of the Incarnate as having 'come down' from heaven: if St. John's theology is that of 'the Word made flesh [1]'; is there room for question that they would have emphasized against Nestorius the continuity and unity of Christ's person?

Finally, if St. John is emphatic against all attempts to explain away the reality, and the permanent reality, of Christ's flesh: if he asserts a Christ not only come, but still 'to come in the flesh': if St. Paul takes the present glorified state of Christ as the prototype of our own spiritual body: if the manhood of Christ in heaven is a truth proclaimed under different forms in the Acts of the Apostles and in the epistle to the Hebrews [2]; is it really open to question that the apostolic writers would have regarded Monophysitism or the absorption of manhood into Godhead, as inconsistent with right belief? When once these four problems were really presented to them, though they must have deplored the necessity for formal legislation, they could not, I contend, have refused to answer them, and they must have answered them in one way.

It is then a fact of the most astonishing kind, that the Hibbert Lectures recently published [3],—which result in the position, that the theological propositions of the creed are no part of original Christianity and need be no part of the Christianity of the future, which speak of Christianity as passing from being a rule of life in the beginning

---

[1] Phil. ii. 7 ; 2 Cor. viii. 9; Eph. iv. 9, 10; St. John i. 1 14.

[2] See app. note 32, p. 259.

[3] See app. note 25, p. 252.

to a creed in the process of centuries,—should actually
have left out of consideration the theology of the apostolic writers. Is there theology in St. Paul, St. John, and
even St. James? Does that theology represent or mis-
represent the religion of Jesus Christ? These questions
are not considered. Is the theology of the Nicene creed
any more metaphysical, or only more technical, than the
theology of St. Paul or St. John? This question again
is not considered. Now it seems to me that a book
written about the development of Christian theology,
which omits any real examination of the New Testament writers, is like a work written to account for the
later French empire which should omit any serious consideration of the great Napoleon.

It may then be said with undoubted truth, that between the period of the apostles and the period of the
councils there was a great development of theology.
The Church was gradually learning to use that exact
terminology with which the Greek genius supplied her, to
enshrine her creed. In the process of learning to express their thoughts the Christian theologians made
abundant mistakes; phrases can be produced from
Justin Martyr, or Tertullian, or Dionysius of Alexandria,
or Gregory of Nyssa, which by comparison with accurate
standards must be pronounced inexact or verbally heretical. But these have either to do with the precise statement of truth, or, much less frequently, express some
exceptional opinion adopted by this or that individual
but, on reflection, repudiated by the 'common sense' of
Christians. All along, the traditional faith which men
are endeavouring to express, from Athanasius and
Augustine back to Origen and Tertullian, from Origen

and Tertullian back to Ignatius and Clement, in an un-
broken stream of tradition, is the same faith in the
realities of the Trinity and the Incarnation. Gradually
the most exact and fitting language to express these
verities is elaborated in testing, sifting controversy. A
theory which, like Gnosticism, denied the unity of God
and of the universe, or, like Ebionism, denied the pre-
existence of the Son, can never put in any fair claim to
represent the teaching of the apostles or the tradition
of the churches. As we look back at the issues raised
all down the line of controversy, we see plainly enough
that the rejected heresies do in fact represent, like
Ebionism, a deterioration from the original teaching, or,
like Gnosticism, a subversive and alien doctrine, or,
like Sabellianism and Arianism, a one-sided logic; the
church dogma meanwhile has held the balance and
preserved the apostolic type.

What the Church then borrowed from Greek thought
was her terminology, not the substance of her creed.
Even in regard to her terminology we must make one
important reservation, for Christianity laid all stress on
the personality of God and of man, of which Hellenism
had thought but little. Thus the phrases, ' hypostasis '
or ' persona,' used to express personality, have an altogether new shade of meaning given to them to meet
new needs of thought. Thus even in regard to phraseology, Christianity, in its intense consciousness of personality, had to infuse its own meaning into the terms it
borrowed. Still Greek philosophy did supply the terms,
but the truth to be expressed in them is the original
faith in Jesus Christ the Son of God made Son of man ;
it is nothing else than this which at last, amid the tumult

of controversy, wins its way to clear and impressive
utterance, which rings down the ages in dominant and
unmistakable notes.

## V.

The notes of the catholic creed still ring on, for the
Christian dogmas claim the same permanence as the
Christian Church.

In considering their title to permanence, a great
deal depends on the spirit in which they are approached.
It is necessary that they should be fairly criticised,
but also that they should be appreciated before they
are criticised.   One is inclined to ask, ' breathes there
a man with soul so dead ' as not to feel the title to
veneration which attaches itself to our ancient creeds
merely because they are ancient?   Necessarily a great
deal in human life changes ; science grows, criticism
advances, institutions vary, society makes its way to new
forms of organization, the outward fashions of life pass.
All this is obvious, and inevitable, and the ground of hope
for the future ; but it causes all of us, who are not shallow-
hearted, only to love more intensely anything in human
life which does not change.   For there is underneath
what is variable an unchanging region in man.   It is one
main pleasure in the study of an ancient classical literature
that it enables us to shake hands across the ages with
men of other days and other races, on the basis of a
common manhood.   This common manhood is especially
apparent in the region of poetry and in the region of
religion.   A great poet gets down below the surface,

to what is permanent in us : 'deep in the general heart of men,' Wordsworth says, ' his power survives.' What delights us in the verse of Homer, for instance, is in great measure the simple, noble expression which the poet of so long ago gives to the radical, fundamental passions, sorrows, joys, of men all over the world. Now what is true of poetry is true also of religion—pre-eminently true of the religion founded by Jesus Christ. ' Deep in the general heart of men *His* power survives '; for He evoked into consciousness, and then satisfied, the deepest needs and instincts of human life. Thus He founded a catholic religion, capable of infinite adapta-tion in different societies, but appealing to the manhood which does not change, in the name of an unchanging revelation of God to man, in the person of Jesus Christ, ' the same yesterday, to-day, and for ever.' As a matter of fact, this religion has found expression in creeds which have already during fifteen centuries shown their capacity for permanence through very different states of society. I say then, that any one who is not shallow-hearted in his love of what is modern, must be well-disposed towards the catholic creeds, merely because they are old, because they represent so wide and permanent an assent of the redeemed humanity, because they offer an unchanging basis of definite religious instruction, and a form of religious confession which unites us, as we repeat it, with a great catholic communion of many ages and many nations.

I am not now putting the claim of the creeds to permanence on any ground of authority; all that I am asking is that their value should be first recognised and felt, before they are criticised. When once they are thus appreciated, they can, I feel sure, justify their claims to be legitimate interpreters and guardians of the apostolic faith for the time to come.

Is there, I ask, anything in these dogmas, considered in themselves, which disqualifies them as permanent safeguards of the Christian faith. Surely not, unless they are liable to be superannuated in respect of the questions they raise, or the answers they give, or in respect to the phraseology in which they give their answers. But the questions they raise are the permanent questions, of as vital moment to-day as ever before. Is Christ indeed, as Son of God, really God? Is His character God's character, His love God's love? Or again, is He really man in human sympathies and human faculties, really tempted, really tried? Or again, is He God incarnate, made man for our redemption, not a splendid example merely of one man deified? Or again, is He still truly human in nature and sympathy? These are living problems, vital to the preaching of the gospel, vital to the general heart of man. Their solution in the creeds is the solution necessary to safeguard apostolic Christianity. To answer them in the opposite sense, or not to answer them at all, is, in different degrees, to allow the foundations of the Christian gospel to be undermined. Lastly, the language in which they express their decisions shows no signs of being antiquated.

It may be truly said of the dogma of transubstantiation that it is couched in terms of a distinction of substance and accidents which belongs only to a particular moment in philosophy: or again of a popular doctrine of the atonement, that it is couched in language which does violence to man's moral sense ; but the dogmatic language of the Council of Chalcedon is open to no such objection. Its language is permanent language, none the less permanent because Greek. The Greek language was in fact fitted, as none other ever has been, to furnish an exact and permanent terminology for doctrinal purposes. The ideas of substance or thing, of personality, of nature, are permanent ideas ; we cannot get rid of them ; no better words could be suggested to express the same facts ; the same creeds have been found equally dear to the heart of Greek and Roman and Teuton, in the age of Greek philosophy, in the age of mediaeval barbarism, among the scholastic philosophers, in the modern nations since the reformation. In our own country they have regained their ancient value since the 'seculum rationalisticum' of the last century : they show no signs of losing their importance in the mind of those who hold, or desire to teach, the truths of the New Testament.

But we need always to distinguish the permanence, from the adequacy, of our dogmatic language. It is as good as human language can be, but it is not adequate. Human language never can express adequately divine realities. A constant tendency to apologize for human speech, a great element of agnosticism, an awful sense of unfathomed depths beyond the little that is made known, is always present to the minds of theologians who know what they are about, in conceiving or expressing God. ' We see,' says St. Paul, ' in a mirror, in terms of a riddle ;' ' we know in part.' ' We are compelled,' complains St. Hilary, ' to attempt what is unattainable, to climb where we cannot reach, to speak what we cannot utter : instead of the mere adoration of

faith, we are compelled to entrust the deep things of
religion to the perils of human expression [1].'

## VI.

Let me conclude by asking you to entertain three
considerations, calculated not to diminish, but to re-
strain within just limits, our sense of the value of the
dogmatic decrees of the councils on the subject of the
person of Jesus Christ.

(1) The form of these dogmas, as distinct from the
creeds, is negative rather than positive. They are intended to say 'no' rather than 'yes,' to deny rather
than to teach. This is apparent from their history. Certain interpretations of the old faith had been suggested,
calculated to undermine its foundations, and the Church
met them with a negative. Test-words, selected to embody these negations, were adopted to guard the old faith,
without adding to it, by simply blocking off false lines
of development or explanation on this side or on that.
An indirect positive influence these negations undoubtedly had, but it was indirect and unintended. The old
sources of positive information remained the same, the
creed to initiate and the Scriptures to give further
enlightenment. Nothing in fact can exceed the urgency
with which the Fathers press upon all Christian people
the obligation of building themselves up in the knowledge of the faith by intercourse with Scripture. This
was a principle of great importance. Would that it had
been continuously borne in mind! But in fact the

---

[1] S. Hil. *De Trin.* ii. 2, 4.

dogmatic decisions of the Church, like other good things, have been greatly misused. And how? By being treated as sources of our positive information about Christ, practically overriding the Gospel picture.

Thus the Gospels present us with a Christ, divine and human, whose personality, if complex and difficult to analyze, yet presents a marvellous and impressive unity. The four great dogmas are our guides in contemplating the picture, and the Gospels respond to the anticipations which they raise, and fill up the meagre outline into a living whole. They show us a Christ, really one with God and really made man; Himself God, but acting in love to us under conditions of growth and experience and limitation and suffering and victory, which really belong to the manhood which He took— took, not as the veil of His glory merely, but as the real sphere of His action. But take up a mediaeval or later dogmatic treatise on the Incarnation, and follow the course of the argument. It lays down first of all the fundamental dogmas, and then proceeds to argue that such and such results must follow. As the manhood is taken into personal union with the Godhead, so as man, Jesus Christ must have possessed, infused into His manhood, all that it is capable of receiving, and that from the first; but manhood is capable of enjoying the fulness of the beatific vision, the knowledge of all things past, present, and future; therefore the manhood of Christ had all knowledge of past, present, and future, and the fulness of the beatific vision; therefore, He can never have been ignorant even in His human mind. He can never have grown to know what He did not know before. He can never have experienced any break in the vision of

God. Athwart the course of such abstract argumentation occur interjected certain isolated texts of Scripture : ' Of that day and that hour knoweth no man, no, not the Son.' ' He grew in wisdom.' He cried, ' My God, my God, why hast thou forsaken me ? ' Rapidly they are explained away. Alternative ' interpretations ' are suggested, which in fact do not interpret, but contradict ; and we are assured that our Lord only seemed to grow in wisdom, but really had no need for growth, or said He did not know, meaning only that He would not tell, or cried out as if He were desolate, while in fact He was never really deprived of the consolations of the Father's presence. Thus we are led on through a series of deductions, drawn syllogistically from the abstract dogmas considered as positive sources of information—the isolated Bible texts being used only as illustrations, or as supplying material to be explained away. This is the misuse of dogma, not its use. The dogmas are only limits, negatives which block false lines of development, notice-boards which warn us off false approaches, guiding us down the true road to the figure in the Gospels, and leaving us to contemplate it unimpeded and with the frankest gaze.

(2) In the idea of the Fathers of the councils it was only necessity which justified their dogmatic decisions : it was not supposed that the Church was better off for religious knowledge, in virtue of these specific requirements, in advance of the old baptismal creed, or that it was the Church's function to develop them, to God's glory and man's good. It was simply that an insidious form of misbelief appeared within the Church, calculated to undermine her life, and that circumstances facilitated,

and prudence suggested, a particular way of meeting the danger. A new word, a new formula, like the ὁμοούσιος, was, as such, an object of suspicion. We, with our experience, may shrink from calling these dogmatic decisions 'necessary evils,' because we may feel, not only that they have acted as safeguards of true Christian belief through dull and irreligious periods, but also that the faith has really been better expressed in their terms and in consequence better understood. But we shall not fall into the error of supposing that the test of a Church's spiritual power, the test of its vital development, is the amount of its dogmatic requirement. It is very possible that a framework of dogma was necessary for the Church, but that it is a real good only within very moderate limits. On the basis of a moderate amount of central dogma, it may be the discipline intended for every Christian, that he should grow according to the measure of his opportunity and capacity into a fuller and fuller perception of the meaning of the faith. If we consider that in society a little government, a certain amount of external enactment regulating life, is a good, but over-legislation is an evil, it is obvious that a similar reserve of theological legislation may be the ideal for the Church. It may have been desirable to guard dogmatically the central truths of Christ's person, but undesirable, quite apart from questions of truth or error, to do the same for the dependent doctrines. All the Church's positive teaching need not be made matter of dogmatic requirement. At least it is a fact, that the dogmas which have the assent of the whole Church and which are imposed in the English Church, are few in number, and we can see in this the hand of providence.

(3) As concerns the method of the conciliar action, I would ask you to note how the appeal of the Church is apparently less intellectual than that of the different heretical teachers, but issues in a deeper, more rational, position.

Arius appealed chiefly to logic: of a shallow sort we feel, but still logic: as that 'a son must be younger than his father.' Apollinarius appealed to certain abstract conceptions of the divine unchangeableness, and to a current psychology of human nature. Nestorius took his stand on an extreme doctrine of human liberty or indeterminateness. The Church in all cases made its appeal to tradition, Scripture, and the practical needs of redemption : when she was satisfied as to the result of this threefold appeal, she spoke decisively, and left it to theologians and philosophers afterwards to show the reasonableness of her action. Her function was only to guard a deposit. But in the result it is not hard to see that the logic of Arius, or Apollinarius, or Nestorius, was one-sided and very far from final, while a far deeper philosophy underlies the *via media* of the Church. 'The foolishness of God is wiser than men.'

This will become plainer as we go on, but I ask you to notice before we separate that the reproof given to a hasty logic in these ecclesiastical decisions is specially wholesome in the sphere of the Incarnation. St. Paul in the passage which I made my text, as elsewhere, teaches us that the right way to understand the action of God in the Incarnation is to contemplate it morally. It is an act of moral self-denial such as can be an example to us men in our efforts at sympathy and self-sacrifice. 'Let this mind be in you which was also in Christ Jesus.'

But after all, all such efforts on our part do more or less defy logical analysis. The power of sympathy is a power of self-abandonment, or self-effacement, which enables a man to abjure the platform of a rightful superiority, and enter into the conditions of another person's experience, thinking with his thoughts, seeing with his eyes, feeling as he ought to feel, and so raising him, as it were, from within. Of such self-abandoning sympathy the Incarnation of God is the prototype: it is more intelligible to the heart than to the head: but this is exactly what is true of all self-sacrifice and sympathy. Logic cannot analyze the phrases, 'self-surrender,' 'entering into another's pain,' yet they express realities. We cannot get far with logic, then, in understanding the method of divine love. Its value is negative rather than positive. It is not the platform of the schools on which we must take our stand for an effective vision ; it is not the abstract consideration of divine attributes, to which we must trust for insight into the mystery, whether applied on the side of rationalism or of dogmatism. We must approach the matter rather with the moral conception of deliberate sympathy, such as does not save *de haut en bas* by acts of power from its own vantage-ground, but comes down into another's condition to lift him from below. 'Let this mind be in you which was also in Christ Jesus, who, pre-existing in the characteristics of God, thought not equality with God a prize to be clutched at, but emptied Himself, and took the characteristics of a servant, and was made in the likeness of men : and being found in fashion as a man, He humbled Himself, and became obedient, unto death, even the death of the cross. Wherefore God also highly

exalted Him, and bestowed upon Him the name that is
above every name, that at the name of Jesus every
knee should bow, of things in heaven, and things in earth,
and things under the earth; and every tongue should
confess that Jesus Christ is Lord, to the glory of God the
Father.'

# LECTURE V.

## GOD REVEALED IN CHRIST.

*Neither doth any know the Father, save the Son, and he to whomsoever the Son willeth to reveal him.*—St. Matthew xi. 27.
*He that hath seen me hath seen the Father.*—St. John xiv. 9.

MANY passages in the apostolic writings form a commentary on these words of our Lord about Himself. 'No man hath seen God at any time,' says St. John; 'God only begotten, which is in the bosom of the Father, he hath declared him[1].' He is 'the image of God,' or 'the image of the invisible God,' says St. Paul[2]. He is 'the express image of his substance,' writes the author of the Epistle to the Hebrews[3]. These words of our Lord and of His apostolic interpreters convey the same impression. The Son reveals the Father, the apparent Christ reveals the unapparent God. He alone does this, or can do this; and He can do it without any risk of mistake, because He is essentially the Father's image. We can contemplate therefore the intelligible lineaments of the human character of Jesus, and in Him indeed behold the very God. 'We beheld his glory,' St. John bears witness, 'glory as of the only begotten from the Father'; 'the glory of God in the face of Jesus Christ,' says St. Paul[4].

---

[1] St. John i. 18 (R.V. marg.).
[2] 2 Cor. iv. 4; Col. i. 15.
[3] Heb. i. 3.
[4] St. John i 14; 2 Cor. iv. 6.

1

## I.

When the fathers of the council of Nicæa insisted so strenuously on the doctrine of the one substance of the Son and the Father—the doctrine, that is, that the Son belongs to the Father's eternal nature, and is not a mere subsequent creation of His will—they were influenced by no consideration more seriously than by the practical needs of redemption.  Christ is our salvation, because in being united to Him, we are united to nothing less than God Himself.  But a most important element of salvation is revelation.  Man in being united to God is to know God, and here again everything depends upon the truth about Christ's person.  For the Christian revelation is not a mere message about God, it is the unveiling of God.  We are to contemplate Christ, that human character, so profound yet so intelligible, its methods, its motives, its principles—and we are to know that it is not the character of any mere creature, but of God Himself.  A creature can never be complete.  One quality belongs to one, another to another ; no one occupies the whole ground of possible existence.  If Christ is only a creature, His qualities can only occupy a certain space in the area of God's revelation of Himself.  We have not got to what is ultimate and all-embracing in getting to Him.  But if He is God, it makes all the difference ; in Him dwells, not one quality of God, but 'all the fulness of the Godhead bodily [1].'  His love is the ultimate love.  The relation which love holds to justice or to any other quality in Him, is the relation which it

[1] Col. ii. 9.

holds in the ultimate reality; His aims are God's aims; His will God's will; His victory God's victory. No different or more real power lies behind Him. Here is the ultimate secret. This is, St. John says, the genuine God, made intelligible and interpreted in the manhood of His Son[1].

Some thirty-three years ago, a great controversy was originated in this pulpit by a Bampton lecturer, who took for his subject, ' The limits of religious thought[2].' Dean Mansel held in little esteem the pretensions of the Hegelian school in Germany to criticize by the standard of rationality the contents of divine revelation. Revelation, he held, was a fact. We had evidence that it had really been given, and certificated by miracles. On this evidence all the stress must be laid. Granted that it is cogent, we must accept the revelation as it has been given. We have not the faculties necessary to criticize what God has been pleased to tell us about Himself. ' Nay but, O man, who art thou that repliest against God?'

Unfortunately Mansel did not confine himself to re-emphasizing Butler's strong protest, as valuable to-day as in the last century, against the easy over-estimate of the powers of the human mind to judge *à priori* of what is probable in a divine revelation. He went further, and exposed himself to the charge of denying that we have, or can have, any real and direct knowledge of God Himself at all. ' We cannot know what God is,' he seemed to say, ' but only what He chooses us to believe about Himself.' Thus we cannot, for example, argue against a certain doctrine of the atonement on the ground of its injustice or hardness, because we do not know what

[1] 1 St. John v. 20.       [2] See app. note 33, p. 260.

justice or goodness in God means.  Human qualities are
not necessarily of the same sort as the divine.

   This form of Christian apology produced an indignant
protest from Frederick Denison Maurice, and drew from
John Stuart Mill the passionate exclamation : ' I will call
no being good who is not what I mean when I apply that
epithet to my fellow-creatures, and if such a being can
sentence me to hell for not so calling him, to hell I will
go[1].'  It was an exclamation, not easy to accommodate
to the philosophy of the greatest pleasure, but it finds a
response without a doubt in the Christian conscience.
For if anthropomorphism as applied to God is false, if
God does not exist in man's image, yet theomorphism as
applied to man is true ; man is made in God's image, and
his qualities are, not the measure of the divine, but their
counterpart and real expression.

   Man was made in God's image.  The significance of
this truth from our present point of view is, that in that
original constitution of manhood lies, as the Fathers saw,
the prophecy of the divine Incarnation and the grounds
of its possibility.  God can express Himself in His own
image, He can express Himself therefore in manhood,
He can show Himself as man.  And conversely, in the
occurrence of the Incarnation lies the supreme evidence
of the real moral likeness of man to God.  All along,
through the Old Testament, inspired teachers with growing spirituality of conception had been expressing God in
terms of manhood—taking the human love of the mother
for her child, or of the husband for his adulterous wife, to
explain the divine love : and in the Incarnation all this
finds its justification.  In the person of the Incarnate

---

[1] See *Exam. of Sir W. Hamilton's Philosophy* (Longmans, 1872), p. 129.

we see how true it has been all along that man is in
God's image: for this is man, Jesus of Nazareth ; His
qualities are human qualities, love and justice, self-
sacrifice and desire and compassion ; yet they are the
qualities of none other than the very God.   So akin are
God and man to one another that God can really exist
under conditions of manhood without ceasing to be, and
to reveal, God ; and man can be taken to be the organ of
Godhead without one whit ceasing to be human.   Here
in Christ Jesus, it is man's will, man's love, man's mind,
which are the instruments of Godhead, and the fulness
of the Godhead which is revealing itself only seems to
make these qualities more intensely human.


## II.

We have then in Jesus Christ a real knowledge of
God, expressed in terms of humanity.   What then is it
in our knowledge of God which was brought to light, or
at least finally guaranteed, in His incarnation ?

(1) In the first place let us rank His personality.   Of
course this truth was not first intimated in the Incarnation.   It had been subject-matter of the older revelation.   And, though in fact it is doubtful whether a clear
sense of one personal God has ever been arrived at by
any race, except as an outcome more or less direct of
God's revelation of Himself to Abraham, yet there are
arguments which of themselves strongly suggest God's
personality, and which many modern philosophers, such
as Lotze and Martineau, have found irresistibly cogent.
But in Christ our sense of God's personality is raised at
least to a new level of certainty and intensity, and with

it the corresponding sense of personality in man as well.

Compare Christianity with a system based on an opposite principle, and observe the contrast. To the Buddhist personality is an evil, a hindrance: spiritual progress lies in the gradual evacuation of consciousness, of desire, in a word, of personality. With Christ, the case is the opposite : ' I am come,' He said, ' that they may have life—full personal conscious life—and may have it abundantly.' 'Whosoever shall lose his soul, or life, for my sake, the same shall save it[1].' For the elimination of selfishness is only to strengthen personality. So Christ attends to, respects, developes, educates personality in His little band of apostles ; and that because to become like Him, they must realize personality in its depth, its fulness, its distinctiveness. In Him it was no accident, nothing which He had assumed for a time or of which He could rid Himself; it belonged to His eternal nature ; over against the Father in the eternal world, He stood person with person, a son with His father. It was because He was eternally personal that He had been able to give personality to a human nature[2]. Yes, as we gaze at the personal Christ, incarnate God, we are sure that whatever else God is, above and beyond what we understand by personality, —and we can depend upon it that He is infinitely above and beyond what we can comprehend,—yet He is at least personal; for He has manifested His personality to us, and made it intelligible, in a human nature, while on the other hand the human nature loses

---

[1] St. John x. 10 ; St. Luke ix. 24.
[2] See app. note 34, p. 260.

not one whit of its humanity because the personality which is acting in it is the personality of very God.

(2) Secondly, we are taught by the Incarnation that the quality of the divine personality is love.

The thought of the fatherhood of God, in that moral sense which implies His love, is so familiar, at least superficially, to us, that the less thoughtful among us are apt to assume it as something self-evident; as if it were a matter of course apart from Christ's revelation. But it does not require much thought to enable us to perceive, or much bitter experience, or much sympathy, to enable us to feel, that the world apart from Christ gives us no adequate assurance that God is Love. The Psalmist indeed argues, 'He that made the eye, shall He not see?' and Robert Browning has taught us to add: 'He that created love, shall He not love?' But, if love in man argues love in God, whose offspring he is, yet there is much on the other hand to give us pause in drawing such a conclusion. Not only the inexorable, remorseless aspect of physical nature seems against it, but also the fact that love even in humanity, as we contemplate it 'writ large' in history, appears often feeble and helpless by the side of his lust, his bitterness, his cruelty, his selfishness, his untrustworthiness. That God is love means, of course, not merely that there exists such a thing as love in the world, nor merely that it represents something in God. It carries with it also the assurance that love is the motive of creation, and the realization of the purpose of love its certain goal: that love exists in that supreme perfection in which the universality of its range over all creatures diminishes nothing from its particular

application to each individual. That love is God's motive ;
that love is victorious ; that love is universal in range
and unerringly individual in application, in a word that
*God is love*—it is this that our Lord guarantees, because
He has translated divine love into the intelligible lineaments of the corresponding human quality.  We behold
in Jesus love the motive, love individualizing, love impartial and universal, love victorious through death ; and
he that hath seen Him, we know, hath seen the Father ;
His love is the Father's love ; there is nothing behind
it to overcome it, nothing outside it to escape it, nothing
below it to be too small for it.  This is the Christian
gospel.

We must observe that this revelation of the love of
God is not like a scientific discovery, which once made
and published is independent of its originator, and would
be in no way affected if his personality were to fade into
darkness or oblivion.  For Jesus Christ did not satisfy
our minds with arguments, He did not solve objections,
or show us why pain and sacrifice are necessary throughout creation ; nay He did not even declare God's love as
a dogma and prove it by miracles.  The gospel lies in
His person.  He took upon Himself all that tells against
divine love, all that has ever wrung from men's hearts
the bitter words of unbelief, or the more chastened cry
of agonizing enquiry, ' My God, My God, why hast thou
forsaken me ? '  He took all this upon Himself, and as
the man of sorrows, made it, in His bitter passion and
death upon the cross, the very occasion for expressing
the depth of the divine self-sacrifice.  Thus the satisfaction that He gives us lies in His proving to us, out of
the very heart of all that might seem to speak against

such a conclusion, that behind all the groaning and
travailing of creation lies the love of God, and beyond it
all the victory of God ; and the demonstration consists in
the fact that Jesus as essential Son of the Father reveals
no other love than God's, and by His resurrection from
the dead manifests that love triumphant through all
seeming failure. If He was not God, He manifested no
more than any other good man, namely, that there is
such a thing as goodness and self-sacrifice to be set
against the selfish treachery of Judas, and malice of
Caiaphas, and weakness of Pilate, and indifference of the
Jews ; and if He did not rise from the dead we have lost
altogether the thrilling security which His life has
afforded to the weakest of the faithful of final victory.
Certainly, it is only because Jesus is God that we have
our gospel for the world ; but grant that, and love is, not
the first word, but the last word, in God's disclosure of
Himself ; love is God's motive ; love forgets no single
individual ; love goes all lengths of sacrifice ; love in the
universe works on through all failures to its victorious
issue [1].

(3) Thirdly, we look again at the love of God as Christ
manifests it, and we notice that it is in no isolation from
those other qualities of God His justice, His truth —
which belong, we may say, to His earlier revelation of
Himself. The love of God is no mere benevolence
which simply desires to make man happy anyhow, in
any condition. God's love created man for fellowship
with Himself. 'The glory of God,' Irenaeus grandly
says, ' is the living man; the life of man is the vision of
God [2].' Thus, as God's love created man for fellowship

---

[1] See app. note 35, p. 260.          [2] St. Iren. c. haer. iv. 20. 7.

with Himself, so His love goes out in redemption to bring men back, by boundless self-sacrifice, into that fellowship, when it had been lost. 'God was in Christ reconciling the world unto himself.' *Unto Himself*: thus love goes out to call men back; it goes out as a summons, a claim, an invitation, to something high and holy, even God's presence. This it is that makes love awful. 'The sinners in Zion,' cries Isaiah, 'are afraid; trembling hath surprised the godless ones. Who among us shall dwell with the devouring fire? who among us shall dwell with everlasting burnings[1]?' This fire, this everlasting burning fire is nothing else than the divine holiness, which forces men to feel 'they could not breathe in that fine air, that pure severity of perfect light.'

Thus it is that Christ's love, God's love, contains in itself, as it goes forth to redeem, the element of severity, of judgment. God will go all lengths of self-sacrifice to supply us with the motives and means to return to Him. His mercy interposes with His justice, it interposes delays, it tries all expedients: 'let the barren fig tree alone this year also,' it pleads, 'till I shall dig about it, and dung it; and if it bear fruit thenceforth, well'; but at the last issue justice must prevail, 'if not, thou shalt cut it down[2].' Thus mercy, rejoicing against judgment, must prepare for judgment at the last; because in God there is perfect reality, unalterable truth. We can trust Him utterly to give to all men in this life, or beyond it, a real chance of knowing God as He is, and of accepting His love. Christ, in fact, has proved that He wills all men to be saved and come to

---

[1] Is. xxxiii. 14.    [2] St. Luke xiii. 8, 9.

the knowledge of the truth, that He is infinitely considerate of the cases and circumstances of individuals :
but on the other hand Christ has proved, and we must
take account of it, that 'mercy and truth meet together,'
and that 'righteousness turns again to judgment'; that
God deals in justice at the last with the use that each
soul has made of its opportunities.

For listen to the Christ of the Gospels.  He speaks
plain words as to our unfitness, in the present condition
of our nature, for His spiritual purposes.   He cannot
commit Himself to any man, because He knows what
is in man ;  He demands conversion ;   He requires a
new birth.   He is indeed infinitely encouraging to all
who will make a start for good, to the adulterous
woman, to the penitent thief :  He is infinitely patient
with slow and timorous progress like that of Nicodemus or of His own Apostles :  He is royal-hearted in
the recognition which He gives to ignorant goodness
like that of the heathen who ministered unknowingly
to Him in the least of His brethren, or that of the man
who was casting out devils in His name, but followed
not with the apostolic company; but, none the less, He
is terrible in His severity to those who are obsti-
nately deaf to calls, who are stereotyped in a routine of
respectability and satisfied with themselves as they are ;
who are outwardly professors of religion, but selfish and
covetous within.   'Woe unto you,' he cries, 'scribes and
Pharisees, hypocrites, . . . how shall ye escape the judgment of hell[1] ? '  Yes, He who sets such value on human
life, who sacrificed Himself so utterly for it, shrinks not a
whit from announcing the inexorable penalties of wilful

---

[1] St. Matt. xxiii. 29, 33.

sin, of the wilful repudiation of the light; 'this is the judgment, that the light is come into the world, and men loved the darkness rather than the light; for their works were evil.'  Men may repudiate an external message and be comparatively guiltless, because they may do it ignorantly, not knowing what they do; they may 'speak a word against the Son of man' and be forgiven: but there is an inner visitant to the heart of man, there is a witness of the Holy Ghost within, and there is a point where the deliberate repudiation of this inner light becomes the blasphemy against the Holy Ghost which passes the limits of forgiveness; there is a sin which 'shall not be forgiven, neither in this world, nor in that which is to come.'  Not surely because God loses the willingness to forgive; but (must it not be?) because sin has become the ingrained and inextricable habit of the soul; the man is 'guilty of an eternal sin [1].'

### III.

We touch here upon a moral law, the law of moral deterioration, the law that who will not, at last can not. It is part of that larger law, in accordance with which all acts of will form habits, and habits stereotype into character, and character becomes indelible; and the fact of its recognition by Jesus Christ leads us to notice another element in His revelation of the Father.

He is constantly calling attention to certain laws in accordance with which God works in spiritual matters. It is easy to give examples: 'If ye forgive men their trespasses, your heavenly Father will also forgive you.

[1] St. Matt. xii. 32; St. Mark iii. 29.

But if ye forgive not men their trespasses, neither will your heavenly Father forgive your trespasses.' 'With what judgment ye judge, ye shall be judged: and with what measure ye mete, it shall be measured unto you.' 'Every one that asketh receiveth, and he that seeketh findeth, and to him that knocketh it shall be opened.' 'Whosoever hath, to him shall be given, and he shall have abundance: but whosoever hath not, from him shall be taken away even that which he hath.' 'Except a grain of wheat fall into the ground and die it abideth by itself alone; but if it die, it beareth much fruit.' 'He that loveth his life (or soul) loseth it; and he that hateth his life (or soul) in this world shall keep it unto life eternal[1].' These are divine laws which Christ enunciates.

Law prevails, we learn, as much in the spiritual as in the physical world. This is nowhere more strikingly illustrated than in our Lord's teaching about prayer. Faith, we are led to believe, can obtain by prayer the accomplishment of its desires, but it is the faith which is in union with Jesus, that is to say in deliberate harmony with the mind and method of the Father. 'If ye abide in me, and my words abide in you, ask whatsoever ye will, and it shall be done unto you[2].'

Thus the very sequence of petitions in the Lord's prayer contradicts as forcibly as possible the crude notion that prayer is an arbitrary process, by which we induce God to do what we happen to want, and drag His action down to the level of our short-sighted desires. The very sequence of the petitions forces us first to exalt God's glory—His name, or disclosure of Himself –above

[1] St. Matt. vi. 14, 15; vii. 2, 8; xiii. 12; St. John xii. 25.
[2] St. John xv. 7 10.

man's need, and to make our first prayer, 'hallowed be
thy name'; then it lifts us to the contemplation of a
divine kingdom, yet to be realized, and teaches us to
merge our petty wants in the great purpose of the
Father: 'thy kingdom come.' Next it overshadows us
with the sense of a divine will, the execution of which
is the law of the unseen world, and it forces us to find in
submission to this our true liberty and power: 'thy
will be done as in heaven, so on earth.' Only at this
point are we allowed to express our own need; and,
even so, it is our bare need and not our extravagant
wishes: 'give us to-day our bread for the coming day.'
And because we cannot serve God, unless we are at
peace with Him, therefore we pray for forgiveness of our
debts; not anyhow, but in accordance with the law, that
God deals with us as we deal with our fellow men:
'forgive us our debts, as we also have forgiven our
debtors.' And because we depend utterly upon the
divine protection, therefore we conclude, 'bring us not
into temptation, but deliver us from the evil one.'
Surely the mere sequence of these petitions makes it
impossible to attribute any arbitrary power to prayer.
Its power, we learn,—the power of our sonship—is not
power to override God's law, but to co-operate with it,
it depends on our intelligent co-operation with the divine
method [1].

It was the enunciation of this truth, in the region of
natural philosophy, which has made men think of Lord
Bacon as the prophet of modern science. 'Nature,' he
said, 'can only be controlled by being obeyed.' But
the principle had already found rich expression, in re-

[1] See app. note 38, p. 261.

gard to the whole of God's universe, in the spirit and teaching of Jesus Christ. The truth that God works by law appears not only in His words, but in all the circumstances of His appearance.

Thus His manifestation is the outcome of slow-working forces, 'in the fulness of the time [1].' As manifested, He is a miraculous person, yet, as was pointed out, His miracles are not arbitrary portents, they are the proper phenomena of His supernatural nature. They themselves exhibit a law—a law of correspondence with faith; 'according to their faith it is done' to men, and 'Jesus could do no mighty works,' where there was no belief. Moreover the Christ being what He was, was introduced into the world of law to set new forces at work in it, but as part of the old system. In this sense too, He was 'born under the law.' That is to say, He showed Himself as He was, and then let circumstances take their course with him. Thus the death of Christ was not, as people sometimes seem to have imagined, God's act, it was man's act: it was the crime by which the sin of the world betrayed its true character. Of God it is said in the matter that He spared not His only Son [2]. He suffered all to go on, according to the deep-working order of the world, even to His death; and the Son co-operating with the Father exempted not Himself, evoked no miraculous protection, but gave Himself as the Father gave Him. Nor was this merely the hiding of God's power; it is the method of His power, its constant method.

Thus what is true of Christ, is true of the church which is to represent Him. There is nothing arbitrary

[1] Gal. iv. 4; Heb. i. 1, 2.  [2] See app. note 37, p. 261.

or capricious about our Lord's method of preparing for
the church, by the choice and training of His disciples ;
everywhere He respects the limits which moral character
sets to spiritual influence ; slowly, deliberately, the moral
materials are collected, and adapted, for the spiritual
fabric. Again all the anticipations which our Lord
raised in the minds of His disciples as to the future
method of the kingdom, are in accordance with this
respect for law, and correspond with what has actually
occurred since He left the world. The church has been
at work with a supernatural presence to rely upon, but
bound up with natural processes of the world's order, as
leaven, or salt, or seed operates in physical nature.

The same principle had already appeared in the church
of the Old Testament. As a whole it presents a striking
example of gradual operation, according to a law that
can be traced. When Gnosticism, emphasizing the imper-
fections of the Old Testament and the contrast which it
presents to the New, declared the Old Testament the
work of another and a hostile God, the Christian Church,
with a splendidly true instinct, insisted upon the right
conception of God's gradual method. In the old co-
venant, they said, things 'had their origin and beginning,
with us their extension and completion [1].'

Such is the 'tranquil operation' of God in spiritual
matters, and it is akin to the physical development.
Thus Augustine, with other ancient teachers, anticipates
modern views by suggesting that nature, as we now see
it, represents a gradual evolution from original germs [2].
Of course recent knowledge of natural processes has
greatly emphasized this conception ; slowly, we know, in

[1] See app. note 38, p. 262.　　　　[2] Cf. app. note 39, p. 262.

the struggle for existence, by tentative advances, through painfully-secured results, has the end been realized, and the developed product attained.   There is harmony here, wonderful harmony, between the spiritual and physical methods of God ; and the result of all we know of God's working in nature and in Christ is thus to modify some popular notions of the divine omnipotence.   In accurate theology God has been generally regarded as inherent in nature as well as transcending it ; as working out a divine purpose *in* the whole ordered system.   The system, the laws, are regarded as, in a certain sense, limiting Him, only because they express His mind.   God is limited by no force external to Himself, but by His own being ; and the laws of nature are, therefore, limits in His working, only so far as they express something of that law of perfect reason, that fundamental law, 'against which,' says St. Augustine, 'God can no more work than He can work against Himself[1].'

This conception of a self-limited God, a God whose very being is law, has never vanished from the best theology, but it has been seriously obscured in much theology, and in popular conception.   In part this has been due to the spirit of western imperialism, which led men to conceive of God externally, as the great un-fettered monarch of all worlds.   In part to Calvinism with its doctrine of arbitrary and irrational decrees[2].   In part again it has been due to Lutheranism, with its theory of an unreal imputation of sin and of merit : a theory which represents God's action as lawless and unaccountable.   In part, as the inheritor of these earlier systems, to English eighteenth century theology, with its thought

[1] See app. note 40, p. 263.        [2] See app. note 41, p. 263.

K

of a remote God, whose presence is seen in occasional interventions in the order of nature. More than to all specified systems, it has been due to the tendency always present in the vulgar imagination, to see the Divine rather in what is portentous and unaccountable than in what is orderly and tranquil ; to think of power, not as what works through law, but as what triumphs over it. Thus it is that God's omnipotence has been understood to mean, not His universal power in and over all things which works patiently and unerringly in the slow-moving process to the far-off event, but rather the unfettered despot's freedom to do anything anyhow. Thus it has not been without excuse supplied by Christians that Mr. Cotter Morison has represented the grace, which Christianity proclaims, as an arbitrary or even demoralizing action of divine benevolence[1]. But certainly such a representation is without excuse in the best theology. The action of Jesus Christ before His ascension, and after it to the present moment, is action by law and method, action which is in direct continuity with the system of natural laws, physical and moral. Certainly we cannot contemplate God in the person of Jesus Christ without apprehending that the divine power works, and must work, by law.

## IV.

It is impossible for any person to disclose his mind and will towards others, without at the same time letting them see something of his inner self. Thus it was, as we may say, in the process of revealing God's mind externally towards man, that our Lord gave us also that insight

[1] See Mr. C. Morison, *Service of Man* (Kegan Paul, 1887), pp. 92 ff.

into His inner being which is expressed in the doctrine of the Trinity.

It is important to notice that there is no moment when Jesus Christ expressly reveals this doctrine. It was overheard, rather than heard. It was simply, that in the gradual process of intercourse with Him, His disciples came to recognise Father, Son, and Holy Ghost as included in their deepening and enlarging thought of God. Christ was often speaking of His relation as Son to the Father, nor did He ever allow His disciples to confuse their sonship with His : He spoke of 'my Father' and of ' your Father,' never—except when dictating to them the words of their prayer—of 'our Father.'   His Sonship belonged to that transcendental being of His, which in spite of all the close human fellowship which they enjoyed with Him, the disciples could not fail to recognise and to acknowledge.   In the higher world He stood in the intimate relationship of a son, an only son, to a father. Moreover He spoke not only of the Father, but also of the Holy Ghost as in a sense greater than Himself upon earth, and as a person who, like Himself, could be blasphemed ; plainly as in the fullest sense divine.   In His last discourse, it appeared that the Holy Ghost was to take His own place when He had gone.   He was to be His vicar and substitute in the hearts of the apostles, and in the church.   It appeared also, that though He was to be the divine person with whom the disciples were to be in most immediate contact, yet He was third, not second, among the sacred Three, proceeding from, and sent from, the Father and the Son.   Moreover it became plain that these divine Three were not distinct individuals, who could act separately or apart ; there

appeared an inseparable unity and 'co-inherence' among
them.   Thus the coming of the Holy Ghost was not
merely to supply the absence of the Son, but to complete
His presence.   In the coming of the Spirit the Son too
was to come ; in the coming of the Son, also the Father.
' He will come unto you,' ' I will come unto you,' ' We
will come unto you,' are interchangeable phrases[1].   The
process is not easy to describe, but it came about that
the apostles learned to think of Father, Son, and Holy
Ghost as included in the being of God, and that without wavering for a moment in their sense of the divine
unity.   The name of the one God, as our Lord finally
named it in the formula of baptism, is the name of the
Father and of the Son and of the Holy Ghost.

It is remarkable that the apostles seem to have experienced no intellectual difficulty in regard to this
Trinity in the Godhead.   I suppose this is to be accounted
for, by the fact that difficulties in logic do not trouble
us at all where facts of experience are in question.   Thus
we are often ludicrously at fault in attempting to give a
logical account of quite familiar experiences, for example,
of the inner relations of those three strangely independent
elements of our own spiritual being, will and reason and
feeling[2], or of the relation of mind and body.   But our
inability to explain facts logically goes no way at all to
alter our sense of their reality.   Now the apostles lived in
a vivid sense of experienced intercourse, first with the
Son, then with the Father through the Son, later with the
Holy Ghost, and with the Father and the Son through
the Holy Ghost.   This vivid experience, outward and inward, made logical formulas unnecessary.   When the

[1] St. John xiv. 16-23.          [2] See app. note 42, p. 264.

formula of the Trinity—three Persons in one Substance
—was developed in the Church later on, through the
cross-questioning of heresies, it was with many apologies
for the inadequacy of human language, and with a deep
sense of the inscrutableness of God.   The formula was
simply intended to express and guard the realities disclosed in the person of Jesus Christ, and great stress was
laid on the divine unity.   The three Persons are not
separable individuals, so that it could be argued that
what one of the sacred three does another does not do,
as we commonly argue about persons amongst ourselves,
regarding each person as separate and exclusive of
others.   God in three is inseparably one.   Thus if He
creates, it is the Father through the Son by the Holy
Ghost ; if He redeems, it is the Father who is the
fount of redemption through the Son by the Holy
Ghost ; if the Spirit comes, He brings with Him in His
coming the Son and the Father, for in eternal subordination and order the three are one inseparable God.

I suppose we should almost all of us admit that whatever we can know certainly of the being of God must
be known by God's disclosure of Himself.   We cannot
by searching find out God.   On the other hand, if man
is made in God's image, if man's reason represents the
divine reason, we must expect that even mysteries
will be rational.   Thus St. Thomas declares that we cannot *à priori* prove the doctrine of the Trinity, but that
it is rational, in the sense that once posited, it is found
to be in conformity with reason [1].   The right claim for
reason, in respect to mysteries, seems to me admirably
expressed in the following proposition of Hermann

---

[1] St. Thom. Aq. *Summa Theol.* p. I. qu. 32. ad 2dum.

Lotze: 'If reason,' he says, 'is not of itself capable of finding the highest truth, but on the contrary stands in need of a revelation, still, reason must be able to understand the revealed truth, at least so far as to recognise in it the satisfying and convincing conclusion of those upward-soaring trains of thought which reason itself began, led by its own needs, but was not able to bring to an end [1].'

The doctrine of the Trinity then is, I assert, not discoverable by reason, but agreeable to reason. It corresponds to upward-soaring trains of thought which reason itself originates, but is not able to bring to a conclusion. For the reasons which lead us to believe in God at all, lead us to think of Him as an eternal and spiritual being. Now the life of spirit, the highest life we know, is made up of the action of will and reason and love. In God then, we imagine, is a perfect and eternal life, of will and reason and love. But must not this be a life of relationships? Most surely love is only conceivable as a personal relationship of a lover and a loved. If God is eternal love, there must be an eternal object for His love. Again, the life of reason is a relationship of the subject which thinks to the object thought, and an eternally perfect mind postulates an eternal object for its contemplation. Once more, the life of will means the passage of will into effect: there is no satisfaction to will except in production; an eternally living and satisfied will postulates an eternally adequate product. Thus it is that our upward-soaring trains of thought lead us to postulate over against God in His eternal being, also an eternal expression of that being, which shall be both an object to His thought

---

[1] *Microcosmus* (Eng. trans.), ii. p. 660.

and a satisfaction to His will and a repose to His love, and this is St. John's doctrine of the Logos, the eternal expression of God's being in fellowship with Himself: 'The Word was with God, and the Word was God.'

The *à priori* considerations which suggest trinity, as distinct from duality, in God, are apt to appear fanciful and unreal at first sight ; more so perhaps than on further consideration they prove themselves to be.   But it is enough, surely, if we can be rationally satisfied that God cannot be a monotonous unity, that the one life of God must contain within itself distinctions of a personal sort. If this is the verdict of reason, we, knowing how little way reason can go in *à priori* anticipations, should be justly called rationalistic if we refused to accept, as in fact disclosed in Christ, God's triune being [1].

Thus the Christian, taught of Christ, lifts up his mind in reverent awe, and yet in confidence, to catch some glimpse of the eternal Being.   Back then, behind all the forms of life, all the laws and subordinations of parts and manifold relationships and processes, physical and spiritual, which characterize this complex universe, his mind penetrates to an eternal Being in whom lies the explanation of all this created world, an eternal pro- ductiveness, an eternal law, an eternal subordination, an eternal process, an eternal relationship of will and thought and love.   He beholds by faith God, self- contained, self-complete, as the Father moves for ever forth in the begetting of the Son, and the Father and the Son in the procession of the Spirit.   There lies an eternal fellowship, in which the Father finds in the Son His adequate word or utterance, the satis-

[1] See app. note 13, p. 264.

fying expression of His being, and object of His thought and will and love ; in which the Son eternally receives and communicates the fulness of the divine life ; in which the Spirit, the life of the Father and the Son, is the product and joy of both, and the bond of communion of the one with the other.

That this high doctrine is in fact rational is made perhaps most evident by carrying the war into the enemy's country.   Let me then briefly endeavour to substantiate the position that this Christian doctrine of God alone makes permanently possible a rational theism, by holding together the extremes of pantheism and deism at a middle point of balance.

Pantheism gives noble expression to the truth of God's presence in all things, but it cannot satisfy the religious consciousness : it cannot give it escape from the limitations of the world, or guarantee personal immortality, or (what is most important) give any adequate interpretation to sin, or supply any adequate remedy for it.   On the other hand, unitarian deism, with its eternal uni-personal God, distinct from the world, is involved in insuperable difficulties.   How can any conception be formed of a God, really alive, with a life of will and reason and love, yet in blank monotonous solitude, without product or object or response ?   The difficulty is so great, that it would seem as if unitarianism must almost inevitably tend to pass either into pantheism, which makes the world as necessary to God as God is to the world ; or as with Coleridge, and Maurice, and Hutton, into Christian theology [1].

For Christian theology is the harmony of pantheism

[1] See app. note 44, p. 264.

and deism.  On the one hand, Christianity believes all
that the pantheist believes of God's presence in all
things.  'In him' we believe 'we live and move and
are': 'in him all things have their coherence[1].'  All
the beauty of the world, all its truth, all its goodness, ·
are but so many modes under which God is manifested,
of whose glory nature is the veil, of whose word it is
the expression, whose law and reason it embodies.
But God is not exhausted in the world, nor dependent
upon it; He exists eternally in His triune being, self-
sufficing, self-subsistent.   His Spirit is moving in the
world and His Word is sustaining and governing it,
but before creation and beyond it, the Spirit and the
Word dwelt in the bosom of God.   God is not only in
nature as its life, but He transcends it as its Creator, its
Lord,—in its moral aspect—its Judge.   So it is that
Christianity enjoys the riches of pantheism without its
inherent weakness on the moral side, without making
God dependent on the world, as the world is on God.
On the other hand, Christianity converts an unintelligible
deism into a rational theism.   It can explain how God
became a Creator in time, because it knows how creation
had its eternal analogue in the uncreated nature; it was
God's nature eternally to produce, to communicate itself,
to live.   It can explain how God can be eternally alive
and yet in complete independence of the world which He
created, because God's unique eternal being is no solitary
and monotonous existence; it includes in itself the fulness
of fellowship, the society of Father and Son and Spirit.

[1] Acts xvii. 28; Col. i. 17.

## V.

It is a splendid heritage, a magnificent possession, that of faith in God, as it is bestowed upon the Christian. To believe in God is to move about the world—increasingly as we realize God's presence better—in the spirit of a worshipper. For the spirit of worship is derived from the recognition of God in all things and all things in God. God is in all things. There is no creature so small, but represents something of His goodness. He is disclosed in all the grades and kinds of life: under the divers modes of beauty, and truth, and goodness, each with its own intrinsic value: through the ministries of artist and thinker, labourer, craftsman, statesman, reformer, priest. He is living in the life of nature and of man. One and unchanged He is revealed in all varieties of loveliness, all fragments and elements of knowledge, all traits of worthy character. Thus the Christian touches all things with a loving reverence, for within them God is hidden. And because wherever He is, He is to be adored, therefore to the believer in God all joy in what is beautiful, all satisfaction in ascertained truth, as all delight in human fellowship, is for ever passing back into worship of Him, whose essence it is that touches with glory all desirable things, that is, in their fundamental nature and true application, all things that are. ' Holy, holy, holy, is the Lord of hosts : the whole earth is full of his glory [1].'

Worship, I say, is the recognition of God in all things, and also of all things in God. For no created thing adds to His essential good. All things that are, do but

---

[1] Is. vi. 3.

represent in a lower form what exists eternally in God. ' By faith we understand that the worlds have been framed by the word of God, so that what is seen hath not — been made out of things that do appear[1].' Not out of things that do appear have the worlds been framed, but they do represent unapparent and eternal realities, for the whole universe is the expression in gradual evolution of what existed beyond time in the divine — mind. ' What has come into being,' says St. John, ' was life in Him[2].' So that if all created things should pass into the nothingness out of which they sprang, there would be no loss of essential good. They but express imperfectly a perfect archetype. To see all things in God, then, is the crown of worship. We shall behold through eternal ages more and more of God, not only in His perfected creatures, but in Himself. In endless progress of felicity without weariness we shall see further and further, on and up, into the depths of beauty and holiness and truth in Jesus, incarnate and glorified, and in the triune God ; and as we see God we shall adore, not for the sake of anything we get from Him, but for the sake of His own supreme worthiness. 'We praise Thee, we bless Thee, we worship Thee, we glorify Thee, we give thanks to Thee for Thy great glory.' Blessed indeed are the pure in heart, for no other reason than that they shall see God.

The Christian then, as believing in God, finds this earth a temple for adoration, and looks forward to entering the inner shrine. He sees God in all things and all things in God. And because in one half of his nature he is thus beholding God, so in that part of his nature which he

---

[1] Heb. xi. 3.          [2] St. John i. 3.  See R. V. marg.

turns towards men and in view of the world's vicissitudes
he is as one who 'is not afraid of any evil tidings, for
his heart standeth fast and believeth in the Lord.' Men
in their wilfulness, though never in mere ignorance, may
destroy themselves : they may make it impossible that
they should individually attain the end for which God
created them ; but they cannot destroy God's work. The
world about us with its lawlessness, its disunions, its
jarrings, seems sometimes as if it could attain to no
great end ; like a restless sea of many waters, aimless,
barren, unprogressive. But there is purpose in it. The
tossing sea we shall behold one day shot with the fires
of the divine judgment, as St. John beheld it, 'a sea
of glass mingled with fire' ; and beyond the judgment
again, as the sea of glass clear as crystal, which mirrors
in its calm surface the throne of God before which it is
spread. 'For though the waves toss themselves they
shall not prevail.' All things move on to the divine
event. The nations of the earth shall walk in the light
of the holy city, and the kings of the earth shall bring
their glory and honour into it. All things in heaven and
earth, and under the earth, shall bow and adore Jesus,
the heir of the whole world's movement and fruitfulness.

Thus the goal of all things is unity, subordination,
worship.

'The four living creatures,' who with their wings and eyes
symbolize the manifold forces and vital powers of nature,
'rest not day and night, saying, Holy, holy, holy, is the
Lord God, the Almighty, which was and which is and
which is coming. And when the living creatures shall
give glory and honour and thanks to him that sitteth on
the throne, that liveth for ever and ever, the four and

twenty elders—that is, the representatives of redeemed
humanity—shall fall down before him that sitteth on
the throne, and shall worship him that liveth for ever
and ever, and shall cast their crowns before the throne,
*saying,* Worthy art thou, our Lord and our God, to receive the glory and the honour and the power, for thou
didst create all things, and because of thy will they
were, and were created [1].'

[1] Rev. xv. 2 ; iv. 6; xxi. 24 ; iv. 8 11.

# LECTURE VI.

## MAN REVEALED IN CHRIST.

*Wherefore it behoved him in all things to be made like unto his brethren.
. . . For in that he himself hath suffered being tempted, he is able to
succour them that are tempted.*—HEBREWS ii. 17, 18.

JESUS CHRIST is not only the revelation of Godhead,
He is also the revelation of manhood. 'As He shows
God to man,' says Irenæus, 'so He exhibits man to
God [1].' He exhibits man to God, and to himself. For
over against all false and meagre ideals of man's capacity
and destiny, He represents the great reality; He is the
Son of man.

## I.

The dogmatic safeguards of this revelation of manhood in the person of Jesus Christ the Church has
abundantly provided on three distinct occasions. First
when she condemned, in Apollinarius, all attempts to
curtail our Lord's complete humanity, or to secure
His sinlessness by denying to Him the reality of
human spirit. Secondly, when she condemned in
Eutyches the false reverence which would merge His
humanity in His Godhead, and affirmed that He is
'of one substance' with us in His manhood as with
God in His Godhead. Lastly when, against the
Monothelites of the seventh century, she repudiated

---

[1] Iren. *c. haer.* iv. 20. 7.

renewed attempts to deny in Christ the real action of human faculties, and asserted as certain truth that in the person of Jesus Christ is to be found unimpaired the distinctive action of human will, the distinct operation of the properly human energies.

Our Lord Jesus Christ, then, is truly and completely man, and He acts as man through the exercise of distinctive human faculties: this is the Church's dogma. Nothing perhaps shows more plainly the hand of God in these ecclesiastical decisions than the fact that they were framed with such emphasis on the human nature of Jesus in an age when the tendency of catholic thought was certainly not humanitarian.

But though anti-humanitarian tendencies were not allowed to impair the formal doctrine of the Church, they have more or less dimmed the apprehension of its meaning at more than one epoch. In part this has come about, because the exigencies of theological controversy in the period of the later ecumenical councils overclouded, not in the best minds, but in many of the most active and representative minds, that vivid realization of Christianity as a way of life for man—' *the way*[1],'—and of Christ as 'the living law of righteousness[2].' which characterized early times. In part, because mediaeval theology viewed the Incarnation metaphysically rather than ethically, and treated it by the aid of syllogisms rather than of a genuine study of the Gospel records. In part because with the Reformation, when controversial interest reappeared in absorbing power, discussions about justification, predestination, and the atonement, were allowed a disproportionate

---

[1] Acts ix. 2 ; xxii. 4.    [2] Lactantius, *Divin. Instit.* iv. 25 ; cf. iv. 17.

share of attention. The late Dean of St. Paul's describes thus the theological tendencies in this country at the period immediately previous to the Oxford movement. ' Evangelical theology had dwelt upon the work of Christ and laid comparatively little stress on His example, or the picture left us of His personality and life. People who can recall the popular teaching which was spoken of then as " sound " and " faithful " and " preaching Christ," can remember how the Epistles were ransacked for texts to prove the sufficiency of Scripture, or the right of private judgment, or the distinction between justification and sanctification, while the Gospel narrative was imperfectly studied and was felt to be much less interesting [1].'

In different ways then it has come about that the reality of our Lord's human example, and therefore the true meaning of His manhood, have not been so much in view in the Christian Church as, to judge from the New Testament, they should have been, in their bearing on the life of individuals and of society. We need again and again to go back to the consideration of the historical Jesus. The dogmatic decisions of the Church Catholic afford us guidance and warning in the undertaking : they are notice-boards to warn us off false lines of approach to Him, but they are not, as has already been explained, meant to be anything more. To fill up the dogmatic outline into a living whole, to know the meaning of the Incarnation, and the conditions of the humanity of the Son of God, we must go back to scrutinize the figure in the Gospels.

---

[1] Church, *The Oxford Movement* (Macmillan, 1891), pp. 167–8.

## II.

The conditions of our Lord's early childhood are veiled from us. Nothing is told us about His education, nor are we given any glimpse of Him at the period when men learn most from those outside them, but He grew so truly as a human child that Joseph and His mother had not been led to expect from Him conduct incompatible with childhood, when they took Him up with them to the temple in His thirteenth year. This must mean that He was taught as the young are taught; and in the temple courts He impressed the doctors as a child of marvellous insight and intelligence. Not but what, even then, there was present to Him the consciousness of His unique Sonship: 'Wist ye not,' He said to His parents, 'that I must be about my Father's business[1]?' but that consciousness of divine Sonship did not interfere with His properly human growth. 'The child grew and waxed strong,' says St. Luke, 'becoming full of wisdom, and the favour of God was upon him.' Again, 'Jesus advanced in wisdom and stature, and in favour with God and men[2];'—the phrase being borrowed from the record of Samuel's childhood, with the specifications added, 'in wisdom and stature.' There was a real growth in mental apprehension and spiritual capacity, as in bodily stature.

The divine Sonship is impressively asserted at the baptism in the river Jordan. Again, Jesus Christ manifests His consciousness of it in His relation to John the Baptist; and henceforth throughout our Lord's ministerial life, it is not possible for one who accepts, even generally,

---

[1] St. Luke ii. 49.          [2] St. Luke ii. 40, 52; cf. 1 Sam. ii. 26.

L

the historical character of the Synoptic Gospels and of St. John's, to doubt that He knew His eternal pre-existence and Sonship: but the consciousness is not allowed to interfere with the really human development of life. He receives as man the unction of the Holy Ghost; He was led as man 'of the Spirit into the wilderness,' and hungered, and was subjected as man to real temptations of Satan, such as made their appeal to properly human faculties, and were met by the free employment of human will. He was 'in all points tempted like as we are, apart from sin[1].' When He goes out to exercise His ministry, He bases His authority on the unction of the Spirit according to Isaiah's prophecy. 'The Spirit of the Lord is upon me,' He reads, 'because he anointed me to preach[2].' 'God,' comments St. Peter, 'anointed Jesus of Nazareth with the Holy Ghost and with power: who went about doing good, and healing all that were oppressed of the devil; for God was with him[3].' Thus if His miraculous power appears as the appropriate endowment of His person, it was still a gift of God to Him as man. 'The power of the Lord was with him to heal,' says the evangelist: 'by the Spirit of God' He Himself declared, He cast out devils[4]: and St. John, in recording the words of Jesus before the raising of Lazarus, would teach us to see at least in some of His miracles, what is suggested also elsewhere by our Lord's gestures, a power dependent on the exercise of prayer. 'Father, I thank thee that thou didst hear me[5].'

[1] Hebr. iv. 15.    [2] St. Luke iv. 18.    [3] Acts x. 38.
[4] St. Luke v. 17; St. Matt. xii. 28.
[5] St. John xi. 41; St. Matt. xiv. 19; St. Mark vii. 34.

Once more, while as very Son Jesus knows the Father as He is known of Him, and reveals Him to whom He will, He does not appear to teach out of an absolute divine omniscience, but rather as conditioned by human nature. It is, of course, beyond question that our Lord's consciousness, not only towards God but towards the world, was extraordinary. Thus He frequently exhibits a supernatural knowledge, insight, and foresight. He saw Nathanael under the fig-tree, and knew the incident in the life of the Samaritan woman, and told Peter how he would find the piece of money in the fish's mouth, and the disciples how they would find the colt tied up in the village, and the man bearing a pitcher of water to take them to the upper chamber. He discerned 'from the beginning' the heart of Judas [1], and prophesied the denial of Peter, and had in view His own passion, death, and resurrection the third day. But all such supernatural illumination is, if of higher quality, yet analogous to that vouchsafed to prophets and apostles. It is not necessarily Divine consciousness. And it coincides in our Lord with apparent limitations of knowledge. The evidence for this we may group under four heads.

1. There are attributed to our Lord constantly human experiences which seem inconsistent with practical omniscience. Thus he expresses surprise at the conduct of His parents, and the unbelief of men, and the barrenness of the fig-tree, and the slowness of His disciples' faith [2]. He expresses surprise on many occasions, and therefore, we must believe, really felt it, as on other

---

[1] St. John vi. 64.
[2] St. Luke ii. 49; St. Mark vi. 6, xi. 13, iv. 40, vii. 18, viii. 21, xiv. 37.

L 2

occasions He asks for information and receives it[1].    It is in agreement with this, that as St. Luke especially teaches us[2], He lived in the constant exercise of prayer to God, which is the characteristic utterance of human faith and trust, that human faith and trust of which the Epistle to the Hebrews sees in Jesus the supreme example[3].

This reality of human faith becomes more obvious as the anxieties and terrors of the passion close in upon Him.    He shows us then the spectacle of true man, weighted with a crushing burden, the dread of a cata-strophe awful and unfathomed.    It was only because the future was not clear that He could pray: 'O my Father, if it be possible, let this cup pass away from me[4].'    Boldly simple is the language of the inspired commentator on this scene of the agony: 'Christ,' he says, 'in the days of his flesh, having offered up prayers and supplications with strong crying and tears unto him that was able to save him from death, and having been heard for his godly fear, though he was a Son, yet learned obedience by the things which he suffered.'    No language less than this would correspond with the historical narrative, but it is language which implies very strongly the exercise of human faith in our Lord's case; nor is it possible that He could have cried with real meaning upon the cross, 'My God, my God, why hast thou forsaken me?' unless He had really entered into the experience which originally prompted that cry

---

[1] St. Luke viii. 30; St. Mark vi. 38, viii. 5, ix. 21; St. John xi. 34.

[2] St. Luke iii. 21, v. 16, vi. 12, ix. 18, 28, xxii. 32, 42, x. 21.

[3] Hebr. ii. 13, 'I will put my trust in him': xii. 2, 'the captain of our faith,' i.e. leader in the life of faith; see Westcott *in loc.*

[4] St. Matt. xxvi. 39.

of the Psalmist, into the trial of the soul from whom God hides His face, the trial of the righteous man forsaken.

2. Though our Lord knew so well, and told so plainly, the moral conditions of the great judgment to come, and discerned so clearly its particular application in the destruction of Jerusalem, yet He expressly declared, as St. Matthew as well as St. Mark assures us, that of the day and the hour of His second coming, no one knew except the Father, not even the angels which are in heaven, neither the Son [1];—and we cannot hold this declaration apart from the other indications that are given us of a limited human consciousness.

3. A similar impression is left on our mind by the Gospel of St. John. Unmistakably is our Lord there put before us as the eternal Son of the Father incarnate, but it also appears that the Son of the Father is living and teaching under human conditions: He speaks the words of God, St. John tells us, because God 'giveth not the Spirit by measure,' that is, because of the complete endowment of His manhood. He Himself says, that He accomplishes 'what the Father taught Him': that He can do only ' what He sees the Father doing': that the Father makes to Him a progressive revelation, ' He shall show Him greater works than these': that the Father 'gave Him' the divine 'Name,' that is, the positive revelation of Himself, to communicate to the apostles : that He has made known to them ' all things that He had heard of the Father,' or ' the words which the Father had given Him [2].' The idea is thus irresistibly suggested

---

[1] St. Matt. xxiv. 36 ' R.V.'; St. Mark xiii. 32.
[2] St. John iii. 34, viii. 28, v. 19, 20, xvii. 11, 8, xv. 15.

of a message of definite content made over to our Lord
to impart.  Now, even though we bear in mind to the
fullest extent the eternal subordination and receptivity
of the Son, it still remains plain that words such as have
been quoted express Him as receiving and speaking
under the limitations of a properly human state.

4. Lastly, there is the argument from silence, coincident
with these indications.  Our Lord exhibits insight and
foresight of prophetic quality.  He exhibits towards all
facts of physical nature the receptiveness of a perfect
sonship, so that, for example, the laws of natural waste
and growth are pointed out by Him with consummate
accuracy in the parable of the sower.  But He never
enlarges our stock of natural knowledge, physical or
historical, out of the divine omniscience.

The recognition of these phenomena of our Lord's life
leads us to the conclusion that up to the time of His
death He lived and taught, He thought and was inspired and was tempted, as true and proper man, under
the limitations of consciousness which alone make possible
a really human experience.  Of this part of our heritage we
must not allow ourselves to be robbed, by being ' wise
above that which is written.'  The evidences that our
Lord really lived under human limitations are as plain
as the evidences that in and under the properly human
nature, He who spoke, and worked, and suffered, was
the Son of God, one with the Father.  But then, you
will say, how are the phenomena to be reconciled in one
conception? how can we imagine the consistency of the
Godhead with the manhood?

### III.

Before we approach the consideration of this question, let us determine at any rate to be true to the facts which the Gospels supply, even though in doing so we have to part company, more or less, with two much opposed classes of theologians.

I have already spoken of the method of the scholastic and later dogmatic theologians, of whom no more capable representative is to be found than the learned Jesuit De Lugo [1]. He of course accepts all the decrees of the general councils, and the few decisions which have been given by popes, on the subject of the Incarnation. And he has in mind all the opinions of the theologians, on each point that comes under review. These decrees, decisions and opinions form the material on which he works, and out of them he elaborates a conception of Christ's person, coherent indeed and exact enough to satisfy any mind, but strangely unlike the picture in the Gospels. It is a picture of a human Christ, who, if He was as far as His body is concerned in a condition of growth, was as regards His soul and intellect, from the first moment and throughout His life, in full enjoyment of the beatific vision. Externally a wayfarer, a 'viator,' inwardly He was throughout a 'comprehensor,' He had already attained. Thus, from the first instant of its existence, His humanity possessed at least perfect actual knowledge of all reality past, present, and future, in virtue of its union with the Divine Word; and over and above this, an infused knowledge, covering for practical purposes

---

[1] See app. note 45, p. 205.

the same range, so that it is stated to be a matter almost
of indifference whether He be supposed to have acquired
knowledge gradually or at a bound, and in fact such
acquisition of knowledge loses all reality when His
manhood was by other means fully equipped with all
possible knowledge from the first. It is denied that He
used the discursive reason, or was ever subject to priva-
tion of knowledge, or was in a condition of uncertainty;
it is denied that He can strictly be called 'the servant of
God' even as man, in spite of the direct use of that
expression in the Acts of the Apostles. He is spoken
of at the institution of the eucharist as offering sacrifice
to His own Godhead.

Now on each of these points the position of De
Lugo stands in more or less striking contradiction
to what the New Testament would lead us to believe
to be true. Yet one finds, one is almost irritated to
find, that these positions are regarded as only statements of what was true in fact; it being admitted,
for example, that it was possible in the abstract, for
the humanity of Christ to have contracted even actual
error, where such error would not have affected the purpose of His mission, if the divine power had allowed it
to err. These positions then are supposed to be only
statements of what was true in fact: they are mostly
admitted at the last resort to be not 'of faith.' Yet in
spite of this *à priori* freedom in abstract possibility, and
this comparative liberty in the region of dogma, the
facts of the historical Gospels are never really examined
at all. All that we have given to us is an *à priori*
picture of what an Incarnation may be thought to have
involved; which yet, in the region of the later western

theology, so preoccupies the mind, as in great measure
to deprive it of contact with the historical Christ. Surely
we have a warning here against *à priori* methods ; surely
we are justified in feeling that those who give the highest
meaning to the inspiration of holy Scripture as a doctrine, may be least at pains to pay attention to what it
actually says.

But there are others, belonging to very modern ways
of thought, who assure us that Christ, because He was
man, must have been at least peccable or liable to sin,
and fallible or liable to make mistakes. Now something will be said in the next lecture in regard to the
position that our Lord actually committed Himself to
an error of fact in regard to the authorship of the 110th
Psalm. Assuming for the moment, that our Lord's allu-
sion to the Old Testament in this case, as in others, affords
no ground for attributing to Him erroneous teaching ; assuming this, and looking at the matter in general, must we
not admit that the idea of a fallible or peccable Christ, in
the ordinary sense of those terms, has the same abstract
character as the doctrine of the later dogmatists ? Place
yourself face to face with the Christ of the Gospels ; let
His words, His claim, His tone, make upon you their
natural impression ; and you will not, I believe, find that
He will allow you to think of Him as either liable to sin,
or liable to mislead. He never fears sin, or hints that
He might be found inadequate to the tremendous charge
He bore ; He does not let us think of Him as growing
better or as needing improvement, though He passes
through each imperfect stage of manhood to completeness. He challenges criticism. He speaks as the invincible emancipator of man, the deliverer who binds the

strong captor and spoils his goods. He appears in no
relation to sin, but as the discerner, the conqueror, the
judge of it, in all its forms and to the end of time. In
the same way, whenever and whomsoever He teaches,
it is in the tone which could only be morally justifiable
in the case of one who taught without risk of mistake ;
claiming by His own inherent right the submission of
the conscience and will and intellect of men. 'Heaven
and earth,' He said, 'shall pass away, but my words shall
not pass away[1].' 'Lo,' said His apostles, amazed at
the openness and security with which He spoke before
His passion, discerning their hearts and satisfying their
doubts, 'now know we that thou knowest all things, and
needest not that any man should ask thee : by this we
believe that thou camest forth from God[2].'

Indeed, when men suggest fallibility in our Lord's
teaching, or peccability in His character, it is as much in
the teeth of the Gospel record as when on the other
hand they deny Him limitation of knowledge, or the
reality of a human, moral, trial, in the days of His flesh.
We will be true to the record, then, at all costs ; and
resolved on this, let us approach the question how the
two sides of the evidence are to combine into a unity in
our conception of Christ's person.

IV.

As we look at the history in the Gospels we see side
by side in Jesus, a life of one who dwells in the Father
and manifests the Father, and a truly human life of joy
and sorrow, sympathy and antagonism, trial and victory

[1] St. Matt. xxiv. 35.         [2] St. John xvi. 30.

faith and prayer. These two lives, as we think of them apart, are in strongly marked contrast, but they are not incompatible. We find something analogous to them in the case of a prophet like Jeremiah. In his case, too, there is the life of divinely-given certainty in insight and foresight, based upon the divine word communicated and the vision of God vouchsafed: and, side by side with it, the life of intense personal trial and dismay. Here again the lives are contrasted as we think of them separately:—of Jeremiah with God's words in his mouth, set over the nations and over the kingdoms, and of Jeremiah, the man of sorrows and complaints, crying 'O Lord, thou hast deceived me, and I was deceived. Thou art stronger than I and hast prevailed: I am become a laughing-stock all the day, every one mocketh me.' But the two lives fade into one another in the record, and present the picture of the one person. In the case of our Lord the eternal Sonship necessarily gave to His teaching a personal tone, unmistakably distinct from that of any of the prophets. But the analogy of the prophets is sufficient to show us that the plenary authority of our Lord's teaching, and on the other hand the limitations of consciousness exhibited in His experience of human trial, are not incompatible elements, arbitrarily put into juxtaposition, any more than parallel phenomena in the case of God's lower messengers.

They are not in themselves incompatible elements, but our perception of their unity, that is our power of interpreting the Incarnation, will depend chiefly on our having clearly in view its *motive* and its *method*.

A divine motive caused the Incarnation. It was a

deliberate act of God 'propter nos homines et propter
nostram salutem': it was a 'means devised' for our
recovery and for our consummation, a means, therefore,
directed and adapted in the divine wisdom, to serve
its purpose. That purpose included on the one side a
clearer revelation of God's mind and being to man in
terms intelligible to him, and on the other hand the exhibition of the true ideal of human nature. Now for the
first part of the purpose, for the unveiling of the divine
character, what was necessary was that the humanity
should reflect, without refracting, the divine Being whose
organ it was made. It could not be too pure a channel,
too infallible a voice, provided it was really human and
fitted to man. Thus in fact, in becoming incarnate, the
Son of God retained and expressed His essential relation
to the Father; he received therefore, as eternally, so in
the days of His flesh, the consciousness of His own and
of His Father's being, and the power to reveal that which
He knew. 'No man,' He said, 'knoweth the Son save
the Father; neither knoweth any man the Father' (not
*knew*, but *knoweth*) 'save the Son, and he to whomsoever
the Son willeth to reveal him.' Limited moreover, as
we shall have occasion to remark, as is His disclosure of
the unseen world, what He does disclose is in the tone
of one who speaks 'that he doth know, and testifies that
he hath seen:' for example, 'I say unto you, that in
heaven the angels of the little ones do always behold
the face of my Father which is in heaven.' 'In my
Father's house are many mansions; if it were not so I
would have told you[1].' Plainly the continuous personality of the Son carried with it a continuous con-

[1] St. Matt. xviii. 10; St. John xiv. 2.

sciousness, which if the human nature was allowed to
subject to limitation, it was not allowed to deface or
to distort.   What He teaches, He teaches so that we
can depend upon it to the uttermost, and the fact is
explained by the motive of the Incarnation.

On the other hand, our Lord is to exhibit a true example of manhood—tried, progressive, perfected.  For
this purpose it was necessary that He should be without the exercise of such divine prerogatives as would
have made human experience or progress impossible.
He could not, as far as we can see, abiding in the
exercise of an absolute consciousness, have grown in
knowledge, or have prayed, 'Father, if it be possible,'
or cried, 'My God, my God, *why*'—He could not, that
is, have passed through those very experiences, which
have brought Him closest to us in our spiritual trials.

So far the facts of the Incarnation are accounted for
by the divine motive which underlay it; but they are
interpreted further by the divine *method* or principle of
action as St. Paul unfolds it to us.  He describes it as a
self-emptying [1].  Christ Jesus pre-existed, he declares, in
the *form* of God.  The word 'form' transferred from physical shape to spiritual type, describes—as St. Paul uses
it, alone or in composition, with uniform accuracy—the
permanent characteristics of a thing.  Jesus Christ then,
in His pre-existent state, was living in the permanent
characteristics of the life of God.  In such a life it was
His right to remain.  It belonged to Him.  But He
regarded not His prerogatives, as a man regards a prize
He must clutch at.  For love of us He abjured the prerogatives of equality with God.  By an act of deliberate

---

[1] Phil. ii. 5-11 ; see Lightfoot *in la*.

self-abnegation, He so emptied Himself as to assume the permanent characteristics of the human or servile life : He took the *form* of a servant.  Not only so, but He was made in outward appearance like other men and was found in fashion as a man, that is, in the transitory quality of our mortality.  The ' form,' the ' likeness,' the ' fashion ' of manhood, He took them all. Thus, remaining in unchanged personality, He abandoned certain prerogatives of the divine mode of existence in order to assume the human.

Again, St. Paul describes the Incarnation as a ' self-beggary[1].'  The metaphor suggests a man of wealth who deliberately abandons the prerogatives of possession to enter upon the experience of poverty, not because he thinks it a better state, but in order to help others up through real fellowship with their experience to a life of weal.  ' Ye know the grace of our Lord Jesus Christ, that, though he was rich, yet for your sakes he beggared himself, that ye through his poverty might be rich.' This is how St. Paul interprets our Lord's coming down from heaven, and it is manifest that it expresses something very much more than the mere addition of a manhood to His Godhead.  In a certain aspect indeed the Incarnation is the folding round the Godhead of the veil of the humanity, to hide its glory, but it is much more than this.  It is a ceasing to exercise certain natural prerogatives of the divine existence ; it is a coming to exist for love of us under conditions of being not natural to the Son of God.

The act, which on the part of the Son is thus represented as an abandoning of what He possessed, is

---

[1] 2 Cor. viii. 9.

on the part of the Father also represented as a real
surrender, a real giving-up of the Son, as a father
among us might give up his son to be a missionary:
'So God loved the world that he gave his only-begotten
Son.'   'He gave him up for us [1].'

We must dwell, more than we are apt to do, on the
principle or method of divine action thus exhibited to us.
What is revealed is, that for our sakes the Son of God
abandoned His own prerogatives in God, in order as
man to merit and win, by gradual and painful effort, a
glory which in right might have been His all along, the
glory which He had with the Father before the world
was.   Of the results of this self-emptying we can only
judge by the record in the Gospels.   That our Lord
could not lose His personality, or essential relation to
the Father, is indeed certain *à priori* and is confirmed
in the record.   The personality is, then, throughout the
same; but in regard to the divine attributes, what He
retained in exercise and what He abandoned—whether
He abandoned only the manifest glory, or also, for example, the exercise of the divine omniscience—we could
hardly form any judgment *à priori*; but the record
seems to assure us that our Lord in His mortal life was
not habitually living in the exercise of omniscience.

Is then such a self-emptying intelligible?   It is easy
to see that it involves no dishonouring of the eternal
Son, no attribution to Him of failing powers.   'It was
not,' says St. Leo, 'the failure of power, but the condescension of pity [2].'   There was conscious voluntariness
in all our Lord's self-abnegation; 'I have power to lay

---

[1] St. John iii. 16; Rom. viii. 32; 1 St. John iv. 9.
[2] St. Leo, *Ep.* xxviii. 3.

down my life,' He said, 'and I have power to take it
again :' 'Thinkest thou that I cannot beseech my
Father, and he shall even now send me more than
twelve legions of angels[1]?' This same deliberateness
belongs, we must suppose, to the limitation of consciousness under which our Lord is found. And God
declares His almighty power most chiefly in such an
act of voluntary self-limitation for the purposes of sympathy. It is physical power which makes itself felt
only in self-assertion and pressure ; it is the higher
power of love which is shown in self-effacement[2]. The
power to think one's self into another's thoughts, to
look through another's eyes, to feel with another's
feeling, to merge one's self in another's interests,—this
is the higher power, the power of love, and we owe it
to the Incarnation that we know God to possess and
to use, not only the power to vindicate Himself, but
the power also of self-limitation.

'But,' it may be asked, 'is such a process as that of
abjuring the exercise of consciousness really thinkable ?'
In a measure it is, because it is realized in all sympathy.
There are two ways of helping others. We may help
them from the secure platform of a superior position ;
we may give them information from the vantage-ground
of superior knowledge in the form which that knowledge naturally takes. But we may help them also by
the method of sympathy, and this means a real en-
trance into the conditions of another's consciousness.
By this method the grown teacher accommodates himself to the child's mind, the educated to the mind of
the savage ; and thus, mind acts upon mind by the

---

[1] St. John x. 18 ; St. Matt. xxvi. 53.    [2] See app. note 46, p. 265.

way of force infusing itself from within, rather than
of alien information conveyed simply from without.  In
such action there is involved a real abandonment of
the prerogatives which belong to a superior state of
consciousness, and those will most easily understand
this who have been at most deliberate pains to culti-
vate the life of sympathy.  Beyond this we can readily
conceive that the attributes and powers of God must
be more wholly, than is the case with us, under the
control of the will.  They must be less mechanical and
more voluntary.  God cannot act against the perfect
law of reason, but what the divine love and reason ·
demand, that the divine will can make possible.

But after all, we shall not, if we are wise, expect to
understand the whole matter.  It has been well said
that 'we must all be agnostics, if we only put our agnosticism in the right place.'  We do know God really ;
our own best methods teach us really the methods of
God ; but not adequately, not completely.  The methods
of God are of the same kind, but inconceivably more intense and more far-reaching.  Thus, if our own deliberate
acts of sympathy have in them something analogous to
the act of God in incarnation, they do not reach all the
way to the explanation of it ; for sacrifice ourselves as
we may we cannot enter into a new state of being, or
pass through any transition comparable to that involved
in the incarnation of the Son of God.  It must have
involved an act of self-limitation greater than we can
fathom, for the eternal to begin to think and act and
speak under conditions of humanity.

Thus far, however, we can see our way.  The Incarnation involves both the self-expression, and the self-

M

limitation, of God.  God can express Himself in true manhood because manhood is truly and originally made in God's image ; and on the other hand, God can limit Himself by the conditions of manhood, because the Godhead contains in itself eternally the prototype of human self-sacrifice and self-limitation, for God is love.


## V.

Let me state in other terms the result we have arrived at.  We conceive that in the Incarnation the eternal Son really so assumed our manhood in its completeness in the womb of the blessed Virgin, as to be to it its centre of personality and to use all its faculties as His own in every stage of their development.  We conceive that He thus assumed our manhood, in part in order to make through it a revelation of the character and being of God, such as should be both true and intelligible to us, as expressed in the language of our own nature : in part also, in order to set the example of a true human life in its relation both towards God and towards man. We conceive further that, in order to this true human example, the eternal Son so far restrained the natural action of the divine being as, in St. Cyril's phrase, ' to suffer the measures of our manhood to prevail over Him[1]:' so that He passed through all stages of a human development, willing with a human will, perceiving with human perceptions, feeling with human feelings, receiving, and depending upon, the illuminating and conse-

---

[1] St. Cyril, *Quod unus Christus*, ed. Pusey, vol. vii. pt. i. p. 399.

crating unction of the Holy Ghost; and thus fathoming
to their depths the experiences which can come upon
man in accordance with God's will.

In forming such a conception as this, we must necessarily set many questions aside which we cannot answer.
We make no pretence—God forbid that we should—
to exhaust the depths of a divine mystery [1]. But so far as
we go we seem to be moving within the lines of dogma
and doing justice to all the intimations of Scripture.
Throughout the Incarnation the person of the Son is
unchanged; and since the Incarnation, He is at every
moment and in every act both God and man; but the
relation of the two natures is different at different
epochs. Before His resurrection, He, very God, is acting under conditions of manhood; since His glorification
He, very man, is living under conditions of Godhead.
First the Godhead exhibits itself under conditions of
manhood, and then the manhood is glorified under
conditions of Godhead.

In so conceiving of our Lord in His Incarnation, we
are, as I have said, well within the limits of those pre-
scribed dogmas which were intended as restraints on
error, rather than as sources of information. Further
than this, we receive a great deal of sanction from the
best early theologians [2], from St. Irenaeus to Theodoret,
and from some of the best theologians of the Anglican
Church since the Reformation. On the other hand, it
is true that many of the Fathers, beginning with Hilary
and Augustine, and almost all mediaeval theologians,
decline to allow in our Lord's humanity any such limi-

---

[1] See app. note 47, p. 265.          [2] See app. note 48, p. 267.

tation of consciousness as the New Testament seems
to postulate.   In view of such a fact there are three
considerations which should not be omitted.

In the first place, it was much easier intellectually
for them, than it is for us, to explain away the plain
meaning of words, as in other books, so equally in the
New Testament.   Exact interpretation is, more or less,
a growth of recent times, which brings with it corresponding responsibilities.   If mediaeval writers surpass
us in subtlety of theological perception, we have better
opportunities than they, of understanding what the
writers of Scripture actually meant.

Secondly, it was easier morally for churchmen of
past ages than it is for us, to suggest that when our
Lord said, 'He did not know,' He meant that He
knew but would not tell.   The indignant protest of
Theodoret against such an interpretation would find an
echo in almost every modern conscience [1].

Thirdly, there were causes, which have not been sufficiently taken into account, tending to make mediaeval theologians depreciate the real significance of our
Lord's truly human condition.   Of these, not the least
considerable was the almost apostolic authority attributed to the writer who was believed to be Dionysius
the Areopagite, the convert of St. Paul; but who was in
fact a fifth or sixth century writer, of unmistakably
monophysite tendency, in whom the Incarnation was
viewed almost exclusively as a theophany.   Thus it
was said of St. Thomas Aquinas, with not more than
an exaggeration of truth, that 'he drank almost his

[1] See app. note 49, p. 267.

whole theological doctrine out of the most pure wells of Dionysius [1].'

In view of such considerations it is no exaggeration to say that the real pressure of the problem we have been considering in this lecture, exegetical, moral, and theological, was not felt by mediaeval writers as we cannot fail to feel it. Thus in asking men to fall back upon the Church's formal decisions about our Lord's person and upon the text of the New Testament, and to reconsider, on this basis, the moral and human meaning of the Incarnation, we are not asking them to re-open a problem which can be represented as either dogmatically decided or fairly considered.

## VI.

Jesus Christ then is the Son of man : and as we approach to accept from Him the standard of our manhood, we are struck both by His likeness, and by His unlikeness, to ourselves. Let us devote the concluding portion of this lecture to considering three respects in which Jesus, because His humanity is perfect, presents features of unlikeness to other men.

(1) In the first place in Him humanity is sinless. He is represented to us in the wilderness as being assailed by the three great typical temptations before which our race has succumbed : by the lust of the flesh in its most subtle form ; by worldliness in the form calculated to make the most brilliant appeal to the imagination ;

---

[1] See Westcott's *Religious Thought in the West* (Macmillan, 1891), p. 152 ff.

and by pride in the form which spiritual and powerful minds have found most seductive. In every form temptation was rejected, not because He had not real human faculties to feel its force, but because His faculties acted simply under the control of a will, which followed unhesitatingly the movement of the Holy Spirit, in other words, which existed only to do the Father's will. And this representative victory summarizes His whole human life in its moral aspect. 'The prince of this world came and had nothing in him.' He was in all points tempted as we are, apart from sin; that is, so far as a sinless nature can be tempted, so far as one can be effectively assailed who has not, as we have, the traitor within the camp.

To say that He was sinless is to say that He was free. Moral freedom—in the sense in which Scripture and the higher moralists use the term; in the sense in which Shakespeare speaks of 'hot passion' as opposed to 'the *free* determination 'twixt right and wrong'— means not an indeterminate power to choose this or that, to do good or bad, but the power to vindicate the mastery of will and to realize the rational law of our being. 'That man has true freedom,' said St. Leo, 'whose flesh is controlled by the judgment of his mind, and whose mind is directed by the government of God[1].' Such was the liberty of manhood in Jesus Christ. He did not sin, because none of His faculties were disordered, there was no loose or ungoverned movement in His nature, no movement save under the control of His will. He could not sin, because sin being what it is, rebellion against God, and He being what He was,

---

[1] S. Leo, *Serm.* xxxix. 2 ; cf. xlii. 2.

the Father's Son in manhood, the human will which was His instrument of moral action, could not choose to sin. It is right, as St. Augustine and St. Anselm assure us[1], to say that Christ could have refused obedience if He had willed; what was impossible was that He should will to sin.

The summary proof, then, that sin is not according to man's true nature, that it is rebellion and not nature, lies in the fact that in Christ, the true man, sin had no place. He viewed sin in no other way than as the disease which He came to remedy, the havoc of the intruder whom He came to expel. He is ' the lamb of God which taketh away the sin of the world.' And we look forward, through Him, to a liberty like His: to a blessed time, when acts of resistance in the power of the divine Spirit shall have accumulated into habits, and habits shall have become fixed as character, and the liberty of the blessed shall be ours: which is, the inability any longer to find attraction in what is not of God.

(2) In Jesus Christ humanity was perfect. We have no reason to think that man was originally created perfect[2]. Irenaeus and Clement expressly deny it. We believe that when the body of man was first made the dwelling-place of a self-conscious, free personality, man might have developed on the lines of God's intention, not without effort and struggle, but without rebellion and under no curse. But in any case, all the process of development of all human faculties lay before him. He was imperfect, and only adapted to develope freely.

---

[1] See app. note 50, p. 268.
[2] See app. note 51, p. 268.

But in Christ, humanity is not only free from taint, but, in the moral and spiritual region, also at the goal of development. In Him first we see man completely in the image of God, realizing all that was in the divine idea for man. He was perfect child according to the measure of childhood, boy according to boyhood's measure, man according to man's standard; and He was perfected at last according to the final destiny of manhood in eternal glory. That which without Him could have been no more than a hope of immortality, a dim expectation of final perfecting, becomes in Him a realized certainty. He has 'shed the light on life and immortality [1].' We behold Jesus, not only the captain of our faith, but its consummator in glory.

(3) Jesus Christ is the catholic man. In a sense all the greatest men have overstepped the boundaries of their time.

'The truly great
Have all one age, and from one visible space
Shed influence. They both in power and act,
Are permanent and time is not with them,
Save as it worketh for them, they in it.'

But in a unique sense, the manhood of Jesus is catholic; because it is exempt, not from the limitations which belong to manhood, but from the limitations which make our manhood narrow and isolated, merely local or national. Born a man, and a Jew, in a carpenter's family, He can be equally claimed by both sexes, by all classes, by all men of all nations. This is apparent, in part, in the broad appeal which Jesus makes to man as man, in His teaching and in His institutions. We observe that while He explicitly and

[1] 2 Tim. i. 10.

unhesitatingly legislated in regard to marriage, which is
an institution purely human and catholic, He refused to
express any judgment which could have been held to
sanction merely national customs, such as the Jewish
law of inheritance[1].   He would not put the new wine
into the old bottles.   Again, He converted the Jewish
Passover into a catholic sacrament with symbols common
to all men.   Once more He used the Scriptures, as all
men may use them.   'When we compare,' says Dr.
Edersheim, ' the long discussions of the Rabbis on the
letter and law of Scripture with His references to the
word of God, it seems as if it were quite another book
which was being handled [2].'

But this rich truth of our Lord's catholic manhood
has only been gradually apparent in the history of
the world.   Each race has its special aptitudes, its
'glory and honour[3]'; and as the glory and honour of
each nation has been brought within the light of 'the
holy city,'—the versatility and intellect of the Greeks,
the majestic discipline of the Romans, the strong individuality of the Teutons—each in turn has been able
to find its true ideal in Jesus of Nazareth, not as a
dream of the imagination, but as a fact of observation,
and has marvelled how those that were in Christ before
them could be blind to the presence in Him of what
they so especially value.   Thus it is only gradually
that the true moral ideal of Christianity is appre-
hended.   No doubt, for example, many early Christians had an imperfect perception of the obligation of

---

[1] See Latham, *Pastor Pastorum*, p. 404.

[2] Edersheim, *Jesus the Messiah* (Longmans, 1884 , i. p. 234.

[3] Rev. xxi. 26.

truthfulness, but when Augustine vigorously asserted it to be a part of Christian morality, he asserted what is undoubtedly true. Christ did lift all conversation to the level of absolute truthfulness, to the level formerly held only by statements under oath: 'Let your yea be yea, and your nay nay.' We in our time, to take only one more example, have learnt to give great prominence to the virtue of considerateness. The rough and summary classifications of men in groups, the equally rough and summary condemnations of them, the inconsiderate treatment of heretics and even of speculators, these facts in Church history strike us as painful and unworthy. Considerateness, we say, is a Christian virtue. 'Let your considerateness be known unto all men [1].' We look back to our Lord, and are astonished that any can have failed to see His intense respect for individuality, His freedom from fanaticism, in a word His considerateness. Certainly, it is there. Only lest we should be arrogant, we need to remember that other ages and other races have caught more readily in Him what we ignore—His antagonism to pride or to the selfish assertion of property,—and that the whole is not yet told. Only altogether, all ages, all races, both sexes, can we grow up in one body, 'into the perfect man'; only a really catholic society can be 'the fulness of him that filleth all in all [2].' Thus we doubt not that, when the day comes which shall see the existence of really national churches in India and China and Japan, the tranquillity and inwardness of the Hindu, the pertinacity and patience of the Chinaman, the brightness and amiability of the Japanese, will each

[1] Phil. iv. 5.     [2] Eph. iv. 13; i. 23.

in turn receive their fresh consecration in Christ, and
bring out new and unsuspected aspects of the Christian
life; finding fresh resources in Him in whom is 'neither
Jew nor Greek, neither male nor female, barbarian,
Scythian, bond nor free, but Christ all in all[1].'

We contemplate Jesus Christ, the Son of man, in the
sinlessness, the perfection, the breadth of His manhood,
and in Him we find the justification of our highest hopes
for man.  There is much in human nature to disgust us,
to dishearten, to dismay.  'We see not our tokens.'
'There is none that doeth good.'  We say in our haste,
' All men are liars.'  ' What is man,' we cry out to God,
' that thou art mindful of him, or the son of man that
thou visitest him?'  In very truth we do not see a satisfactory manhood about us, nor do we find it within us.
But we see Jesus, born, growing, living, dying, suffering,
glorified; and in Him we find what is both the condemnation of what we are, and the assurance of what we
may be.  As Son of man, he claims and exercises over
us a legitimate authority, the authority of acknowledged
perfection : as Son of man He shows us what human
nature is to be, individually and socially, and supplies
us with the motives and the means for making the
ideal real.  The consideration of these functions of the
Son of man as authority, example, new life, will occupy
us in the two remaining lectures.  It is enough for
us to recognise at this point in how large and full a
sense Jesus Christ is really man, made in all points
like His brethren, sin apart ; and to confess, with a
full assurance of conviction, that the clue to progress, social and individual, lies with those, and only

[1] Gal. iii. 28 ; Col. iii. 11.

those, who in simplest loyalty, with calmest delibera-
tion and completest courage, take His teaching to
guide them and His character to mould them—'looking unto Jesus.'

# LECTURE VII.

## CHRIST OUR MASTER.

*All authority hath been given unto me in heaven and on earth. Go ye therefore, and make disciples of all the nations, baptizing them into the name of the Father and of the Son and of the Holy Ghost: teaching them to observe all things whatsoever I commanded you: and lo, I am with you all the days, even unto the end of the world.*—St. MATTHEW xxviii. 18.

THERE is no subject more in dispute at present in religious circles than the reality, the function, the seat, of authority in religion. Now neither as to the reality of religious authority nor as to its seat in the first instance can any Christian be in doubt. Jesus Christ is the summary authority in religion. He is this because He reveals God, as being His very image, and every revelation of God must come upon men with authority, as from above; He is this, again, because He is perfect man, and therefore exercises over humanity the control which is always exercised by acknowledged perfection

### I.

Our Lord's method as a teacher, as it is exhibited to us in the Gospels, is unmistakably the method of authority. 'Verily,' He said, 'I say unto you.' 'Heaven and earth shall pass away, but my words shall not pass

away.' 'He taught as one having authority, and not as
the scribes.'    It is obvious to contrast this method, in
harmony as it is with that of all God's prophets, with the
method of Greek teachers such as Socrates and Plato. ·

Socrates was content to stimulate thought by questions.   His object was not so much to inculcate a positive
system as to make men exact and critical in their understanding and their speech.   He believed, strangely as
it seems to us, that right action would follow almost
necessarily on right thought.   He was ready to go anywhere where the argument led him.   Plato, by a process
now of Socratic criticism, now of positive construction,
made it his aim to erect an edifice of life and thought
on a basis purely rational; and appears to us to have
attained after all, so far as the positive attempt was concerned, such a very moderate measure of success.

God forbid that we should depreciate these methods.
When the average carelessness of men in thought and
speech is forced upon our notice, not least in the religious
world of to-day, we are tempted to echo the cry, 'Oh,
for one hour of Socrates!' to question our teachers in
public places as to the meaning of their words.
Further, we notice that when our Lord used argument,
it is occasionally in the Socratic manner.   Once more, if
St. Paul is an inspired apostle, the method of dialectic
is certainly justified in Christian theology.   We must
not, then, depreciate the method of argument, but we
must recognise that it is not the basis of the Christian
system; it is not the primary method of Christianity.
It will avail to prepare the way for religion, to formulate
it, to defend it, to keep it true to type; but it will not
establish it in the first instance, or propagate it in the

world.   Religion goes out from the lips of Christ and
of all who represent Christ as a word of God, appealing
to men because they believe in God and have ears to
hear ; a word of God to be first of all received in faith.
' This is the work of God, that ye believe on him whom
he hath sent [1].'

It is not, then, open to question that the Christian
religion—whether as imparted by a teaching Church,
or as contained in a volume of inspired writings, or as
presented in, what lies behind both these subordinate
instruments, the person of Jesus Christ Himself—the
Christian religion is an authoritative word of God,
and Christians are men under authority.   ' A prince,'
says Bishop Andrewes, on Christmas day, as he comments on the prophecy of Isaiah [2], ' so is Jesus styled,
" born " and " given " to establish a " government," that
none imagine they shall live like libertines under Him,
every man believe and live as he list.   It is Christ not
Belial that is born to-day, He bringeth a government
with Him ;  they that be His must live in subjection
under a government ; else neither in Child nor Son, in
birth nor gift, have they any interest.'


## II.

Authority in religion obviously implies some considerable discipline of private judgment, that is, of the
uncontrolled opinion or inclination of the individual.
In part this belongs to all reasonable education, and

[1] St. John vi. 29.
[2] *Sermons of the Nativity*, Serm. ii. on Is. ix. 6.

ought not to present any difficulty to us in connection with religion.   It is not intended that each generation or each individual should start afresh in life, and exercise the unassisted intellect or imagination *de novo* on the matter of human sensation and experience and thought.   The heritage of the past, the truth at which mankind has already arrived, is to be first of all received, as a communicated doctrine which is to mould the mind of the generation that is rising, and is to be assimilated with the reverence due to the 'testimony of the elders.'   Only out of such submission to be taught, such subjection to an external lesson to be received and assimilated, can any right originality have its origin.   So philosophers have been at pains to assure us, from Plato and Aristotle down to Hegel and Goethe.

And in the things of God authority has necessarily a more permanent place than in the affairs of men. In religion, even when a man has got to the level of his fellow-men—when he has learnt what they can teach him, and as 'a spiritual man' is 'judged of none'—still at this level he is hardly less than before under authority.   For 'God is in heaven and man upon earth,' man has never discovered Him aright or found out His true being ; at every stage man's knowledge of God has come through God's disclosure of Himself.   Whether by the 'categorical imperative' which appeals to the will through the conscience, or by the word of God through the prophet, or by the mission of the Son, but always by the way of revelation from above, has the real knowledge of God been gained.   Thus the oldest and the wisest of men must still remain in an attitude of acceptance, of adoration, of faith ; faith which, however sure it is of its rationality—though it cry through the lips of St. Anselm, 'having begun by believing I have grown into understanding,'—yet never ceases to be faith; faith which, in the case of a Christian, rests unceasingly on the person of Jesus, the very reason and word of the Father.

Partly then because it is an educational system, partly because it is a revelation of the most high God, Christianity is authoritative ; but, granted this, we are only at the beginning of our enquiry, for authority is of different types. Broadly we may distinguish two, the despotic and the fatherly. The aim of despotic authority is to produce unquestioning obedience, at least in that department of life to which it applies—and it is worth noticing that it can be content with part of a life more easily than parental authority. The aim, I say, of despotic authority is to produce in the intellect simple acceptance, and in the conduct unquestioning obedience. It works therefore through explicit commands and dogmas, which cannot in fact be too explicit, or leave too little to the imagination and thought of the subject. If the end is simply to produce obedient servants, the directions cannot be too clear or too exact. But parental authority works by other means. Its end is to produce conformity of character, sympathy of mind, intelligent co-operation in action. It is never satisfied with blind obedience. For this very reason, it delights in the stimulus of half-disclosures, in directions which arrest attention and suggest enquiry, but leave much to be done in the mind of their recipients. For education in sonship, it is easily possible for information to be too full, and directions too explicit, because such fulness and explicitness may tend to suppress rather than to stimulate, and secure blind obedience rather than co-operation.

Now the authority of the Mosaic law, or rather of those portions of it which St. Paul treats as characteristic of the whole, is of the despotic sort. It consists of directions, moral and ritual, explicit, exact, calculated to secure scrupulous obedience, and that is all. But the higher authority of our Lord is characterized by being more moderate, not in respect of the thoroughness of the claim made, but in the mode of its presentation. The discipline of the Old Testament is that of the master, the authority of the New that of the father. No doubt there must always be place and occasion in Christianity for blind obedience. There are moments in all lives, and not only in crushed and ruined lives, when men must be content to be slaves that they may become sons ; as there was place even in our Lord's life for the characteristic Old Testament virtue of εὐλάβεια[1] : 'He was heard for his godly fear.' But the characteristic note of the New Testament authority is that of the father over the son, and for this very reason it is moderate. This moderation is noticeable both in its range and in its method.

We might have imagined antecedently that God's completer revelation of Himself, which belongs to the New Testament, would have been characterized by the wide area over which it ranged; that there would have been a letting loose of the divine omniscience ; that the multitude of the disclosures would have been in proportion to the power exhibited and the benefit received. But the actual method of the Incarnation contradicts such a supposition. However our Lord's silence is to be in-

[1] See Trench, *Synonyms of the N. T.* (7th ed., Macmillan, 1871), p. 164.

terpreted, at any rate it did not fall within the scope
of His mission to reveal His omniscience by disclosures
in the region of natural knowledge, or His eternity
by information about history, otherwise inaccessible, in
the past or in the future. He came neither to make a
display of omniscience nor to relieve us from the
effort of acquiring knowledge. Moreover, within the
spiritual region how reserved are His communications.
What is given is primarily the disclosure of God's
mind and will towards men. Even His triune being
is rather overheard, than heard as a distinct and separate
announcement. About the life beyond the grave, while
the thoughts of men are rectified, spiritualized and moral-
ized, very little positive information is given. The old
metaphors of 'Abraham's bosom,' 'the unquenchable fire,'
'the undying worm,' the names Hades, Gehenna, Heaven,
are filled with new moral meaning, but supplemented
by hardly any disclosure to satisfy the imagination
or curiosity. Once again, however the belief in good
and bad spirits had come to take its place in the
Jewish creed, that belief is accepted and used by our
Lord in positive teaching with such explicitness and
emphasis that there is, I think, no room for a Christian
to doubt—as why in reason should he doubt?—that such
spirits really exist and exercise influence in the life of
nature and man. But again, how little information
is given. If, as St. Paul says, we Christians who live
in the light of revelation, yet see 'in a mirror, darkly,'
'know in part and prophesy in part'—this is a direct
consequence of the limits set by the divine wisdom
upon our Lord's prophetic office [1].

---

[1] See on the above paragraph app. note 52, p. 268.

The reserve which is noticeable in the content, is notice-able also in the method, of our Lord's communications. One of the most observant and suggestive of recent writers about the Gospels, Dr. Latham, says, 'Among the great teachers of the world there is hardly one whose chosen pupils have received so few tenets in a formulated shape, as those of Christ [1]'; and if Dr. Martineau is exaggerating when he says that 'the sublimest things which he told the people he assumed that they in their secret hearts must know[2],' even the exaggeration is suggestive of the truth. Obviously our Lord knew that revelation might be too full, too explicit in answers to questions, too easily intelligible; and that because such fulness, explicitness, and plainness, would not leave men enough to do for themselves.

Our Lord, then, trained His disciples to do a great deal for themselves in the way of spiritual effort in apprehending truth. Thus, when He finally elicited from St. Peter the confession of His own name—'Thou art the Christ, the son of the living God,'—He elicited, as the utterance of the disciple's own slowly formed conviction, what He might have dictated from outside. We have further evidence of our Lord's refusal to do too much for His disciples in His use of paradoxes. The Mosaic law says exactly what it means, you have only to take it and obey it: but the Sermon on the Mount sets a man thinking: it perplexes, it almost baffles; it is only by patient effort to appreciate its spirit, that it can be reduced to practice. The same is true of the parables which our Lord used to teach the people. They stimulate thought, they suggest principles, they

---

[1] *Pastor Pastorum,* pp. 271-2.     [2] *Seat of Authority,* p. 322.

arrest the attention, but they do not give men spiritual information in the easiest and most direct form. Our Lord then taught, and especially taught His disciples, so as to train their characters and stimulate their intelligences ; He worked to make them intelligent sons and friends, not obedient slaves. He would have them set ends above means, and principles above ordinances ; as when He said that 'the sabbath was made for man, and not man for the sabbath.' And His own ordinances, such as baptism and the eucharist, are Christian sacraments and not Jewish laws—the sacraments of sons and not the ordinances of servants—because they carry with them their own justification, because they convey a declared and intelligible grace. They are obligatory, but as food is obligatory ; for to know their secret is to desire their use, as a son desires food and fellowship in his father's household.

There is then an ideal of paternal authority, the authority which exists to develope sonship ; and this is the authority of Christ.   St. Augustine describes well the character of authority as thus conceived, when he says, that ' authority is prior to reason in order of time, but reason is prior to authority in essence [1].'   In other words, all legitimate authority represents the higher reason, educating the development of the lower.  Legitimate religious authority represents the reason of God, educating the reason of man and communicating itself to it.   Now man is made in God's image : he is in his fundamental capacity a son of God, and he becomes so in fact, and fully, through union with Christ.  Therefore in the truth of God, as Christ presents it to him, he can recognise his own better reason :

---

[1] S. Aug. *de ord.* ii. 9 (26).

to use Plato's beautiful expression, he can salute it by force of instinct as something akin to himself, before he can give intellectual account of it [1]. He begins by accepting it on faith, and in obedience, but the very thing that he accepts quickens and satisfies his faculties, and he grows from faith to intuition, from love to knowledge, till as the developed 'spiritual man' he 'judges all things,' till by the 'unction of the Holy One' he 'knows all things [2],' and what was once an external 'mould of doctrine' has become the ineradicable conviction of his own mind.

We may then characterize Christian authority in two respects ; first, that as a higher sort of reason, it stimulates and developes in each of its subjects not conscience only—though it appeals first to conscience, and the way of conversion is the true beginning of enlightenment—nor only the faculties of obedience and worship, but also the faculty of reason and free judgment. While developing human reason into the image of the divine it also frees it and satisfies it on its own level.    It is above our reason, not below it.    Thus, so far as history enters into the things of faith, and with history the occasion for criticism and investigation, authority must be able to present its historical credentials in a shape which corresponds to the requirements of reason.    Its historical supports must be as satisfactory as historical supports can be.    It must encourage its votaries to test all things. It must set no premium on credulity; it must make no virtue of mental blindness, as if the refusal to investigate were in any way connected with reverence and faith.    It is the test of Christianity's legitimate tenure, that it can encourage free enquiry into its title-deeds.

---

[1] *Republic* 402 A.                [2] 1 Cor. ii. 15 ; 1 St. John ii. 20.

Secondly, as Christian authority educates men for sonship, so it is not satisfied with bare acceptance of dogmas
and obedience to rules.   It is not satisfied that one or
two of the Christian community should do the positive
work of religion for the rest.   It desires to see the whole
community an organized body in active co-operation, a
royal priesthood in consecrated service.   It is because it
thus desires to enlist all men, and the whole man, in
positive service, that the best kind of authority refuses to
do too much for men, refuses to be too explicit, too
complete, too clear, lest it should dwarf instead of
stimulating their higher faculties.


## III.

At this point, then, I cannot but ask you whether the
mind of the Church of England does not give a very
fair expression of the Christian ideal of authority.   Our
church would have each of its members educated,
through childhood and youth, in a catechism which contains the creed as a summary of theology, the Lord's
prayer as the type of prayer, the ten commandments
with their explanation as a rule of duty, the teaching
about the sacraments as a law of church membership.
This preliminary instruction would be somewhat supplemented by the services intended for everybody's use.
Here is a dogmatic basis for education, clear and distinct
up to a certain point, but leaving a great deal for the
individual churchman to do.   He is to grow into a
clearer apprehension of what he has been taught by
familiarity with the Scriptures ; on points left doubtful
in the explicit formulas he is to form his own judgment

with the help of such information as God puts within his reach. Thus his relation to Christian truth is gradually to become that of personal conviction and enlightenment, not of mere passive acceptance.

There are some who would destroy this ideal by removing the basis of obligatory fundamental dogma. This would be equivalent to destroying altogether the ideal of a church, as a society based upon an authoritative message. There are many more who, nominally accepting the ideal, in fact ignore it. Perhaps there is no part of the Church which has sinned as the English Church has sinned, in the neglect of definite religious teaching. Nor can one who desires her welfare aim at anything better than the recovery and promotion of simple dogmatic teaching, based on the catechism and appealing to Scripture, not least among the youth of the educated classes.

Our ideal, we admit, has been grievously neglected; but where it is put in practice, with its dogmatic teaching, its scriptural appeal, its encouragement of enquiry, may we not maintain that it is truer to the type of our Lord's method than a system which does much more by authoritative dogma and leaves much less for the individual to do for himself? It is untrue to say that such a system as ours is inapplicable to the poor. And in fact it is not the poor who complain of Anglicanism on the score of indefiniteness. Their complaints, expressed or unexpressed, are of a different sort. Those who resent the incompleteness of the dogmatic teaching of the English Church and contrast it with the dogmatic system of Rome are in fact men and women whose opportunities of education are much greater, but who disapprove that so much should be left for them to do for themselves.

For there is another dogmatic system with which the Church of Rome is identified, the ideal of which is very different from what I have been describing. It aims at being as explicit and complete in dogmatic instruction as possible. It rejoices simply in clear and definite answers to all questions. The 'peradventure' of an Augustine as to a purgatory for the imperfect after death—*non redarguo*, he says, *quia forsitan verum est*[1]—has become a positive teaching about purgatory, full of exact information. This system leaves the individual churchman simply to accept what the Church teaches, and to practise what the Church enjoins, and so to secure his everlasting salvation. Now it is plain that such a peremptory and complete system of dogma may by its very clearness and explicitness represent a lower level of discipline than our Lord intended for His disciples. It is not in fact at all agreeable to the method which He and His apostles actually pursued, while by its very existence it makes far more difficult of execution the truer ideal, attracting men as a short and easy method of solving difficulties, just at the time when perhaps they most need the more troublesome discipline.

But the Roman system not only does not encourage personal investigation, it positively discourages it. It regards the free appeal to history or Scripture in verification of church dogmas as a mark of distrust ; it calls it rationalism or implied heresy[2]. And that for a plain

---

[1] See app. note 53, p. 269.
[2] See further, *Roman Catholic Claims*, pp. 12-14, 53 f.

reason. Some of the special dogmas of Rome are below reason rather than above it, at the point where the things of faith come into the area of historical enquiry. For the Roman Church is formally tied to the old catholic position that there can be no new doctrines in the Church. 'First of all,' wrote Cardinal Newman, many years after he joined the Roman Church, '*ex abundanti cautela*'—that is as something almost too obvious to need stating—'every Catholic holds that the Christian dogmas were in the Church from the time of the apostles : that they were ever in their substance what they are now[1].' But this is exactly what is not true, for instance, of the immaculate conception of the mother of our Lord : of the treasury of merits to be dispensed in indulgences : of the papal infallibility. If there is such a thing as history, it bears unmistakable witness that those beliefs were not in substance part of the original Christian faith. Again, the Roman Catholic celebrates with the dignity which belongs only to the greatest festivals the assumption to heaven of the body of Mary; but this supposed event has nothing which can be called respectable historical evidence to support it. It is thus because of the substance of some of her dogmas and beliefs, that the Roman Church is by her very principles forced to put a certain premium upon credulity; to make the refusal to enquire a mark of reverence, and to pursue towards the critical reason the same lines as orientalists of old pursued towards the physical flesh—to cast it out as evil.

I am not concerned here to be controversial, but only to maintain that the Anglican ideal of authority represents

[1] See app. note 54, p. 269.

satisfactorily enough the method of our Lord, in respect
of that very thing which is often imputed .to it as an
objection; namely that it leaves so much for the individual
to do for himself, and lays so much stress on historical
verification, if not by every individual, at least in the
society as a whole.    I may add that this ideal represents
also the method of the early Church.    Certainly, among
Christians of the first four centuries, in the Church of
Irenaeus and Origen, in the Church represented by the
catechetical lectures of Cyril of Jerusalem or Gregory
of Nyssa, there was a requirement made on the intelligence and patience of the individual, at least as great as
that made by the English Church even in its present
condition.    And it needs to be remembered, that in
appealing across the ages to the Church of the first
centuries we are not appealing merely to a Church which
is primitive, but to one which existed under intellectual
conditions comparatively like our own.


## IV.

But if such be the character of Christian authority,
where does it reside?

In discussing the nature of the authority exercised by
Christ, and to be exercised in His name, I have already
used words which imply that that authority is outwardly
represented to us at the present time by two instru-
mentalities, the Church and the Bible.    The Christian is
first to be brought under instruction by the Church,
and then is to deepen, develope, verify, purge his faith
by the study of Scripture.    This is commonly recognised

as the Anglican view,—'the Church to teach, the Bible
to prove,'—and it is, I may say, unquestionably the view
of the ancient Church [1]. It does not fall within the scope
of this lecture to enlarge upon it or to vindicate it, but
I may endeavour to bring out some of its meaning and
show its relation to the authority of our Lord.

The Christian authority is simply Jesus Christ; but
for the external knowledge of our Lord, the knowledge
of what He taught and was, we are dependent, by His
deliberate intention, upon the witness of His apostles.
Now the testimony of the apostles holds good for us
simply on its natural basis as testimony, because, as I
have had occasion to point out, they were such good
witnesses, morally and intellectually, and because we have
such strong grounds for believing that their testimony
remains to us in the New Testament narratives.   Nor
do we need anything else than their evidence, fairly
estimated, to justify our own belief in Jesus Christ or
to suggest to others the grounds for believing.

But when men have once become believers in Jesus
Christ, as the incarnate Son of God, they will recognise in the apostles something more than witnesses,
namely, witnesses qualified for a unique function by a
special inspiration.   St. John records how in His last
discourse our Lord promised them that the Holy
Ghost whom the Father would send in His name should
teach them all things and bring all things to their remembrance whatsoever He said to them.   This special
gift of the Holy Ghost was to qualify the apostles as
witnesses of Jesus.   He was to lead them into all the
truth, He was to take of what belonged to Jesus, and

---

[1] See lect. iv. app. note 25, p. 252.

declare it to them [1].  'This section' in St. John's Gospel,
says Dr. Westcott, 'marks the position of the apostles
with regard to revelation as unique ; and so also by
implication the office of the apostolic writings as a record of their teaching.'   Christians believe then that
the apostles were specially enlightened to present to
us without distortion the person and teaching of our
Lord, and familiarity with their writings through nine-
teen Christian centuries has confirmed the belief.   We
cannot as a matter of historical enquiry go behind the
apostles, for our Lord wrote nothing Himself ; as a
matter of faith we do not need to go behind it.   In
the apostolic teaching, then, we find the ultimate court
of appeal in respect of 'the faith once delivered to the
saints.'   He that heareth them, heareth Him.

How then are we to be taught by the apostles ?   You
answer, ' By reading the New Testament.'   Undoubtedly,
but not primarily.   The books of the New Testament
bear upon the face of them the evidence that they were
not meant for primary instruction ; they were addressed
to men who were already Christians, that is to say,
men who as members of a definite society, the Church
or the Churches, had already received oral instruction [2].
It is matter of historical fact that the Christian teaching
was not first of all written down, but was originally
committed to a confederation of societies as a 'tradition'
which they were to hold, or, as it was afterwards called,
a rule of faith : and ever since that day, through all
vicissitudes, this society or group of societies has been

---

[1] St. John xiv. 26, xvi. 13, 14, and Westcott *in loc.*
[2] See St. Luke i. 4 ; 1 Cor. xi. 23, xv. 3 ; Gal. i. 6 8 ; Heb. v. 12 ;
James i. 19 [R.V.] ; 2 Peter i. 12, iii. 1 ; 1 John ii. 20 ; Jude 3.

in the world teaching the Christian creed. The primary depositary of the Christian tradition, then, is the Christian Church. It has been, and it is, 'the pillar and ground of the truth[1].'

But the tradition of a society, however powerful a factor it is in human life, is not, as every one knows, trustworthy unless it can be checked. Thus the Christian tradition, instead of being miraculously exempted from the ordinary tendencies of a tradition, was provided with checks, partly in its own earlier records, but especially in the New Testament. Thus the New Testament is not the primary instrument of teaching, but it is the criterion of teaching. 'Do not believe me simply,' says St. Cyril of Jerusalem, speaking even to his catechumens, 'unless you receive the proof of what I say from Holy Scripture[2].'

This view of the Christian Church as the teaching body, with the New Testament as the constant criterion of its teaching, is a view which makes a powerful appeal to our imagination and our mind. On the one hand there is the great catholic society, intended to exist among all nations but to be confined to none and dependent upon none. This is an incomparable instrument for maintaining and propagating religion, calculated to take hold of what is richest and noblest in human nature. On the other hand, in the original Scriptures there is a safeguard provided against the tendency of all religious traditions to deterioration and narrowness. For developments in proportion to their power tend to become one-sided; but the Catholic faith is not meant to become one-sided or narrowed as it passes down the

---

[1] 1 Tim. iii. 15.    [2] Cyr. Hieros. *Cat.* iv. 17.

ages.   Here then should come in the counteracting force
of Scripture.   As there is to be a perpetual development
out of the apostolic teaching in response to new requirements, so there is to be a perpetual return upon it,
a perpetual reversion to type.   The familiarity of all
Christians with the apostolic pattern—the original and
inspired type of Christian doctrine, and the record of our
Lord's life—is meant to prevent either the stereotyping
of one-sided traditions or the erection of current opinions
into articles of faith.   The Church is perpetually to teach ;
the New Testament is perpetually to prove, to verify,
to correct the teaching.   This is the ideal.   It is an
ideal which, sadly enough we admit, cannot be applied
by us to-day in its perfection.   The divisions of Christendom on the one side, and on the other side the habitual
neglect of Scripture as a criterion of doctrine in many
parts of the Church and at many periods of her history,
have marred the presentation of Christian authority in
the world.   But in spite of hindrances, both elements
in the authority are still real.   Every one of us can put
himself to school with the Church's creed and traditional
teaching, more or less perfectly according to his opportunities and means of education; and gaining thus
what Athanasius calls his ' point of view,' he can go,
in the mind of the catholic society, to the study of the
New Testament, and so grow into the more perfect
knowledge of Him in whom are hid ' all the treasures
of wisdom.'

## V.

Both the New Testament and the Church represent to us in different ways that original authority with which our Lord endued His apostles. 'All authority hath been given unto me.' He said to them, 'Go ye therefore and make disciples of all the nations, baptizing them into the name of the Father and of the Son and of the Holy Ghost, teaching them to observe all things whatsoever I commanded you ; and lo, I am with you all the days.' In this and parallel commissions lie the title-deeds of the authority both of the Church and of the New Testament. But there is another part of the Bible, namely the Old Testament, which already existed in our Lord's day, and which He is found to have treated as already possessing divine authority.

Our Lord primarily used the Old Testament as God's word to the Jews. Thus He brings out its witness against Sadducean rationalism. 'Ye do err, not knowing the scriptures nor the power of God[1].' He brings out its witness, again, against the spurious orthodoxy and false expectations of the Pharisees.

The 'Psalms of Solomon,' which appear to be the work of a Pharisee. writing some fifty years before our Lord's birth, give us probably a good idea of the Messianic expectation which was held by the religious world of our Lord's day. If the picture of the Messiah, given in these psalms, is compared with the ideal of the canonical books, especially of Isaiah, it is found to have lost two important elements. First, it has lost the divine

---

[1] St. Matt. xxii. 29.

element. The Messiah is David's son, and apparently he is
nothing more. We are never reminded of the 'Wonderful
Counsellor, Mighty God, Everlasting Father,' of the first
part of Isaiah. Secondly, the idea of the second part of
Isaiah, the idea of the suffering servant of Jehovah redeeming God's people through his sacrifice, has altogether
vanished and left no trace. There is no other image
presented than that of the victorious king who shall
expel the Roman intruders and overthrow the Sadducean
sinners[1]. From this lower ideal then, which had its hold
not only on His opponents, but also on His disciples,
our Lord makes His appeal to the Old Testament Scriptures with their witness to a higher righteousness, to a
diviner king, to a suffering redeemer. 'Ought not the
Christ to have suffered these things and to enter into
his glory? And beginning from Moses and from all the
prophets, he interpreted to them in all the scriptures
the things concerning himself[2].'

Thus if our Lord claimed to supersede, He claimed
also in the fullest sense to fulfil, the Old Testament
ideal. 'Ye search the scriptures,' He said, 'because ye
think that in them ye have eternal life ; and these are
they which bear witness of me[3].' That our Lord thus
recognised in the Old Testament a special authority and
inspiration there can be no doubt. He contrasts the
law, as 'the word of God,' with the traditions and
commandments of men ; He declares that no jot or
tittle of it is to pass away unaccomplished[4]. Again, the
revelation of the Old Testament is recognised in all

---

[1] See Ryle and James, *The Psalms of Solomon* (Camb., 1891), pp.
lii-lix.

[2] St. Luke xxiv. 26, 27.                [3] St. John v. 39.

[4] St. Mark vii. 13 ; St. Matt. v. 18.

the chief stages of its development, the original revelation of man's creation, the revelation to Abraham, the
giving of the law by Moses, the teaching of prophets
and of psalmists.   All is regarded as the divine preparation for Himself.   'Your father Abraham rejoiced
to see my day': 'Moses wrote of me': 'these are the
words which I spake unto you, while I was yet with you,
how that all things must needs be fulfilled which are
written in the law of Moses, and the prophets, and the
psalms, concerning me.   Then opened he their mind
that they might understand the Scriptures[1].'   His own
language is full of Old Testament allusions.   In His
temptation, in His prophecy of the last things, on the
cross, He appropriates again and again the language of
righteous Israel.   He declares that the messianic forecast
must be fulfilled in Himself.   'How then,' He asks,
'should the scripture be fulfilled that thus it must be?[2]'
At least on one occasion He is believed by the evangelist
to have deliberately acted so as to fulfil a detail in the
picture given in the Old Testament[3].

I have said that our Lord used the Old Testament
primarily as God's word to the Jews, so that He regards
its primary function as ended with the fulfilling of
Israel's vocation.   'The law and the prophets were
until John : from that time the gospel of the kingdom
of God is preached[4].'   But the function of the older
scriptures was not exhausted towards the Jews.   The
Apostle of the Gentiles still commends them to us as

---

[1] St. Matt. xix. 4–8 ; St. John viii. 56, v. 46 ; St. Luke xxiv. 44, 45.
   St. Matt. xxvi. 54.
[3] St. John xix. 28.
[4] St. Luke xvi. 16 ; St. Matt. xi. 13.

'given by inspiration of God' and 'written for our ad-
monition upon whom the ends of the world are come [1].'
For us they stand not as adding anything to what is
revealed in Christ, but, in part, as giving in adequate
perfection some elements of the perfect religion—as the
psalms express for ever the relation of the soul to God,
and the prophets, the eternal principles in the divine
government of the world—in part, as showing us the
stages and elements through which and out of which
the complete fabric of divine truth was reared.   Nor do
I think that any one who starts from the platform of
belief in Christ can fail to see in the Old Testament
a special action of divine inspiration, a divine movement
towards the Incarnation, a divine preparation for the
Christ.

But it has been usual to go beyond this, and to
assert that the authority of our Lord binds us to the
acceptance of the Jewish tradition in regard to the
authorship and literary character of different portions
of the Old Testament—for example, that the use by our
Lord of such a phrase as 'Moses wrote of me' binds us
to the Mosaic authorship of the Pentateuch as a whole,
and that His reference to the flood, or to Jonah's three
days' entombment in the fish's belly, binds us to receive
these narratives as simple history.   To this argument
I do not think that we need yield [2].   The lessons incul-
cated by our Lord can be shown to inhere in the narratives even if we cannot be sure of their exact authorship
or literary character.   That special assistance of the
Holy Ghost, which we call inspiration, may have been

[1] 2 Tim. iii. 16 ; 1 Cor. x. 11 ; cf. Rom. xv. 4.
[2] See further *Lux Mundi*, Pref. to 10th ed., pp. xix ff.

O 2

given to a Jewish writer in any literary undertaking which the conscience of his age would have approved, as His assistance certainly was given to Jewish agents in imperfect forms of moral action : and what the divine Spirit could inspire, Jesus, in that same Spirit, could recognise and use. Further, He must have alluded to the books of the Old Testament by their recognised names,—the names by which men always will refer to them when they are speaking ordinary human language ; just as men will always speak of the poetry of Homer even if the composite origin of the Iliad and the Odyssey comes to be universally recognised.

There is however one reference by our Lord to the Old Testament which raises a special difficulty, and about this I propose to say something in detail, because of the important lesson which seems to emerge out of it :—the argument from Psalm cx. To show the Pharisees the inadequacy of the idea of the Messiah as 'the son of David,' our Lord argues with them on the assumption of the Davidic authorship of this psalm. 'The Lord said unto my Lord.' Now if the inspired David himself calls the Messiah 'Lord,' how can it be right to describe him as his son[1] ? This argument certainly in some sense depends upon David's personal authorship. Well then, it is urged, can it be reverent to hesitate in accepting this on the authority of Jesus Christ, when all you have to set against it is a literary probability? Let it be said at once that we could not, consistently with faith, hesitate to accept anything on any subject that our Lord meant to teach us. But on the one hand there are reasons which draw us back

[1] St. Mark xii. 35-37. See app. note 55, p. 270.

from accepting the conclusion that He did in fact mean to teach us the authorship of a psalm ; and on the other hand there is another reasonable and indeed illuminating interpretation to be given to His words.

On the one hand, then, an increasing number of Old Testament students find the Jewish tradition by itself a quite inadequate ground on which to assign any writing to a particular date and author ; while this psalm, judged by itself as a piece of literature, presents all the appearance of being not written by a king, but, like the 45th, a psalm in which a king is addressed, under the customary title of ' my lord.' There is therefore no reason for assigning this psalm to king David as its author, unless we suppose that our Lord interposes to support, with an infallible guarantee, the Jewish tradition. But such an interposition would be a unique phenomenon in His revelation. And if we do not ourselves feel any difficulty about the matter, it is surely right that we should be very loth to ask men, who do feel the difficulty, to accept as matter of revelation, what seems to them an improbable literary theory. Such a demand lays a heavy burden on consciences specially sensitive to the claims of truth. There are critical positions in regard to New Testament books which are intimately bound up with our Christian faith, but they stand upon their own critical merits. They are matters of evidence, not of faith.

On the other hand there is an interpretation—I think, a natural interpretation—of our Lord's words which involves no difficulty of the kind we have been considering.

Whenever our Lord teaches, it is with plenary authority.

'He whom God hath sent speaketh the words of God.'
But at times He does something besides teaching, He
asks men questions such as will lead them to examine
themselves closely in the light of their own principles.
It is not difficult to select examples : ' If I by Beelzebub
cast out devils,' he challenges the Jews, ' by whom do
your sons cast them out [1] ? '   Here it is not necessary to
say that any positive truth is being taught as to Jewish
exorcisms, but an appeal is made to our Lord's adver-
saries to be fair and just in view of their ordinary
assumptions.   Again, ' Why callest thou  me  good ?
there is none good but one, that is God [2].'   Our Lord
is not here really disclaiming, as He appears to disclaim, identity in moral goodness with God, but He
is leading a young man to cross-question himself as to
the meaning of his words, to ask himself what reason
he had to address our Lord with a title of deference.
It is probable that our Lord was using a similar method
in His appeal to the Jews about Psalm cx.   On the
face of it, the argument suggests that the Messiah
could not be David's son,—' if David calleth him Lord,
how is he his son ? '—but in fact its purpose is not to
prove or disprove anything, to affirm or to deny anything, but simply to press upon the Pharisees an
argument which their habitual assumptions ought to
have suggested to them : to confront them with just
that question, which they, with their principles ought
to have been asking themselves.

It is easier to conceive of our Lord using this sort of
argument, if we accept the position maintained in the
last lecture—that He, the very God, habitually spoke,

---

[1] St. Matt. xii. 27.                    [2] St. Mark x. 18.

in His incarnate life on earth, under the limitations
of a properly human consciousness. Though speaking
habitually under such limitations, our Lord never yielded
Himself up to fallible human reasonings. As He taught
only the divine word, so only upon that did He repose.
He knew that human reasoning could never generate
religious certitude. He let Peter know that 'flesh and
blood' had not revealed to him the truth about Himself,
but His Father in heaven. And Peter learnt the lesson.
Many years later he wrote, 'If any man speak,' that is
as a religious teacher, 'let it be as speaking oracles of
God[1].' But though human reasonings cannot attain
the highest certitude, they have yet a great function in
human life, and high responsibilities are attached to them.
Thus though our Lord lives as man and as teacher in
the higher region of the divine word, He still can
stimulate and take an interest in the 'reasonings of
men.' He can feel indignation at wrong arguments,
and careless thought, and shallow self-deception.

Now it seems to me that we have got here to a very
important principle : that, if I am interpreting rightly
our Lord's argument with the Pharisees, it shows us the
Son of man fulfilling an important function towards
human life, which we have been inclined to overlook.

The critical and argumentative methods of men
change considerably from age to age, from nation to
nation. Consequently they cannot form part of the
substance of a catholic religion. Christian apologetics
have never the permanence or the universality of the
creeds. But criticism and argument have their value in
relation to divine truth, and their responsibilities. Our

[1] 1 St. Peter iv. 11.

Lord then does not bring to bear on men's intellectual equipment in any generation the divine omniscience so as to crush it, any more than He did upon the Pharisees. But He does bring to bear upon it the moral claim that it should be used rightly, honestly, and impartially. He does teach us, by His question to the Pharisees, that He expects of us all that Socrates expected of his contemporaries, while He supplies us with a great deal more than Socrates could ever supply.

For our Lord does not only, or chiefly, question. He teaches with infallible certainty the words of God, which redeem and strengthen, illuminate and satisfy, human life.

We all remember the pathetic words of Simmias in the argument with Socrates about the immortality of the soul. 'I dare say,' he says, 'that you, Socrates, feel as I do how very hard and almost impossible is the attainment of any certainty about questions such as these in the present life. And yet I should deem him a coward who did not prove what is said about them to the uttermost, or whose heart failed him before he had examined them on every side. For he should persevere until he has attained one of two things: either he should discover or learn the truth about them; or if this is impossible I would have him take the best and most irrefragable of human notions, and let this be the raft upon which he sails through life—not without risk, as I admit, if he cannot find some word of God which will more surely and safely carry him[1].' 'Some word of God': it has come to us: crowning the legitimate efforts, supplying the inevitable deficiencies, of human reasonings;

[1] Plato, *Phaedo* 85 C, D.

satisfying all the deepest aspirations of the heart and
conscience. It has come to us, and not as a mere spoken
message, but as an incarnate person, at first to attract,
to alarm, to subdue us ; afterwards, when we are His
servants, to guide, to discipline, to enlighten, to enrich
us, till that which is perfect is come, and that which
is in part has been done away.

In this generation very many of us feel, like Simmias,
the unsatisfactoriness of human reasonings, when we are
not sure of the faith. We feel their unsatisfactoriness,
even while we make it our custom—

> ' With others whom a like disquietude
> At the like crisis of their lives now keeps
> Restless, with them to question to and fro
> And to debate the evil of the world,
> As though we bore no portion of that ill,
> As though with subtle phrases we could spin
> A woof to screen us from life's undelight :
> Sometimes prolonging far into the night
> Such talk, as loth to separate, and find
> Each in his solitude how vain are words,
> When that which is opposed to them is more.'

Through such a frame of mind—if we are sincerely
honest in our reasonings, if we anxiously rid ourselves
of vanity, if morally we hold fast to Jesus Christ,—through
such a frame of mind we may hope to pass to the recognition of the divine Word, coming down upon our manhood, to rebuke and to satisfy it,—to crown its fallible
reasonings. ' Lord,' we shall cry, ' to whom shall we go ?
Thou hast the words of eternal life.'

# LECTURE VIII.

## CHRIST OUR EXAMPLE AND NEW LIFE.

*God was pleased to make known what is the riches of the glory of this mystery among the Gentiles, which is Christ in you, the hope of glory: whom we proclaim, admonishing every man and teaching every man in all wisdom, that we may present every man perfect in Christ.—* COLOSSIANS i. 27, 28.

### I.

OUR Lord, as Son of man, set the standard of human life; but He did this by exhibiting a specific moral character, a character involving certain moral principles, rather than by the enunciation of rules of conduct. What detailed rules of conduct He did lay down, have to be interpreted in their principle rather than in their letter. Thus after washing His disciples' feet and wiping them with the towel, He bade His disciples do as He had done: for if He, their Lord and Master, had washed their feet, they ought also to wash one another's feet[1]. But we should rightly feel that an exact fulfilment of this precept—such as finds a place in the ritual of the Roman Catholic Church on Maundy Thursday—if it has in certain states of society a considerable symbolical value, yet goes a very little way in real obedience to our Lord's command. It need not involve practically anything of that spirit of humility and willing service which is what our Lord was intending to inculcate.

[1] St. John xiii. 12–15.

The rules of life then which our Lord lays down must not be merely obeyed in the letter: the meaning or principle which lies behind them has to be grasped and reapplied in each fresh set of circumstances. It is because our Lord thus puts principles above rules, and the spirit of life above its practices, that the example which He sets is a universal example, and His teaching is valid for all time and in all states of society. But there is a great danger which attaches to this highest sort of obedience—obedience, as we call it, by a very familiar misapplication of a phrase of St. Paul's, 'in the spirit and not in the letter[1].' The danger is that the spirit of a precept shall be taken to mean something vague and unexacting. It was not surely without a purpose that our Lord gave His injunctions so detailed and definite a form. He meant that the moral principle is to be translated into outward action just in those details of life where it becomes exacting. To apply a precept under changed circumstances—for example, the precept as to washing one another's feet—ought not to mean to give it an application less public, less actual, less troublesome than its original application. For the publicity, the definiteness, the troublesomeness, belong to the principle of the action. They contribute to its moral value. Yet in fact, what has been called obedience to 'the spirit of our Lord's words' has sadly often meant no obedience at all: so that generations of Christians have lived as if He never said to His disciples generally, 'If any man would go to law with thee, and take away thy coat, let him have thy cloke also'; or 'It is easier for a camel to go through the eye of a needle, than for a rich man to

_____
[1] See app. note 56, p. 271.

enter into the kingdom of God'; or to one, 'If thou wouldst be perfect, go, sell that thou hast, and give to the poor, and thou shalt have treasure in heaven: and come follow me'; or to some, 'There are eunuchs which made themselves eunuchs for the kingdom of heaven's sake. He that is able to receive it, let him receive it [1].'

It is in fact the spirit and principle of our Lord's life and words, and not merely a particular application of them, which lays upon us so exacting a claim. Let any one who would be a sincere disciple contemplate steadily the moral character expressed in the words of Jesus Christ and exhibited in His actions, and though he cannot but be attracted by Him who spake as never man spake, he needs must also be filled with a great dread, on account of the tremendous standard which is there before him. Let me ask you to have the courage and the faith to pursue with me for a while the line of thought here opened out to us.

For instance, the whole life of Jesus Christ was one continuous act of obedience. It was, 'Lo I come to do thy will, O God.' But such persistent and genuine obedience to God occupies but a very little part of most human lives. We men, and more particularly we Englishmen, have transferred the virtue of independence out of its proper region—the region of human opinion, where it has legitimate exercise—into that region where it is simply the principle of all sin, the region of our relation to God. We keep God at arm's length; we let religion be an occasional restraint on conduct, rather than its constant and dominant motive. But we look to Jesus; and in Him, the Son

---

[1] St. Matt. v. 40, xix. 24, 21, 12.

of man, we see a manhood which was never allowed
to retain the initiative to action within itself, but found
its perfection, its liberty, its glory, in obedience and in
obedience only, so that each opening sphere of life was
only one new scene in which to learn more of what it
meant to obey.  'He learned obedience'; 'He was obedient unto death.'  Set then the standard of our Lord's
life in this respect over against our current ideas of
human independence, and, I say, it makes us tremble.
It is easy to deepen this impression.  We may go on to
contrast the self-restraint of the Son of man—in whom
no human passion or appetite was allowed to act, except
under the control of the will, which in its turn waited
unintermittently upon the movement of the Spirit—with
our habitual glorification of what is merely impulsive
and undisciplined in word and action.  Or we may think
of those thirty years of silent preparation for the divine
work, by the side of our careless and rapid acceptance
of the highest and holiest trusts, our light-hearted confidence in improvised solutions of unconsidered difficulties.  Side by side with our shrinking from pain,
passing as it too often does from a legitimate instinct
into an allowed habit of self-indulgence, we may set
His considerate bearing of the burdens of others, His
willing acceptance of pain.  Side by side with our pride
we may set His meekness ; by our selfishness, careless
or calculating, His calculated and deliberate self-sacrifice.  Ecce homo! we cry.  But truly if this is the Son of
man, if this manhood is the only satisfactory manhood, if
'by this man God will judge the world in righteousness [1],'
we have, most of us, not appreciated at all adequately

---

[1] Acts xvii. 31.

the amount of deliberate self-discipline and inward recreation, which must be necessary to bridge the gulf between what we are and what we are to be.

## II.

But as soon as we deliberately contemplate the moral standard which Jesus Christ sets up for human life, the thought is sure to rise in our minds—is it possible that a standard of devotion, of purity, of thoughtfulness, of sacrifice such as this, can appeal to any but a few men or women in any society or any age? The answer to this question is not a simple one. We know that on the whole, and in the long run, nothing does appeal to every man's conscience like the life and teaching of a thorough Christian, and nothing does exercise so permanent or widespreading an influence. But so far as it is true that the Christian standard, on account of its very loftiness, appeals only to the few, the most earnest, men, the contingency is one which Jesus Christ beyond all question had steadily in view. 'Narrow is the gate and straitened is the way,' He said, 'that leadeth unto life, and few be they that are finding it.'

The standard of Mohammedanism, by contrast to Christianity, may be described as a standard deliberately adapted to the average moral level of the men to whom it was meant to appeal. 'If one had to express in a short compass,' says a very discerning writer[1], 'the character of its remarkable founder as a teacher, it would be that that great man had no faith in human nature.

---

[1] Mozley, *On Miracles* (Longmans, 3rd ed. 1872), pp. 140–1.

There are two things which he thought man could do and would do for the glory of God, transact religious forms and fight ; and upon these two points he was severe ; but within the sphere of common practical life, where man's great trial lies, his code exhibits the disdainful laxity of a legislator, who accommodates his rule to the recipient, and shows his estimate of the recipient by the accommodation which he adopts. . . . The writer of the Koran does indeed, if any discerner of hearts ever did, take the measure of mankind': that is, the measure of men, on the average, whom he came in contact with, and he legislates accordingly. 'Human nature is weak,' he said.

It is this spirit of moral accommodation which has made Mohammedanism at once so successful among its votaries, in securing conformity to its rules and also so destitute of really progressive power. The method of Christ is in striking opposition. He, before Mohammed, said, 'The flesh is weak'; but from the starting-point of this acknowledgment He proceeds by a quite different path. No book exhibits so profound a contempt for majorities, so startling a refusal to consider the conditions of success on the average, as the New Testament. Jesus Christ makes His appeal to the best : upon the selected disciples He spends His efforts : for them He prays : them He trains in His own school as the nucleus of a redeemed humanity, to act upon the world as 'salt,' or 'light,' or as a 'city set upon a hill'': that is, as a body acts, the savour or appearance of which is distinct, emphatic, unmistakable. So the Christian Church in the world is to be a body coherent, based

---

' St. Matt. v. 13-16; 1 Peter ii. 11, 12.

upon distinctive principles, exhibiting a striking and emphatic ideal.  It is to be in the world and not of it : making its impression by its very distinctiveness : 'that men might by the good works which they should behold, glorify God,' if not in days of worldliness and prosperity, yet at least ' in the day of visitation.'

Now if, with this intention of the founder of our religion in our minds, we look back over the history of Christianity, we cannot but perceive that nothing has been really more fatal to its influence, than the false methods of diffusion to which the Christian Church has so frequently abandoned itself.  I refer, in the first place, to such wholesale conversions of races as that to which Frankish Christianity owed its origin : conversions such as led to a Christianity in which catholic orthodoxy and ritual practices were combined with a morality which, at least in certain aspects, was frankly pagan.  I refer, secondly, to the tendency which has exhibited itself nowhere perhaps more conspicuously than within the area of the special influence of the Jesuits, but from which those who have been most opposed to that great society have been by no means free—the tendency to transfer the strain of Christian obligation from the life to be lived, to the creed to be believed : to make dogmatic orthodoxy or submission to ecclesiastical authority the 'one thing needful,' and granted that, to rest content with the very least degree of moral effort, as if submission to the Church could compensate for it.  Now there is no doubt that if we take mankind generally within our view, we must recognise that intellectual submission and ritual conformity are very much more easily obtained than moral effort. But in the New Testament, if Christianity appears as a religion making a definite demand upon the intellect, as well as a definite claim upon the life, the latter is unmistakably the more severe and the more prominent. It is assumed throughout that he that 'willeth to do God's will,' he who makes up his mind to moral self-committal, shall 'know of the doctrine': it is assumed that the difficulty of being a Christian is practically over, when the will is right, and the courage of self-committal won. In the Bible the antithesis to faith is not reason but sight—that is, the vision limited by the world, the worldly and selfish temper. Now by contrast to this I do not think it is possible to contemplate the Christian Church of the middle ages or of modern times, without seeing what great need there has frequently been to redress the balance. The theological and moral claims have shown a tendency to change places, and, in consequence, a very imperfect representation has been given of the claim of Jesus, or of the claim of Christianity before it became the nominal religion of the world, upon the lives and consciences of men.

There is one more false principle of diffusion which I must notice: it is that identification of the church with the nation which was the outcome of the Reformation as it took place in England, and which in its best form is represented in the ecclesiastical theory of Hooker[1]. I say, it is found in Hooker in its best form, but still in a form which we can now perceive, in the light of experience, to have been profoundly dangerous. For, however noble is the idea of a 'Christian nation,' the

---

[1] See *Eccl. Pol.* b. viii. cc. 1. 7, 4. 6. 8. 9.

church has no right to commit itself to the state, on
the assumption that the state has committed itself to
the church.   The assumption is unwarranted, and the
identification of church and state which is grounded
upon it, results in an almost inevitable confusion between
the province of civil order and civil obligation, and the
province of spiritual authority and spiritual obligation.
What the state sanctions, is assumed to be the sufficient
rule for the Christian: and what the state sanctions
must in the long run, as is increasingly manifest, represent the judgment of the majority, or the wishes of 'the
average man.'   Thus it has come about that it is difficult—to one at all familiar with the language of the
New Testament incredibly difficult—to persuade English
people that there is a law, and a social law, binding
upon Christians, which is not the least abrogated because
the law of the state, representing the will of the
majority, may have come to ignore it ; that in order
to live as Christians they have to look beyond what is
generally expedient, or what appears to be practicable
in state policy, up to the law which came forth from
the lips of Jesus Christ.  ' Every one which heareth these
words of mine, and doeth them, shall be likened unto
a wise man, which built his house upon the rock.'
Why, it is assumed in every page of the New
Testament that a Christian can think of nothing less
than of taking his rule of life from the standard of
the world about him !

   The disastrous results of a diffusion of Christianity
at the cost of its intensity, is very apparent to those of
us who are greatly interested in the social problems
of the present moment.   The remedies proposed for

the evils of society have generally a more or less 'social-istic' character. Now by socialism is commonly meant a certain political theory as to the function of the state in controlling the freedom of individual citizens in the acquisition and employment of wealth. With the group of proposals which come under this head of State socialism, I am not here at all concerned. I may, however, confess myself to be among those who would somewhat jealously set limits to the paternal supervision of the democratic state. But there is another sort of socialism, wholly voluntary, or dependent only upon spiritual sanctions, which the doctrine of the Incarnation seems, beyond all question, to bring with it. There exists what can rightly be called a Christian socialism, by the very fact that the law of brotherhood is the law of Christ. It is quite beyond all question that according to the intention of Christ, the Christian church should at all times represent a body living not only by a certain rule of faith, but also by a certain moral law, which puts the sternest restraints on the spirit of competition, on the acquisition of wealth, on selfish aggrandizement ; which bids every man, in the simplest sense, love his neighbour as himself, which enjoins the bearing one another's burdens, as the only fulfilling of the law of Christ. It is difficult to imagine that a New Testament Christian could have doubted that he had to carry his religion into all the affairs of life, or could have been in the least surprised if his religion involved his being poorer than one of his non-Christian neighbours who was not bound by the obligations of the Church. How is it then that we have reached a condition of things when men can not only utter, as multitudes of men always have done, the maxims of worldliness and selfishness, but utter these maxims without any sense that, by simply giving expression to them, they are repudiating Christianity, as far as words go, quite as really as if they were denying the Christian creed, or as if in the old days of persecution they had offered incense to the divinity of the Roman emperor?

What I am complaining of, what I want you to complain of, with a persistence and a conviction which shall make our complaint fruitful of reform, is—not that commercial and social selfishness exists in the world, or even that it appears to dominate in society: but that its profound antagonism to the spirit of Christ is not recognised, that there is not amongst us anything that can be called an adequate conception of what Christian morality means. The prophetic function of the church, as it seems to me, at the present moment, is not so much, in the first instance, to expand Christian influence as to concentrate it : to see to it that all men, whatsoever be their own convictions and practices, shall at least acknowledge what it is that a Christian must believe, and how it is that a Christian must live and act at all the points where he touches human life.

There must be produced a clear acknowledgment of what it is that a Christian must believe. We must strive to purge from all accretions the current presentation of the Christian creed, and to rid it of all that can bring it into conflict with the legitimate claims of reason, or seem to limit the freedom of enquiry or of criticism. We must so preach our creed, as to 'commend ourselves to every man's conscience in the sight of God.' But when we have done our

best to effect this, the Christian creed will stand
out, as in past history and in Scripture, so in the
preaching of to-day, as a distinctive intellectual position,
in regard to which a man may be in one of many
different attitudes, but the general meaning of which
he can hardly fail to apprehend.  In the same way we
must have all men acknowledge how it is that a Christian
must live.  We want the Christian moral law, the law of
purity, of brotherhood, of sacrifice, to be as intelligibly
presented and as clearly understood, as the dogmas of
the Christian creed.  We want it worked out with
adequate knowledge in its bearing on the various de-
partments of human life.  In a word, we want a fresh
and luminous presentation of the Christian moral code
and some adequate guarantee that one who is deliberately, persistently, and in overt act, repudiating its
plainest obligations shall cease to belong to the Christian
body.  'Do not ye,' writes St. Paul to the Corinthian
Church, 'judge them that are within, whereas them that
are without God judgeth?  Put away the wicked man
from among yourselves [1].'

For Jesus Christ is the same yesterday, to-day, and
for ever.  The claim which He made on the contemporaries of His life on earth, is the claim which He
makes on His disciples to-day.  Many will come to
Him at the last day—so we cannot but paraphrase
His own words—with manifold pleas and excuses derived
from the maxims of what is called the Christian world :
'Lord, we never denied the Christian creed : nay, we
had a zeal for orthodoxy, for churchmanship, for Bible
distribution, but of course in our business we did as

[1] See app. note 57, p. 271.

every one else did: we sold in the dearest and bought in the cheapest market: we did not, of course we did not, entertain any other consideration, when we were investing our money, except whether the investments were safe: we never imagined that we could love our neighbours as ourselves in the competition of business, or that we could carry into commercial transactions the sort of strict righteousness that we knew to be obligatory in private life. Lord, in all these matters we went by commonly accepted standards: we never thought much about Christianity as a brotherhood.' Then will He protest unto them, 'Did I not say to thee and to thee, in that written word wherein thou didst profess to have eternal life: "A man's life consisteth not in the abundance of the things that he posesseth?" Did not I warn thee, "How hardly shall they that have riches enter into the kingdom of God?" Did I not bid thee seek first the kingdom of God and His righteousness? Did I not tell thee that except a man, in spirit or will at least, forsook all that he had, unless he took up his cross and followed Me, he could not be My disciple? Not every one that saith unto Me, Lord, Lord, shall enter into the kingdom of heaven, but he that doeth, that hath done, the will of My Father.'

Brethren, you may depend upon it that you cannot be Christians by mere tradition or mere respectability. You will have to choose to be Christians. Let the figure of Christ, our Master, personal and living as of old, be before your eyes. He lays upon you a claim of service: varying as His vocations are various, as your faculties are various; as clergy and laity, apostles and disciples, married and celibate, saint and penitent, have their place in His kingdom: but upon all of you He lays the same claim of service, of purity, of sacrifice, of brotherhood. He will make His yoke easy and His burden light, in manifold ways, as His consolations are manifold, but in proportion as you take His yoke and accept His burden with thorough loyalty.  If you will to be His disciple, He will enrich your life, He will purge it of its pollution, He will conquer your lusts, He will enlighten your mind, He will deepen in you all that is generous and rich and brotherly and true and just.  He will make your life worth having, yea, increasingly worth having, as you gain in experience of His power and His love, even to the end.  He will touch your sufferings and your labours with the glory of His sympathy; He will deepen your hopes for yourselves and others with the security of an eternal prospect.  At the last He will purify and perfect and welcome you.  Only do not make the fatal mistake of imagining that your life is Christian anyhow, or that it can be Christian by any other process than by your deliberate and courageous acceptance of the law of Christ, because you desire to be His disciple.

### III.

So far the position has been maintained that Christianity must be identified with a positive and exacting moral standard : that the Church exists as 'the pillar and ground of the truth,' because she is to witness, not only to definite theological positions, but also to a definite moral ideal, which is, as well, a moral claim upon the members of her communion.

Now I think no one can read the Gospels with any

seriousness, or the records of the apostolic church, without acknowledging the truth of what has been said. Further than this, no one can study the history of the Christian church from the apostolic days to our own, without acknowledging that the leavening, transforming power of Christianity on individuals and on societies has been due mainly to the *Saints*—that is, to those who have made the ideal standard the real standard which it has been their supreme aim to follow.    So far as the average standard of society has been raised, it is mainly the saints who have raised it : and conversely it has been found true that 'when the best men stop trying, the world sinks back like lead.'    All this is indubitable. Still, with that mixture of humility and laziness which characterizes so many of us, a man may look seriously at a Christian preacher and ask : 'do you really mean that I in my ordinary life in the world, I with my coarse, common-place temptations, I with my way to make in the world as it is, I with my antecedents, my surroundings, and my prospects, am to set myself up to imitate Jesus Christ or forfeit the title to the name of Christian ? Is the imitation of Jesus really practicable ? '

It is when we are in the frame of mind which this questioning represents that we need to consider steadily a certain prominent aspect of Christianity ; an aspect which makes it, in spite of its apparent hardness, pre-eminently the religion of hope for all who have the courage to begin to try to serve Jesus Christ and the patience to make fresh beginnings after renewed failures.

The Christian Church upholds a moral ideal, and thus teaches men the true end of human life, but her special characteristic is rather that she supplies the means, than that she suggests the end. Philosophers on the whole have been not unsuccessful in proclaiming the ideal of life: they have shown their weakness in providing means for realizing it. Here is the strength of the Christian Church. She is a great system of means to the moral end, the 'means' that 'God devised that his banished should not be expelled from him.'

If we look higher still, we do indeed behold our Lord setting an example : but we observe also that there is something which He appraises higher than this function of example. Had this been His highest work, it would, beyond a doubt, have been expedient for us, if possible, that He should not have gone away. As it was, it was 'expedient' that His disciples should lose His visible example that they might gain a greater gift—the gift of the Spirit. 'If I go not away the Paraclete will not come unto you ; but if I go, I will send him unto you[1].' In fact the Paraclete did come at Pentecost, and in virtue of His coming the Church became a body instinct with a new life, and Christianity a thing 'not in word, but in power.'

Thus if we examine the writings not of St. Paul and St. John only, but of St. Peter and St. James[2], we find the thought expressed everywhere in the New Testament that Christians have been born again : that what distinguishes them from other men is the possession, over and above the ordinary human faculties and powers, of a special power, a special life, derived from a definite act of God upon them by which they became the subjects of a new birth. St. Paul and St. John further explain this new birth[2]. It is the coming of the Spirit into a

---

[1] St. John xvi. 7.          [2] See app. note 58, p. 272.

man's life which constitutes it : but the coming of the
Spirit in a particular manner, namely to introduce Christ.
The persons of the Holy Trinity are not, as was said,
separable individuals[1]. They involve each the others;
the coming of each is the coming of the others. Thus
the coming of the Spirit must have involved the coming
of the Son. But the speciality of the Pentecostal gift
appears to be the coming of the Holy Spirit out of the
uplifted and glorified *Manhood* of the incarnate Son.
The Spirit is the life-giver, but the life with which He
works in the Church is the life of the *Incarnate*, the life
of Jesus[2]. We watch the perfect life of Jesus as our
example : we behold Him and accept Him as the perfect
sacrifice : we contemplate Him raised up, beyond example
and beyond sacrifice, into the glory of the Father, 'separated from sinners and made higher than the heavens,'
spiritualized and glorified—but not dehumanized. In
the glory of the Father He is still the Son of man.
As Son of man He has sent down His Spirit upon
the Church, and that Spirit does not merely supply the
absence, but accomplishes the inward presence of the
incarnate Christ. For this primarily the Church exists :
to be the Spirit-bearing body, and that is to be the
bearer of Christ, the great 'Christopher,' perpetuating,
in a new, but not less real way, the presence of the Son
of man in the world.

In the second of these lectures, the difficulty was
raised[3], that if the Christ represents the emergence of a
new sort of life into the world of experience, as organic
life emerged out of the heart of inorganic, or rational out

---

[1] See above, pp. 132–3.      [2] See app. note 59, p. 272.
[3] See above, p. 50.

of the heart of what was only physical,—then the 'Christ-life' ought to have been perpetuated, and become a permanent element of experience.  It was pointed out in partial solution of this difficulty that in one sense the uniqueness of the Christ is a necessary condition of His existence, that there cannot be more than one incarnate Son of God: but it is also true that what was realized once for all in Jesus, is perpetuated in the world.  The Church is the body of Christ.  It is the extension and perpetuation of the Incarnation in the world.  It is this, because it embodies the same principle, and lives by the same life.

The Church embodies the same principle as the 'Word made flesh,' that is, the expression and communication of the spiritual and the divine through what is material and human.  It is a human and material society.  Its sacraments are visible instruments : its unity is that of a visible organization bound into one at least by the link of an apostolic succession and an historical continuity.  But this visible, material, human society exists to receive, to embody and to communicate a spiritual life.  And this life is none other than the life of the Incarnate.  The Church exists to perpetuate in every age the life of Jesus, the union of manhood with God-head.

No doubt this does not always appear upon the surface, for the Church has a majority of unworthy members.  As I suppose the true English character is to be judged of, not by all Englishmen, but by the best Englishmen, so the Christian character is to be seen in genuine Christians.  But the genuine Christians are the justification in every age of the Church's existence.  In every age there are those of whose life no other account can be given and who could give no other account of their own life, than that it ' is hid with Christ in God.' It is this truth of Christ living in His members by His Spirit, that I would have you consider. The Incarnation did not end in Christ our head : it passed on to the incorporation of us His members. Thus ' when Christ who is our life shall appear, we also shall appear with him in glory.'

Looking at the matter not historically or speculatively but personally—what is it for me to be a Christian ? It is to know that my spiritual life is not an isolated thing, drawing simply upon its own resources. God the Holy Spirit has entered at definite moments of baptism and confirmation, by definite acts of God, into my innermost being. He dwells within the temple of my body; and by dwelling there He links my life on to the great system of the redeemed humanity. I am a ' member incorporate in the mystical body of Christ, which is the blessed company of all faithful people.' And every temptation, every need, every suffering, every disappointment, is meant to drive me more inward and upward to realize and to draw upon the hidden resources of my new life—which is ' Christ in me the hope of glory.'

## IV.

The point upon which I am insisting is that if our Lord is our example and our sacrifice, He is also, by the infusion of His Spirit, our present inward life, ' the life of our life': that if the Church exists to uphold a moral standard, she exists also as a body ensouled by a Spirit who makes that standard practicable: or, in other words, that the one end of Christianity is not the proclamation, but the fulfilling, of the law. 'God,' says St. Paul, 'sending his own Son in the likeness of sinful flesh and as an offering for sin, condemned sin in the flesh: that the requirement of the law might be fulfilled in us who walk not after the flesh, but after the spirit . . . For ye are not in the flesh but in the spirit, if so be that the Spirit of God dwelleth in you. But if any man hath not the Spirit of Christ, he is none of his. And if Christ is in you . . . the spirit is life because of righteousness [1].' This doctrine of the inward Christ, 'Christ in us the hope of glory,' is a doctrine of which the New Testament is full. Mystical as it is, and transcending, as it does, our faculties of intellectual analysis, it has been ridiculed, as fit only for enthusiasts, in a rationalistic age such as the last century; but every revival of vital Christianity brings it to the front again, and roots it anew in the consciousness of serious and devout Christians, though they be 'plain men' and unimpassioned. It will become real to each man in turn, as he meditates and acts upon it: and in it he will find the explanation of three very commonly felt difficulties.

(1) First, let us attend to the difficulty which is raised about the example of our Lord  how can the sinless Jesus be an example for us sinners? When the author of the Epistle to the Hebrews says that our Lord was 'in all points tempted like as we are, with the exception of sin,' or 'apart from sin [2],' he is stating that humanity in our Lord was really exposed to all the trials

---

[1] Rom. viii. 3-10.   [2] Hebr. iv. 15, χωρὶς ἁμαρτίας. See Westcott *in lo*.

which can come upon man from outside, and tempted
by all external solicitations ; but that temptation in His
case was unaccompanied by one condition with which
we are familiar—His nature was without sin.　But after
all this exception is so considerable as to appear at first
sight to destroy the value of His example ; for it is
the presence of sin within—the tyranny of passions, the
disorder of faculties, the inward taint and weakness—
which gives temptation in our case its chief power.
We should not so much fear the outward foe, we feel,
were it not for the traitor within the camp.　Does not
Christ then by His very sinlessness, still more by His
impeccability, fail in the conditions of a profitable
example ?

This difficulty, perhaps, like many others, needs only
to be pressed further to suggest its own solution.　For
after all the limits to the power of mere example are
very soon reached.　Mere example acts most power-
fully where men are living close together and under
like conditions, as among the members of the same
college or school or profession, in the same household,
in the relationship of friends.　Its power is weakened
rapidly by anything that separates one man from
another in conditions of life.　Thus, the sobriety of a
clergyman is not, so far, a powerful example to the
labouring man, or the temperance of an Italian or of
a Mohammedan to an Englishman, or the patience of
the aged to the young, or the feats of ancient heroes
to modern readers.　Once more, whenever we feel the
touch of genius, we reach a limit to the power of
example.　'What man has done, man can do,' is, in fact,
a maxim of very limited applicability.　Quite apart then

from the question of impeccability or even of sinlessness, the mere example of Jesus Christ, as a character
in ancient history, would be singularly destitute of
encouragement to us in our temptations to-day, if He
was only our example.   For at the lowest He would
stand as a supreme moral genius, like a Julius Caesar
or a Shakespeare in other regions of life; and we
should feel that it would be as fallacious to conclude
that we could live as Christ had lived, as it would be
to conclude that we could write a tragedy like 'Ham-
let,' or model our career upon the pattern set us by
the founder of the Roman Empire.

But in fact Jesus Christ is a great deal more to us
than a remote and external figure in history.  He is
a still living person in the closest possible relation to
us.   He is a person who while human, has yet, in
virtue of His Godhead, access into the innermost parts
of our being, into the very roots of our personality;
and He has become, even in His manhood, 'quickening
spirit [1].'   Alive in heaven, He is thus also alive
in us, dwelling in us by the Spirit which He hath
given us.   He is moulding us inwardly and gradually,
in this life and beyond it, into the likeness of that
example, which at the first He set outwardly before us.
We look to His example, we contemplate the pattern
of life which stands for ever before our eyes in the pages
of the Gospels; and we know that the moral forces
which were at work in that life to exempt it from sin,
to overcome Satan, to win the flawless moral victory, are
all without exception, and without deterioration, at work
in our life to-day.   For His Spirit is made our Spirit:

[1] See app. note 60, p. 276.

His life is poured into ours. We look at Him in history to know what we must become : we draw upon His present Spirit in order to its realization.

(2) In this truth of the inward Christ, let us see the explanation of a doctrine which often bewilders us, the imputation to us of Christ's merits. To impute the merits of one person to another, external to him and independent of him, would always be an arbitrary and immoral act. But on the other hand we are none of us isolated individuals. To take true account of any one, we must look at him not merely in himself, but in the light of those larger forces of race, of family, of association, which are at work in him. Fathers and mothers, friends and kinsmen, interpret to us those upon whom their influence passes, and make us think of them with more or less of hope than they, taken by themselves, would kindle. 'Looking at the mother,' wrote George Eliot of Mrs. Garth, 'you might hope that the daughter would become like her—which is a prospective advantage equal to a dowry—the mother too often standing behind the daughter like a malignant prophecy, " such as I am, she will shortly be." ' George Eliot, you see, *imputes by anticipation* to the daughter the merits of the mother, because her life is, so to speak, of the same piece. Now, by new birth and spiritual union, our life is of the same piece with the life of Jesus. Thus He, our elder brother, stands behind us, His people, as a prophecy of all good. Thus God accepts us, deals with us, '*in* the beloved ': rating us at something of His value, imputing to us His merits, because in fact, except we be reprobates, He himself is the most powerful and real force at work in us. So it is that in imputing to us the merits of His

Son, the Father is only dealing with us according to His constant and most righteous method. For He deals with us and He loves us, as St. Augustine says, not as we are. but as we are becoming, ' non quales sumus, sed quales futuri sumus [1].'

In the light of this principle you can understand why it is that our sins can be forgiven us 'in the name of Jesus'; why the sacrament of our incorporation into Christ is also the sacrament of plenary absolution, and we can profess our belief 'in one baptism for the remission of sins.' For consider: God, who is truth, deals with us according to reality. He must deal with things at the last resort as they are. He cannot reckon what does belong to us, as if it did not. Thus at the last He can only 'not impute' our sins to us, if they no longer belong to our transformed characters; as Saul the persecutor's 'kicking against the pricks' belongs no longer to Paul the apostle, 'the slave of Jesus Christ.' We can be absolved then, at the last great acquittal, only because, by discipline in this world or beyond it, we have actually had our sins purged out of us. Here in this world in order at any moment to be the subjects of forgiveness, we must really repent, which means that we really abjure our sins and separate ourselves from them in will and in-tention. Not the best of us however can hope to be com-pletely freed from sin except very slowly and gradually. But God deals with us— this is the great truth   by antici-pation, by anticipation of all that is to come about in us, ' non quales sumus, sed quales futuri sumus '; accepting us *in Christ*, forgiving us *in Christ*, and thus setting us free from the burden of our past sins, as often as, being really

[1] S. Aug. *de Trin.* 1. 10 (21.

Q

members of Christ, we do really, in the sincerity of a good will, unite ourselves to Him and claim to be His servants.   Only if we repudiate our Lord, if we 'crucify the Son of God afresh and put him to an open shame,' do we stand once again in our nakedness, so that God must judge us and deal with us not as in Christ's righteousness and better than we seem, but as the children of darkness and the subjects of judgment.

(3) This truth of the immanence of Jesus Christ by the Spirit in the heart of the believer gives us the right position for appreciating the functions of faith within the area of the Christian life.   Faith, in the documents of the New Testament, addressed as they were to men who had mostly passed into the Christian church from Judaism or heathenism, is frequently spoken of as that initial act by which a man became a Christian. 'Received ye the Holy Ghost,' asks St. Paul, 'by the work of the law or by the hearing of faith[1]?'   This initial act of faith by which men first accepted the offer of God made to them in Christ Jesus, was intellectually the recognition that 'Jesus is the Lord[2]:' morally the committal of the life to Him for pardon, for peace, for government.   This initial justifying faith is itself the gift of God, for 'no man can say, Jesus is Lord, but in the Holy Ghost[3],'-- but it also leads the way to further gifts.   'We have had our access by faith into this grace wherein we stand,' says St. Paul again[4]; access by faith into grace.   The believer is baptized, in the 'bath of regeneration,' 'into Jesus Christ[5].'   He is sealed, by the laying on of hands, with the gift of the Holy Ghost,

---

[1] Gal. iii. 2.   [2] Rom. x. 9.   [3] 1 Cor. xii. 3.
[4] Rom. v. 2.   [5] Tit. iii. 5; cf. Rom. vi. 3.

to dwell personally within the temple of his body. He is fed with the royal food of the body and blood of Christ [1]. Henceforth faith has no further need to ask for any completer bestowal of divine gifts. All that can be given, has been already received. Thus all through the New Testament the language is avoided which would suggest that Christians have need to ask for the supply of the Spirit. They are men who possess the gift and only need to use it. 'Quench not the Spirit,' 'grieve not the Spirit,' 'ye did receive the Spirit,' 'the Spirit of God dwelleth in you,' 'stir up the gift that is in you.' This is the language used, sometimes even to very imperfect Christians at Corinth and elsewhere [2]. Faith then, in those who are already Christians, enters upon a new function—that of realizing and appropriating the truth and grace which has been already won. Intellectually faith is to meditate upon the sacred Name which has been invoked upon the life: morally it is to draw upon and use by repeated acts of the will the vast resources of power which have been put at its disposal in the indwelling of Christ. So by a gradual process of appropriation 'Christ' is to be 'formed within': the Christian is to grow up, in the fellowship of the one body, into 'the perfect man.'

If we would consent to consider this matter anew and appreciate this correlation of the grace which is communicated in sacraments with the faith which appropriates and uses it, we should not only read more intelligently the language of the New Testament, but we should also be less ready to suppose that the Catholic insistance upon

[1] Acts viii. 17, 18, xix. 6; 1 Cor. vi. 19, x. 16.
[2] 1 Thess. v. 19; Eph. iv. 30; Gal. iii. 2; 1 Cor. vi. 19; 2 Tim i. 6.

sacraments is in any necessary contradiction to the Evangelical insistance upon the need of a converted will and
of a faith which is something much more than passive
orthodoxy.   Successful life in any stage of nature's development appears to consist in a vigorous appropriation by a certain organism of what is supplied to it
by its outward environment.   When Jesus came to heal
men's bodies, His physical cures exhibited this same law
of correspondence.   It was the virtue or power which
went out from Him which was the instrument of healing,
but it was the function of faith to appropriate and use
it.   According to men's faith, so was it done to them.
These, our Lord's miracles of healing, were but symbols
of His spiritual action.   Still our spiritual recovery is
to be through our vigorous appropriation, by the activity
of faith, of gifts communicated from without.   Through
the sacraments God bestows the gifts : through them is
secured our spiritual contact with Christ [1].   But this outward supply of grace, independently of any action on
our part, is but the challenge to faith to claim and appropriate its rich heritage.   True, positive apostasy may
forfeit the gift altogether.   Short of that, the gift remains,
but its effect on us is wholly dependent on the faith of
intellect and will, which realizes it and uses it.

Why do we grow so little in grace ?   It is, because
we do not use our intellect to meditate upon the
forces of the unseen world amidst which we live, or our
will to draw upon them.   In the moment of temptation
we fight, sadly often, in our own powers, and we fail.   We
know that we are weak, and sin and Satan are strong,
and we know the truth.   But there is a third power

[1] See app. note 61, p. 276.

stronger than either our weakness or the forces of evil, which we commonly forget, and which will never disclose itself except in our using of it. We must stir up the gift within us. Within us we have the Spirit of power, the Spirit of Jesus, the life of Jesus. It remains to us to appeal to it; in constant acts of faith to draw upon it and to use it. Thus it will become to each of us as much a truth of experience as it was to St. Paul, and no vague language of metaphor, that 'it is no longer merely I that live, but Christ that liveth in me.'


## V.

I have come to the end of my task. My point of departure was that Christianity, whether we accept it or not, is in fact the religion based upon faith in the person of Jesus Christ, considered as the Son of God incarnate [1]. I endeavoured to make it plain that this supernatural Person is no unnatural phenomenon, but is in very truth the consummation of nature's order, or the rectification of it, so far as sin, which is unnatural, has thrown it into disorder [2]. I endeavoured to satisfy you that no legitimate criticism can impair the witness of history to the miraculous personality and strictly divine claim of Jesus of Nazareth [3]. Next it was my task to vindicate the Catholic creeds, as simply interpreting and guarding the record of Christ's person, divine and human, which the New Testament gives [4]. After that, using the creeds as our guides in dwelling on the evangelical records, but never as substitutes for that record. I endeavoured to lead you to dwell upon the person of Jesus, God in manhood,

[1] Lecture i.     [2] Lecture ii.     [3] Lecture iii.     [4] Lecture iv.

We considered together what is the revelation of God, given us there in the intelligible terms of our humanity[1]; and what is the revelation of manhood, which we owe to His self-sacrifice, who emptied Himself of divine prerogatives, that He might truly live as Son of man[2]. Finally, omitting, for lack of space, all consideration of His atoning sacrifice, we have dwelt upon the chief remaining functions of this Son of man, as the spiritual authority over humanity[3]; as erecting by His outward example its moral standard ; as being its inward recreator by spiritual communication of His own life[4].

I have done my task.  I have borne my witness. And yet it is not mine, but the witness of something in comparison of which any single preacher is indeed nothing.  It is the witness of that great movement of the redeemed humanity that links us in spiritual communion across the ages with the first apostles.  They first received the witness and set to their seals to the offer of God—'set to their seals that God was true.' Generation after generation has handed down the offer to us.  Amidst the fires of persecution in days when the world was hostile to the profession of Christ's name ; in the not less searching discipline of the days since the world has endeavoured to evacuate the name of Christ of its meaning, by itself professing it ; still the faithful Christians of each age have 'set to their seals' to the document of God's offer.  And now in your turn it is presented to you.  There is, I think, no responsibility which weighs upon us more heavily as we pass from youth to manhood, from the position of children to that of parents, from the seat of the taught to the chair of

---

[1] Lecture v.     [2] Lecture vi.     [3] Lecture vii.     [4] Lecture viii.

the teacher, than the responsibility for handing on unimpaired to the generation beyond us, this best heritage of our human life—the heritage of religious faith and practice and worship.  The deepest prayer we pray is that nothing of religious truth or life may prove to have been impaired or lost in its passage through us. To you, then, brethren, to you more particularly before whom life yet lies in opening promise, the document of God's offer in Jesus Christ is once again presented.  It is black with the signatures, it is red with the seals, of those who, in the generations that are passed or passing away, have given in their assent 'that God is true,' and have handed on to you the results of their faithful witness. You cannot evade your responsibilities ; you must at the last issue confess or deny; you must sign or repudiate. Summon then to your aid every heavenly power to assist you in the great surrender which they make who, having steadily in view all that is involved in faith in Jesus Christ, 'set to their seals' for time and for eternity 'that God is true.'

# APPENDED NOTES.

———•———

## LECTURE I.

### NOTE 1. See p. 1.

*This is the true God* (1 St. John, v. 20). The word 'this' probably refers to 'him that is true,' i. e. the Father, rather than to 'his Son Jesus Christ': but (as this passage among others makes plain) to know the Son is, according to St. John, identical with knowing the Father, so inseparable is their essential unity, and to be in the Son is to be in the Father: see Westcott, *Epistles of St. John, in loc.*

### NOTE 2. See p. 3.

*Exaggerated devotion to Mary.* The passage from St. Alfonso, *Glorie di Maria*, at the beginning, is as follows [1]:—

'Kings, then, should be employed principally in works of mercy, but not so as to forget to execute justice (when necessary) on the guilty. Not so with Mary, who, though a queen, is not a queen of justice, intent on punishing malefactors, but a queen of mercy, who seeks only to obtain mercy and pardon

[1] The translation is that of the Dublin version of 1876, vol. i. p. 80. But the passage was selected originally from the Italian edition recently published in Rome.

for sinners. Hence the Church wishes that we expressly call her the Queen of mercy. John Gerson, the great Chancellor of Paris, commenting on the words of David "these two things have I heard, that power belongeth to God, and mercy to Thee, O Lord" (Ps. lxi. 12), said that the Lord has divided his kingdom which consisted in justice and mercy: the kingdom of justice he has reserved to himself, and the kingdom of mercy he has, in a certain manner, given to Mary, ordaining that all the mercies which he dispenses to men should pass through her hands and be dispensed as she pleases. Behold the words of Gerson: "Regnum Dei consistit in potestate et misericordia, potestate Deo remanente; cessit quodammodo misericordiae pars Matri regnanti." This is confirmed by St. Thomas, in his preface to the Canonical Epistles, where he says that the holy Virgin, when she conceived in her womb and brought forth the Divine Word, obtained the half of the kingdom of God, by becoming the queen of mercy, as Jesus Christ is king of justice: " Quando filium Dei in utero concepit, et postmodum peperit, dimidiam partem regni Dei impetravit, ut ipsa sit regina misericordiae, ut Christus est rex iustitiae."

'The Eternal Father has constituted Jesus Christ king of justice, and has, therefore, made him universal judge of the world: hence the prophet has said "Give to the king thy judgment, O God, and to the king's son thy justice" (Ps. lxxi. 2). On this passage a learned interpreter has said: " O Lord, thou hast given justice to thy son, because thou hast given thy mercy to the mother of the king." Hence St. Bonaventura says: " O God, give thy judgment to the king and thy mercy to the mother." Ernest, Archbishop of Prague, likewise says that the Eternal Father has given to the Son the office of judging and of inflicting punishment, and to the mother, the office of compassionating and relieving the miserable: " Pater omne judicium dedit filio et omne officium misericordiae dedit matri." '

It will be observed that the passage which I have quoted in the text of the lecture is a citation from St. Thomas, but as it perhaps hardly represents St. Thomas fairly, taken as it is out of its context, I thought it better to make St. Alfonso simply responsible for it. The original in St. Thomas, *Praef. in Sept. Epp. Cath.*, is a comment on Esther v. 3 : ' So Esther drew near and touched the top of the sceptre. Then said the king unto her, What wilt thou, queen Esther? and what is thy request ? it shall be given thee, even to the half of the kingdom.' ' Summitatem eius virgae virgo beata tetigit, quando filium Dei in utero concepit et postmodum peperit, et sic dimidiam partem regni Dei impetravit, ut ipsa sit regina misericordiae cuius filius est rex iustitiae.' The other quotations I have not verified.

The opening chapter of *The Glories of Mary* strikes the key-note of the whole book. And I do not think it is open to doubt that it is a book profoundly representative of current Roman devotion to the Blessed Virgin. Alfonso de' Liguori, who died in 1787, was finally canonized in 1839 and declared a ' Doctor of the Church ' in 1871.


NOTE 3. See p. 7.

*The place of Mohammed and of the Koran in Islam.* The articles of Prof. Wellhausen and Prof. Nöldeke in the *Encyclopaedia Britannica* (s. v. *Mohammedanism*) will suffice to illustrate the statements in the text. ' The personality of the Prophet,' says Prof. Wellhausen (p. 548), ' had given an altogether new impulse to a [monotheistic] movement already in existence ; that was all. To found a new religion was in no sense Mohammed's intention ; what he sought was to secure among his people the recognition of the old and the true. He preached it to the Arabs as Moses had before him preached to the Jews, and Jesus to Christians [i. e. as Mohammed imagined Jesus]; it was all one and the same religion as written in the heavenly book.'

The monotheistic movement, prior to Mohammed, Prof. Wellhausen describes as ' the religion of Abraham.'

Again, Prof. Nöldeke (pp. 597 ff.) writes: ' The Koran is the foundation of Islam . . . To the faith of the Moslems the Koran is the word of God, and such also is the claim which the book itself advances. For except in Sur. 1 . . . the speaker throughout is God.

' The rationale of revelation is explained in the Koran itself as follows:—in heaven is the original text ("the mother of the book," "a concealed book," "a well-guarded tablet "). By a process of "sending down" one piece after another was communicated to the prophet. The mediator was an angel, who is called sometimes the " Spirit," sometimes the " Holy Spirit," and at a later time " Gabriel." The angel dictates the revelation to the Prophet, who repeats it after him, and afterwards proclaims it to the world . . . Mohammed's transcendental idea of God as a Being exalted altogether above the world, excludes the thought of direct intercourse between the prophet and God.'

I am only concerned to justify the positions—which would not be disputed—that Mohammed did not claim to be more than a prophet and that the importance of his personality in his theological system is simply that he is supposed to certificate the reality of the revelations which the Koran contains. The sources of the Koran, and the moral estimate which we must form of Mohammed's character and work, are questions which fall outside the scope of this note, but students cannot make a better beginning of enquiry than with the articles quoted above.

NOTE 4. See p. 8.

*The place of Gautama in Buddhism.* The quotation in the text will be found in *The Sacred Books of the East*, ed. Max Müller, vol. xi. pp. 37–38. In *Encycl. Brit.* art. *Buddhism*, p. 432, Gautama is quoted as speaking thus, just before his death : ' O Subhadra ! I do not speak to you of things I have not experienced. Since I was twenty-nine years old till now I have striven after pure and perfect wisdom, and following the good path have found

Nirvana.' ' When I have passed away and am no longer with
you, do not think that the Buddha has left you and is not still
in your midst. You have my words, my explanations of the
deep things of truth, the laws I have laid down for the society ;
let them be your guide ; the Buddha has not left you.'

On the meaning of Nirvana I cannot do better than refer to
this admirable article (T. W. Rhys Davids); see p. 433 : ' When
Nirvana has been described in glowing terms as the happy seat;
the excellent eternal place of bliss, where there is no more
death, neither decay; the end of suffering; the home of peace
... it has been supposed by some European scholars to mean
a blissful state, in which the soul (!) still exists in an everlasting
trance. There can however now be no longer any doubt on the
point. Buddhism does not acknowledge the existence of a soul
as a thing distinct from the parts and powers of man which
are dissolved at death, and the Nirvana of Buddhism is simply
extinction.'

Professor Max Müller asserts strongly that Nirvana means
simply, extinction, and that ' Buddhism, therefore, if tested by
its own canonical books cannot be freed from the charge of
Nihilism.' *Chips from a German Workshop*, i. pp. 283-284.
His argument against this having represented Buddha's own
mind seems to be chiefly *à priori*, see *l. c.* pp. 234-235, pp.
285 f., and *The Parables of Buddhaghosha*, pp. xxxix ff. Surely
he exaggerates the desire for immortality, *as an alternative to
extinction*, in men in general, especially orientals.

But what would be admitted by Professor Max Müller is
quite sufficient for all the purposes of my argument. The
existence of one who has attained Parinirvana is not a practical
existence, such as would admit of personal conscious relations
of the Buddha to his disciples, parallel to those of the risen
Jesus to His Church. Nor are such relations possible in a
religion without a God.

### NOTE 5. See p. 16.

*Aut Deus aut homo non bonus.* Dr. Latham, *Pastor Pastorum* (Cambridge, 1890), pp. 273 ff., has called the attention of students again to the way in which Jesus Christ trained His disciples to trust Himself with an absolute trust—first in His presence, then in His temporary absences, finally under conditions of His spiritual presence, when He had passed into the unseen world.

The argument to the Divinity of Christ from His claim has been recently put afresh, as part of a personal experience, in *An Appeal to Unitarians*, by ‘A Convert from Unitarianism’ (Longmans, 1890), pp. 41–51. ‘If it is not superhuman authority that speaks to us here, it is surely superhuman arrogance.’ It has, however, been chiefly brought home to men’s minds, in recent times, by Père Lacordaire (*Jésus-Christ*, Conf. 1) and Dr. Liddon.

Dr. Liddon did not himself know, and I cannot ascertain, the source of the epigrammatic summary of the argument ‘aut Deus aut homo non bonus.’ In substance the argument appears from early days: e. g. in Victorinus Afer, writing against Candidus the Arian: ‘haec dicens Deus fuit, si mentitus non est: si autem mentitus est, non opus Dei omnimodis perfectum.’ *De. Gener.* i. p. 1020 C (Migne).

### NOTE 6. See p. 23.

*Pharisaic Ebionites.* This was a sect of Judaic Christians mentioned by Irenaeus (*c. Haer.* i. 26, 2), who retained the characteristics of St. Paul’s opponents in Galatia, ‘who were circumcised and persevered in observing the law and maintaining a Jewish mode of life.’ To them, Tertullian tells us, Jesus was ‘nothing more than a Solomon or a Jonah’ (*de Car. Chr.* 18). He was a man naturally born, but pre-eminently justified by his unique observance of the law, and, therefore, made the Christ of God (Hippolytus, *Ref. haer.* vii. 34). Earlier than this definitely heretical sect, we find traces of an 'untheological' Jewish Christianity, such as appears in the *Teaching of the Twelve Apostles*, and would be exemplified probably by the Jewish Christians, to whom the Epistle to the Hebrews was written, to lift them into a fuller perception of the meaning of the Incarnation (Hebr. vi. 1, 2). Earlier still, we have the Judaizers of the Epistle to the Galatians, who loved their old Jewish, more than their new Christian, privileges, and failed to grasp the greatness of the change involved in the coming of the Christ. The point here insisted upon is simply that this 'untheological' Christianity was unimportant, unprogressive and barren, as Church history bears witness; cf. Stanton, *Jewish and Chr. Messiah* (Clark, Edin. 1886), pp. 166-7. The view that these Ebionites represented the Christianity of the original Apostles is considered Lect. iv. p. 83, and app. note 26, p. 254.

## NOTE 7. See p. 24.

*The need of a clear moral ideal.* See *Natural Religion*, by the author of *Ecce Homo* (Macmillan, 1891), p. 128 : ' Look, then, how the English people treat their children. Try and discover from the way they train them, from the education they give them, what they wish them to be. They have ceased, almost consciously ceased, to have any ideal at all. Traces may still be observed of an old ideal not quite forgotten : here and there a vague notion of instilling hardihood, a really decided wish to teach frankness and honesty, and, in a large class, also good manners ; but these after all are negative virtues. What do they wish their children to aim at? What pursuits do they desire for them ? Except that when they grow up they are to make or have a livelihood, and take a satisfactory position in society, and in the meanwhile that it would be hard for them not to enjoy themselves heartily, most parents would be puzzled to say what they wish for their children. And, whatever they wish, they wish so languidly that they entrust the realization of it almost entirely to strangers, being themselves, so they say—and, indeed, the Philistine or irreligious person always is—much engaged. The parent, from sheer embarrassment and want of an ideal, has in a manner abdicated, and it has become necessary to set apart a special class for the cultivation of parental feelings and duties. The modern schoolmaster should change his name, for he has become a kind of standing or professional parent.'

This sense of the need of a definite moral standard, whether in the education of children, or in society as a whole, is no doubt one of the most powerful motives appealing to men, who are not Christians in positive belief, to keep within the area of the Christian Church, and pay homage to its moral power.

We find men also, who do not call themselves Christians, like John Stuart Mill, acknowledging the moral authority of Jesus Christ on more personal grounds. See *Three Essays on Theism* (Longmans, 1874), p. 255: 'Religion cannot be said to have made a bad choice in pitching on this man as the ideal representative and guide of humanity; nor even now would it be easy, even for an unbeliever, to find a better translation of the rule of virtue from the abstract into the concrete, than to endeavour so to live that Christ would approve our life.' Dr. Pusey's comment on this is, 'If men would set this before themselves, there would be fewer unbelievers.' (*University Sermons*, 1864–1879, 'God and human independence,' p. 10, note 1.)

In my lecture, however, I was thinking chiefly of men who would go further than this—of men, and they are not a few, who call themselves Christians and proclaim the moral sovereignty of Christ, while all the while they deprecate theology.

# LECTURE II.

## NOTE 8.  See p. 29.

*The common ground of Science and Christianity in a belief in Nature.* Cf. *Natural Religion*, pp. 22, 23 : ' Nature, according to all systems of Christian theology, is God's ordinance. Whether with Science you stop short at Nature, or with Christianity believe in a God who is the author of Nature, in either case Nature is divine, for it is either God or the work of God. This whole domain is common to science and theology. When theology says, Let us give up the wisdom of men and listen to the voice of God, and when science says, Let us give up human authority and hollow *à priori* knowledge and let us listen to Nature, they are agreed to the whole extent of the narrower proposition, *i. e.* theology ought to admit all that science says, though science admits only a part of what theology says. Theology cannot say the laws of Nature are not divine : all it can say is, they are not the most important of the divine laws. Perhaps not, but they gain an importance from the fact that they are laws upon which all can agree. Making the largest allowance for discoveries about which science may be too confident, there remains a vast mass of natural knowledge which no one questions. This to the Christian is so much knowledge about God, and he ought to exult quite as much as the man of science in the rigorous method by which it has been separated from the human prejudice and hasty ingenuity and delusive rhetoric or poetry, which might have adulterated it By this means we have been enabled to hear a voice which is unmistakably God's.'

See also p. 10: ' Thus the religious view and the scientific view of the Universe, which are thought to be so opposite, agree in this important point. Both protest earnestly against human wisdom. Both wait for a message which is to come to them from without. Religion says, " Let man be silent, and

R

listen when God speaks." Science says, "Let us interrogate Nature, and let us be sure that the answer we get is really Nature's, and not a mere echo of our own voice." Now whether or not religion and science agree in what they recommend, it is evident that they agree in what they denounce. They agree in denouncing that pride of the human intellect which supposes it knows everything, which is not passive enough in the presence of reality, but deceives itself with pompous words instead of things, and with flattering eloquence instead of sober truth.'

NOTE 9. See p. 30.

*Mind from the point of view of merely physical science.* The following extract from an Address in Medicine by J. Hughlings Jackson, M.D., *On the Comparative Study of Diseases of the Nervous System* (see *The British Medical Journal*, Aug. 17, 1889, p. 358), contains a valuable statement : 'Function is a physiological term, and it is, I submit, improper to speak of states of consciousness as being "functions of the brain"; we can only say that states of consciousness attend functions of the brain, of those parts of it, at least, which are the highest cerebral centres. We can only affirm concomitance, and why immaterial processes always go along with the material processes of our brains is, as yet at any rate, inexplicable . . . . . Here is an express repudiation of any intention on my part to attempt to explain psychical states by anatomico-physiological states. It is not the mind, but the physical basis of mind, which is a product of evolution ; it is the organ of mind, not the mind, which, being an evolution out of the rest of the body, is representative of it. When tracing an evolutionary ascent from the muscles of the hand to the highest cerebral centres, nothing was said even remotely implying that the most complex, etc., representation of these muscles became, or became part of, ideas; it was only said that this most complex, etc., representation was part of the physical basis of those ideas. I know of no evolutionist of repute who has attempted the marvellous feat of "getting the mind out of the body." For my part, I am content with "getting" the organ of mind out of the rest of the body.'

## NOTE 10. See p. 32.

*Theistic arguments.* For the arguments summarized in the lecture, I may give the following references.

(1) For the metaphysical argument, see T. H. Green, *Prolegomena to Ethics* (Clar. Press, 1883), Book I. Chapter i.

(2) For the 'argument from design,' as affected by Darwinism, see J. Le Conte, *Evolution and its Relation to Religious Thought* (Chapman & Hall, 1888), Part III, or Aubrey Moore, *Science and the Faith* (Kegan Paul, 1889), Introduction.

(3) For the 'argument from beauty,' see Mozley, *University Sermons* (Longmans, 1876), Serm. 6.

(4) For the ethical argument, see Martineau, *Types of Ethical Theory* (Clar. Press, 1885), Part II. Bk. II. Branch I.

(5) For the personality of God, see Lotze, *Microcosmus* (Eng. trans., Clark, Edinburgh, 1886), Book IX. Cap. 4: also Seth, *Hegelianism and Personality* (Blackwood, Edinburgh 1887), pp. 214–224.

Cf. also, in these lectures, p. 117.

The recent anonymous work, *The Riddles of the Sphinx* (Swan Sonnenschein, 1891), contains, it seems to me, a great deal of fresh and valuable thought on subjects (1) and (5). This can be adopted without reference to some strange conclusions at which the book arrives.

## NOTE 11. See p. 35.

*Moral life supernatural.* I am anxious not to appear to assume anything in this connection as to the circumstances under which the moral life was developed. I would only assert that, considered as a developed product, it cannot be explained by what lies below it. I do not want more than would, according to Dr. Hughlings Jackson (see above, Note 9), be granted me by all 'evolutionists of repute' in regard to mental phenomena generally.

NOTE 12. See p. 37.

*Mr. Darwin's account of his own mind.* See *Life and Letters of Charles Darwin* (Murray, 1887), vol. i. p. 100.

' I have said that in one respect my mind has changed during the last twenty or thirty years. Up to the age of thirty, or beyond it, poetry of many kinds, such as the works of Milton, Gray, Byron, Wordsworth, Coleridge, and Shelley, gave me great pleasure, and even as a schoolboy I took intense delight in Shakespeare, especially in the historical plays. I have also said that formerly pictures gave me considerable, and music very great delight. But now for many years I cannot endure to read a line of poetry. I have tried lately to read Shakespeare, and found it so intolerably dull that it nauseated me. I have also almost lost my taste for pictures or music. Music generally sets me thinking too energetically on what I have been at work on, instead of giving me pleasure. I retain some taste for fine scenery, but it does not cause me the exquisite delight which it formerly did. On the other hand, novels which are works of the imagination, though not of a very high order, have been for years a wonderful relief and pleasure to me, and I often bless all novelists. A surprising number have been read aloud to me, and I like all if moderately good, and if they do not end unhappily—against which a law ought to be passed. A novel, according to my taste, does not come into the first class unless it contains some person whom one can thoroughly love, and if a pretty woman all the better.

' This curious and lamentable loss of the higher aesthetic tastes is all the odder, as books on history, biographies, and travels (independently of any scientific facts which they may contain), and essays on all sorts of subjects, interest me as much as ever they did. My mind seems to have become a kind of machine for grinding general laws out of large collections of facts, but why this should have caused the atrophy of that part of the brain alone, on which the higher tastes depend, I cannot conceive. A man with a mind more highly organized or better constituted than mine, would not, I suppose, have thus suffered ; and if I had to live my life again, I would have made a rule to read some poetry and listen to some music at least once every week ; for perhaps the parts of my brain now atrophied would thus have been kept active through use. The loss of these tastes is a loss of happiness, and may possibly be injurious to the intellect, and more probably to the moral character, by enfeebling the emotional part of our nature.'

### NOTE 13. See p. 40.

*The unity of 'nature' and 'grace' in the best Theology.* Hoping to find another opportunity of illustrating at greater length the statements of the text, I would content myself here with the following references.

The doctrine of the New Testament will be found chiefly in St. John's Gospel i. 1–14 (cf. the commentaries of Godet or Westcott), St. Paul's Epistle to the Colossians i. 13–20 (cf. Lightfoot's commentary), and the Epistle to the Hebrews i. 1–3 (cf. Westcott's commentary).

On the teaching of the Fathers the following references will be found to justify the statements of the text. (1) St. Athanasius, *De Incarn.* 41 ; St. Gregory of Nyssa, *Catech. Magna* 25. Cf. Humboldt, *Cosmos* (Eng. trans., Longman and Murray, 1848) ii. pp. 25–30 ; Mgr. Landriot, *Le Christ de la tradition* (Paris 1888) i. pp. 191 ff.

(2) St. Greg. Thaumat. *Panegyr.* 8 ; St. Athan. *C. Gentes* 35–44 ; St. Greg. Nyss. *Catech. Mag.* 28. On law in miracles see St. Augustine, *C. Faust.* xxvi. 3 ; Macarius Magnes, *Apocritica* iii. 25.

(3) St. Justin, *Apol.* i. 46 ; St. Irenaeus, iv. 6. 5, 7 ; Origen *in Psalm.* xi. 6.

### NOTE 14. See p. 44.

*The rationale of miracles.* The former part of the argument in the text, pp. 45–46, will be found stated by H. S. Holland in *Christ or Ecclesiastes* (Longmans, 1888). Sermon 3. St.

Augustine's language, referred to in the last note, is well known.

'We may, without incongruity, say that God does in a manner contrary to nature what He does contrary to nature as we know it. For what we mean by "nature" is this well-known and customary order, and it is when God does anything contrary to this that His actions are called miracles or wonders. But as for that supreme law of nature, which is beyond the perception of men, either because they are impious or because they are still weak in knowledge—against this God no more acts than He acts against Himself. And God's spiritual and rational creatures, amongst whom are men, the more they become participators in that immutable law and light, the more clearly they can see what can happen and what cannot; and the further off, on the other hand, they are [from that divine law and light], so much the more are they astonished at what they are not accustomed to, in proportion as they are blind to what is coming.'

If we add to the thought here expressed the additional thought, which we find both in St. Athanasius and St. Augustine, that the miracles or exceptional actions of God are to be accounted for by man's blindness to Him in His normal method, and are thus condescensions to human sin and weakness, we have before us the best ancient rationale of miracles.

Archbishop Trench, in the introductory essay to his work on Miracles, gives an admirable view of the various theories on the subject, held at different times in the Christian Church.

### NOTE 15. See p. 52.

*Prof. Huxley on scientific objections to Christianity.*

Prof. Huxley has kindly allowed me to quote the following words from a private letter addressed by him to the late Dean of Wells, Apr. 27, 1877 :—' I have not the slightest objection to offer à priori to all the propositions in the three creeds. The mysteries of the Church are child's play compared with the mysteries of nature. The doctrine of the Trinity is not more puzzling than the necessary antinomies of physical speculation ; virgin procreation and resuscitation from apparent death are ordinary phenomena for the naturalist. It would be a great error therefore to suppose that the Agnostic rejects Theology because of its puzzles and wonders. He rejects it simply because in his judgment there would be no evidence sufficient to warrant the theological propositions, even if they related to the commonest and most obvious every-day propositions.'

This last sentence seems to me so strongly opposed to the facts of the case that one cannot but believe that, if scientific men generally adopt Prof. Huxley's line, the opposition to the Christian religion on the side of science may be greatly reduced.

# LECTURE III.

## NOTE 16. See p. 55.

*Hume's ' Canon.'* See his *Essays* (edd. Green and Grose : Longmans, 1875), vol. ii. p. 94 : 'The plain consequence is (and it is a general maxim worthy of our attention), "That no testimony is sufficient to establish a miracle, unless the testimony be of such a kind, that its falsehood would be more miraculous, than the fact, which it endeavours to establish : And even in that case there is a mutual destruction of arguments, and the superior only gives us an assurance suitable to that degree of force, which remains, after deducting the inferior." When any one tells me that he saw a dead man restored to life, I immediately consider with myself whether it be more probable that this person should either deceive or be deceived or that the fact, which he relates, should really have happened. I weigh the one miracle against the other ; and according to the superiority, which I discover, I pronounce my decision, and always reject the greater miracle. If the falsehood of his testimony would be more miraculous than the event which he relates, then, and not till then, can he pretend to command my belief or opinion.'

I ought to state that in the imaginary case which I have taken from *Mary Barton* the evidence for the mermaid is not exactly the same as that for the flying-fish.


### NOTE 17.  See p. 56.

*À priori tendencies in Dr. Martineau and Card. Newman.* The reference is of course :—

(1) To Dr. Martineau's *Seat of Authority in Religion* (Longmans, 1890), the latter part of which (b. iv.) is a criticism of the Gospel narrative.

(2) To Card. Newman's *Two Essays on Biblical and on Ecclesiastical Miracles* (Longmans, 1885). I must add that my lecture was written, and perhaps preached, before the appearance of Dr. Abbott's *Philomythus*, with the tone and spirit of which one cannot but disclaim sympathy.


### NOTE 18.  See p. 58.

*The Witness of St. Paul's Epistles.* M. Renan called the epistles named in the text 'undisputed and indisputable.' In the lecture, as delivered, they were described as 'practically undisputed.' They have, however, been recently disputed, with utterly perverse and untenable arguments, by a school of writers headed by Loman in Holland and Steck in Switzerland.

The witness of these Epistles, as summarized in the text, will be found in the following passages :— Rom. i. 7, 1 Cor. i 3, 2 Cor. xiii. 14 etc. (the co-ordination of Christ with the Father), Rom. x. 9–14 (Christ, as Lord,=the Jehovah of the O. T.: cf. 1 Cor. i. 2), Rom. ix. 5 (Christ called 'God over all': for

Pfleiderer's statement on this subject see his *Hibbert Lectures*, Williams & Norgate, 1885, p. 55), 1 Cor. viii. 6 (Christ in creation), 1 Cor. x. 4.(Christ with the Jews in the wilderness), Rom. viii. 3, Gal. iv. 4 (God's own Son, incarnate), 1 Cor. xv. 47 (from heaven), 2 Cor. viii. 9 (by self-beggary), Rom. i. 3-4 (disclosing His Godhead through His manhood). Cf. Prof. Sanday's *What the first Christians thought about Christ* (Oxford House Papers, series 1 : Longmans, 1890).

St. Paul's appeal to an earlier narrative is in 1 Cor. xi. 23, xv. 3. For the record of appearances (1 Cor. xv. 5-7), cf. St. Luke xxiv. 34-36, St. Matt. xxviii. 16-20, Acts i. 14 (where James is already among the disciples), Acts i. 6-11. It must be remembered that St. Luke's Gospel and the Acts constitute two parts of the same work. This makes it, I think, absurd to suggest that the 'forty days' mentioned in Acts i. 3 are excluded in St. Luke xxiv.

## NOTE 19.  See p. 66.

*Synoptic Gospels.* In one lecture it is impossible to do more than touch upon the criticism of these books. Among the most suggestive recent contributions to the subject, I may refer to Dr. Paul Ewald's *Das Hauptproblem der Evangelienfrage* (Leipzig, 1890), Mr. Wright's *The Composition of the Four Gospels* (Macmillan, 1890), Dr. Sanday in *Expositor*, 1891, Jan.-May. The external evidence for the Gospels has been admirably re-stated for the general reader by Dr. Dale, *The Living Christ and the Four Gospels* (Hodder & Stoughton, 1890).

It is hardly necessary to mention Dr. Salmon's *Introduction to the New Testament* (Murray, 1st edit. 1885), or Bp. Lightfoot's *Essays on 'Supernatural Religion'* (Macmillan, 1889).

I believe that in taking St. Mark's Gospel, or the main substance of St. Mark's Gospel, as the starting-point, I am doing what will commend itself to almost all enquirers.

It is important to emphasize, at this point, that the evidential use of the Gospels, as merely historical documents, is to be kept distinct from the (logically) subsequent use of them in the Church (see pp. 188–9) as inspired records.

### NOTE 20.　See p. 68.

*St. John's Gospel.*　The reference in the text is to Archdeacon Watkins' *Bampton Lectures*, 1890 (Murray, 1890), on 'Modern Criticism considered in its relation to the Fourth Gospel.' In the introductions to Prof. Godet's and Dr. Westcott's commentaries on St. John's Gospel, and in Prof. Sanday's *Authorship and Historical Character of the Fourth Gospel* (Macmillan, 1872), the student will find all reasonable doubts as to its authorship set at rest.

### NOTE 21.　See p. 70.

*The 'Logos.'*　In regard to this idea it must not be forgotten that, as found in some of the fathers, e. g. Justin and the Alexandrians, it has much closer affinities to Greek philosophy than it has in St. John.

### NOTE 22.　See p. 71.

*Our Lord's discourses in St. John.*　Dr. Plummer (*Camb. G. T. for Schools, St. John,* 1882, p. 100, as cited by Watkins) gives the following interesting extract from a letter written by Cardinal Newman on July 15, 1878 :—

'Every one writes in his own style. St. John gives our Lord's meaning in his own way. At that time the third person was not so commonly used in history as now. When a reporter gives one of Gladstone's speeches in the newspaper, if he uses the first person, I understand not only the matter, but the style, the words, to be Gladstone's : when the third, I consider the style, etc., to be the reporter's own. But in ancient times this distinction was not made. Thucydides uses the dramatic method, yet Spartan and Athenian speak in Thucydidean Greek. And so every clause of our Lord's speeches in St. John may be in

St. John's Greek; yet every clause may contain the matter which our Lord spoke in Aramaic. Again, St. John might and did select or condense (as being inspired for that purpose) the matter of our Lord's discourses, as that with Nicodemus, and thereby the wording might be St. John's, though the matter might still be our Lord's.'

### NOTE 23.  See p. 75.

*The apostles as witnesses.*  Dr. Latham (*Pastor Pastorum*, pp. 241 ff.) describes their qualifications with admirable freshness and truth.

It must be remembered that each apostle was in a peculiar sense a witness of the resurrection of Jesus.  On this event the chief stress was laid (Acts i. 3, 22, 1 Cor. xv. 5, 8).  This may in part account for the fragmentariness and independence of the various accounts we have of the appearances.  The summary in 1 Cor. xv. 5–7 is the nearest approach to a central record of them.  The 'I received' in ver. 3 probably means that this was the account of the appearances given to St. Paul at his conversion, by those who were in Christ before him.

### NOTE 24.  See p. 79.

*The narratives of the Nativity and Infancy.*  A full defence of these narratives will be found in Godet's commentary on St. Luke's Gospel.  Great stress has recently been laid on resemblances, real and supposed, between the 'birth-stories' of Jesus Christ and of Buddha.  In regard to such resemblances, it may be remarked that

(1) We may set aside as contrary to all the evidence any idea of Buddhist influence on the Gospel narrative.

(2) We may set aside as unsupported by evidence the idea of a Christian influence on later Buddhist tradition.  This leaves us in the position of regarding the Christian and the Buddhist narratives as independent growths.

(3) It may be remarked that no claim to an historical character can be put in, on ground of evidence, for the Buddhist

miracles, nor can the Buddhist scriptures be put in any sort of competition as historical documents with our Gospels. The question, therefore, is simply *whether the resemblance of the Buddhist legend to our Gospels indicates so strong a human tendency to imagine a certain class of incidents under certain circumstances as to invalidate the historical evidence for the actual occurrence of such incidents in any case.*

The solution of this question depends on (*a*) the strength of the historical evidence in the particular case; (*b*) the closeness of the resemblance in the Buddhist legend. As to (*a*) I believe that close and unprejudiced study will give an increasing confidence in the trustworthiness of the Gospels and their freedom from mere legend. As to (*b*) I believe that the widespread impression of resemblance is due to such works as *The Light of Asia*—works which the Germans would describe as *tendenziöse*—and not to a study of the Buddhist books which have been translated for us. Resemblances exist, no doubt—in some cases remarkable resemblances—but not resemblances which create any serious obstacle to the historical character of our Christian records. The subject is dealt with at length, and, as it seems to me, with fairness, in Kellogg's *Light of Asia and Light of the World* (Macmillan, 1885), cc. ii–iv.

## LECTURE IV.

### NOTE 25. See p. 81.

*The relation of dogmas to original Christianity.* On the ancient and Anglican idea I may refer to what is said at greater length in *Roman Catholic Claims* (3rd ed. Longmans, 1890), cc. iii, iv: also to an interesting letter of Cardinal Newman, written to R. H. Froude in 1835. See *Life and Correspondence*, by Anne Mozley (Longmans, 1891), ii. pp. 126–7. 'The more I read of Athanasius, Theodoret, etc., the more I see the ancients *do* make the Scriptures the *basis* of their belief. The only question is would they have done so in another point beside the θεολογία which happened in the early ages to be in discussion? I incline to say the creed is the faith necessary to salvation as well as to Church communion, and to maintain that Scripture according to the Fathers is the authentic record and document of this faith . . . . Now this θεολογία, I say, the Fathers do certainly rest on Scripture as upon two tables of stone. I am surprised more and more to see how entirely they fall into Hawkins' theory even in set words, that Scripture proves and the Church teaches.'

In regard to the more recent Roman idea, of which Card. Franzelin may be taken as chief exponent (see *De Divin. Tradit. et Script.*, ed. 3, Rome, 1882, and cf. *R. C. Claims*, p. 58), it must be remarked that no doctrine of development is of any assistance to the Roman position which does not cover an *actual increase in positive revelation.* The early Church did not know anything of, e. g., the immaculate conception of Mary. But this positive increase in revelation is firmly and finally repudiated by Newman. See *Tracts Theol. and Eccl.* (Pickering, 1874), p. 287, written as a Roman Catholic: 'First of all, and in as few words as possible, and *ex abundanti cautelâ*:—Every Catholic holds that the Christian dogmas were in the Church from the time of the apostles; that they were ever in their substance what they are now; that they existed before the formulas were publicly adopted, in which as time went on they were defined and recorded.' With this cf. Lord Acton's words, *Engl. Hist. Review*, Oct. 1890, p. 723: 'Just then after sixteen years spent in the Church of Rome, Newman was inclined to guard and narrow his theory. . . . . He thought that a divine of the second century on seeing the Roman catechism would have recognised his own belief in it without surprise, as soon as he understood its meaning. He once wrote, "If I have said more than this I think I have not worked out my meaning, and was confused—whether the minute facts of history will bear me out in this view I leave to others to determine."'

The third view mentioned in the lecture is that of the late

Dr. Hatch, *Hibbert Lectures*, 1888, 'The Influence of Greek Ideas and Usages upon the Christian Church' (Williams & Norgate, 1890). The fundamental fault of this work is noticed on pp. 99, 100. The same criticism is made in an admirable review of the work in the *Church Quarterly Review*, July 1891, pp. 380 ff., and by Professor Sanday in *Contemp. Review*, May 1891, pp. 688–690. I cannot but think that the criticisms at the end of this latter article go far to invalidate the praise with which it begins. Dr. Hatch's work seems almost always to have this fatal flaw, when he is dealing with Christian subjects, that he omits the central and positive evidence in favour of what is external, suggestive, and subsidiary. Thus his Hibbert Lectures are in fact little more than an abstract consideration of how we might have imagined the development of Christian theology to have taken place, if the New Testament and the sub-apostolic writers had perished. There is however one sentence in Dr. Hatch's work which does describe admirably the facts of the case (p. 207; the italics are mine): 'We may sum up the result of the influence of Greece on the conception of God in His relation to the material universe, by saying that it found a reasoned basis for Hebrew monotheism. *It helped the Christian communities to believe as an intellectual conviction that which they had first accepted as a spiritual revelation.*'

## NOTE 26. See p. 83.

*The theology of the New Testament.* In my third lecture I argued at first simply from the central epistles of St. Paul (1 and 2 Cor., Rom., Gal.) and the Gospel of St. Mark. These are sufficient to show that the theological conception of the person of Christ, as the incarnate Son of God, is the original conception. It is of course assumed by certain writers that St. Paul is the parent of the distinctively Christian theology, and that the original Christianity is better represented by Ebionism. This view is contrary to the evidence.

(1) The evidence of St. Paul's central epistles shows (see above, p. 61) that on the person of Christ there was no controversy between him and the Judaizers.

(2) St. Mark's Gospel, in which the doctrine of divine Sonship appears (see above, p. 66), is connected historically not with St. Paul, but with St. Peter. The same doctrine appears also in the discourses common to St. Matthew and St. Luke; see St. Matt. xi. 27, St. Luke x. 22.

(3) The epistle of St. James, which is most certainly independent of St. Paul, identifies Christ 'the Lord' with the Jehovah of the Old Testament in a manner which involves the theology of the eternal Sonship. The identification is apparent in v. 4, 7, 8, 10, 11, 14, 15; see also ii. 1; and compare iv. 12, where the 'one lawgiver and judge' is God, with v. 9, etc., where 'the judge' is Jesus Christ.

(4) The evidence, external and internal, refers the fourth Gospel to St. John, and renders its doctrine of the Incarnation of the Son independent of St. Paul.

(5) There is no book less 'Pauline' than the Apocalypse, but also no book in which Jesus Christ, the Son of God (ii. 18; cf. ii. 28, iii. 5), is more plainly conceived of as God: see esp. (a) i. 8, where He that 'is to come' is Christ, as in verse 7, and He is also the Alpha and the Omega (xxii. 12, 13). (b) v. 9–13, where the lamb is worshipped as God. (c) xxii. 1 (cf. iii. 1), where the lamb is with the Father the source of the Holy Ghost.

The language in the New Testament, which is most susceptible of an Ebionite interpretation of the highest sort, is that of the early speeches in the Acts taken by themselves. But the supporters of the view which is being combated are precluded from appealing to these, by the fact that the rudimentary character of the theology in these speeches is the best possible testimony to the trustworthiness of St. Luke's materials, and his accuracy in the use of them. Indirectly this augments the trustworthiness of his Gospel material, in which Christ proclaims Himself the Son of God (x. 22, xxii. 70). More directly it augments the historical trustworthiness of the Acts; and if the Acts is historical, then (a) there was no theological opposition between St. Paul and the older apostles: (b) St. Stephen had learnt to worship Christ as Lord before St. Paul's conversion (vii. 59, 60; cf. i. 24 and 1 Cor. i. 3). The only conclusion, then, that can legitimately be drawn from these speeches (which are in no way incompatible with the fullest doctrine of the Incarnation), is that the Christian Church immediately after Pentecost was simply intent (see pp. 96–7) upon demonstrating that Jesus was the Christ.

On the development of Christian theology between the apostles and Athanasius, I may refer to a summary history by the Rev. A. Robertson, which is forthcoming in *Nicene and Post-Nicene Library*, ser. ii. vol. iv. proleg. cap. ii. § 3 (2). In sub-apostolic days the rich theology of Ignatius, the theology of Clement (whose trinitarian formula, *ad Cor.* 58, certified by the recovery of the end of his epistle, sheds light on the rest of his language), and the unmistakable, if confused, incarnation doctrine of Hermas, hold the ground against the anonymous and uncertified documents of an Ebionite or semi-Ebionite character. Moreover, the strong appeal of all Church theologians, as against humanitarianism or gnosticism, *to apostolic traditions*, must never be forgotten. This appeal can be in large measure verified and justified. It is striking to notice how Origen, in his most speculative work, the *De Principiis*, begins with the statement of tradition. See Dr. Bigg, *Bampton Lectures*, 1887, ' The Christian Platonists of Alexandria' (Clar. Press), pp. 152 ff. ' We have already seen what Origen regarded as the proper task of the Christian philosopher. Tradition, embodying the teaching of the apostles, has handed down certain facts, certain usages, which are to be received without dispute, but does not attempt to explain the why or the whence. It is the office of the sanctified reason to define, to articulate, to co-ordinate, even to expand, and generally to adapt to human needs the faith once delivered to the Church. What, then, is the utterance of tradition? It tells us that there is one God who created all things out of nothing, who is just and good, the author of the Old as of the New Testament, the Father of our Lord Jesus Christ: that Jesus Christ was begotten of the Father before every creature, that through Him all things were made, that He is God and Man, born of the Holy Spirit and the Virgin Mary, that He did truly suffer, rise again, and ascend into heaven: that the Holy Ghost is associated in honour and dignity with the Father and the Son, that it is He who inspired the saints both of the old and of the new dispensation: that there will be a resurrection of the dead, when the body which is sown in corruption will rise in incorruption, and that in the world to come the souls of men will inherit eternal life or suffer eternal punishment according to their works: that every reasonable soul is a free agent, plotted against by evil spirits, comforted by good angels, but in no way constrained: that the Scriptures were written by the agency of the Spirit of God, that they have two senses, the plain and the hidden, whereof the latter can be known only to those to whom is given the grace of the Holy Spirit in the word of wisdom and knowledge.'

### NOTE 27. See p. 85.

*Subapostolic writers.* See Dorner, *Doctrine of the Person of Christ* (Eng. trans., Clark's Libr.), div. i. vol. i. p. 92. 'There is undeniably a very significant distinction between the written productions of the apostolic age and those of the age immediately following; and it is hardly possible to represent the relation of the one to the other more erroneously, than when the apostolic age is called, in a dogmatical respect, a germ and a beginning, while the age of the Apostolic Fathers is regarded as the fruitful unfolding of that germ. It is true that, to a certain extent, on one side such an advance was to be expected in the later age; for this is according to the law of history. But if we try each of these ages by the standard of its Christian knowledge, we shall find beyond all doubt a serious falling off in the age following that of the apostles. What was in the earlier age the actual spiritual possession of the distinguished men whom the Lord chose, trained, and equipped, was far from being all retained by the succeeding age; much less was a higher stage of Christian knowledge attained. Such a retrogression, following times of unusual spiritual elevation and expansion, is quite in accordance with the laws of historical development, as we see in other cases.'

### NOTE 28. See p. 87.

*The formula of Chalcedon.* The following is the most important passage :—

'Wherefore, after the example of the holy Fathers, we all with one voice confess our Lord Jesus Christ one and the same Son, the same perfect in Godhead, the same perfect in manhood, very God and very Man, the same consisting of a reasonable soul and a body, of one substance with the Father as touching the Godhead, the same of one substance with us as touching the manhood, like us in all things, sin except; begotten of the Father before the worlds as touching the Godhead, the same in these last days, for us and for our salvation, born of the Virgin Mary, the Mother of God, as touching the manhood, one and the same Christ, Son, Lord, Only-begotten, to be acknowledged of two natures, without confusion, without conversion, without division, never to be separated, (ἀσυγχύτως, ἀτρέπτως, ἀδιαιρέτως, ἀχωρίστως); the distinction of natures being in no wise done away because of the union, but rather the characteristic property of each nature being preserved, and concurring into one Person and one subsistence, not as if Christ were parted or divided into two persons, but one and the same Son and only-begotten God, Word, Lord, Jesus Christ; even as the Prophets from the beginning spake concerning Him, and our Lord Jesus Christ hath instructed us, and the symbol of the Fathers hath handed down to us.'

### NOTE 29. See p. 88.

*Theological confusion in period of councils.* Cf. Holland's *On Behalf of Belief* (Longmans, 1889), ' The building of the Spirit.' He quotes St. Hilary: ' We determine creeds by the year, or by the month; and then we change our determination; and then we prohibit our changes; and then we anathematize our prohibitions.' St. Hilary is speaking of the authorities in the Church. For more quotations see *R. C. Claims*, p. xii, and pp. 49 ff.

### NOTE 30. See p. 88.

*The Via Media.* This is expounded in the admirable little treatise ascribed to Boetius, *con. Eut. et Nest.* praef. and c. 7; cf. Greg. Nyss. *Cat. Mag.* c. 3. where the action of the Church is described as uniting the good in opposite heresies, while opposing each in turn. See further, *R. C. Claims*, ch. 1.

### NOTE 31. See p. 97.

*Dogmatic passages in the N. T.* These passages, Phil. ii. 5–11, Col. i. 15–18, Hebr. i. 1–3. St. John i. 1–18, 1 St. John i. 1–3. ii. 22, 23. have received full explanation, the two first from Dr. Lightfoot, the rest from Dr. Westcott, in their commentaries. See also the phrase of the Ep. to Titus, ' Our great God and Saviour Jesus Christ,' ii. 13; cf. ii. 10, iii. 4, 6.

St. Basil (*de Spirit. Sanct.* iii. 5) hits the mark when he describes the language of the New Testament, by contrast to the controversial language of his time, as untechnical—ἁπλῆ καὶ ἀτεχνολόγητος τοῦ πνεύματος διδασκαλία.

### NOTE 32. See p. 99.

*Christ's permanent manhood.* The permanence of our Lord's manhood, in body and soul, is no doubt a mysterious subject. It is very necessary not to conceive grossly of ' the spiritual

body'; and St. Paul's language, 1 Cor. xv. 35 ff., is sufficient
safeguard against this error. On the other hand, St. John certainly
asserts that Christ is 'to come in the flesh,' 2 St. John 7 ; cf.
Westcott *in loc.* and Acts i. 11. St. Paul certainly teaches the
resurrection of the body, and makes our Lord's glorified body
the prototype, 1 Cor. xv. 23. The Epistle to the Hebrews also
implies the permanence of our Lord's manhood, cf. vii. 26—
viii. 4, x. 19–21.

# LECTURE V.

## NOTE 33. See p. 115.

*Mansel's Bampton Lectures.* These lectures, and the controversy raised by them, are only referred to in order to emphasize
a positive principle involved in the Incarnation—that human
qualities really can and do express those of God. Mansel's
language did undoubtedly appear to obscure this principle.
Hence the controversy of which I endeavour to gather the fruit
without entering into its exact merits.

## NOTE 34. See p. 118.

*Christ's humanity personal or impersonal ?* The truth which
the phrase 'Christ's impersonal manhood' is intended to guard,
is that the humanity which our Lord assumed had no *independent*
personality. It found its personality in the Son who assumed
it. But as assumed by Him it was most truly personal. See
Petavius, *de Incarn.* iii. cc. 12 (§§ 4–7), 13, v. cc. 5–7; and De
Lugo, *de Myster. Incarn.* dispp. x. and xiii. § 2.

## NOTE 35. See p. 121.

*God's love revealed first in Christ.* Cf. Robert Browning, *The
Ring and the Book,* iv. p. 60 :—

'Conjecture of the worker by the work:
Is there strength there?   Enough: intelligence?
Ample: but goodness in a like degree?
Not to the human eye in the present state,
An isoscele deficient in the base.
What lacks, then, of perfection fit for God
But just the instance which this tale supplies
Of love without a limit?   So is strength,
So is intelligence; let love be so,
Unlimited in its self-sacrifice,
Then is the tale true and God shows complete.
Beyond the tale, I reach into the dark,
Feel what I cannot see, and still faith stands.'


### NOTE 36.  See p. 126.

*Prayer in accordance with law.*   Cf. in Gerhard, *Meditationes Sacrae*, med. 25: 'Placet Deo oratio, sed debito modo instituta ; qui ergo exaudiri desiderat, is oret sapienter, ardenter, humiliter, fideliter, perseveranter et confidenter.  Oret sapienter, ut scilicet oret ea, quae divinae gloriae et proximorum saluti serviunt.  Omnipotens est Deus, ergo non statuas ei in precibus modum: sapientissimus est, ergo non praescribas ordinem: non temere prorumpant, sed fidem praeeuntem sequantur, fides autem respicit verbum: quae ergo absolute Deus in verbo promittit, absolute ores; quae cum conditione promittit, ut temporalia, ea itidem cum conditione ores; quae nullo modo promittit, ea etiam nullo modo ores; saepe Deus dat iratus, quod negat propitius.  Sequere ergo Christum, qui suam voluntatem plene Deo resignat.'


### NOTE 37.  See p. 127.

*The death of Christ not God's act.*  Cf. Acts ii. 22-24: 'Jesus of Nazareth, a man approved of God unto you by mighty works and wonders and signs, which God did by him in the midst of

you, even as ye yourselves know; him, being delivered up by
the determinate counsel and foreknowledge of God, ye by the
hands of lawless men (or 'men without the law') did crucify
and slay: whom God raised up.' Here, as elsewhere in the
New Testament, the manifestation of the Christ and the raising
up of the Christ from the dead are assigned directly to God. On
the other hand, the crucifixion of the Christ is man's act, which
God foresees, bears with and works through to His own ends.

It is to put this in other words, to say (with St. Anselm, *Cur
Deus Homo*, i. 9) that God willed, primarily, the obedience of the
Christ: and in a secondary sense the death of the Christ,
because under the sinful conditions of the world, obedience
led to death. 'Potest enim dici quia praecepit illi mori Pater
cum hoc praecepit unde incurrit mortem.'

## NOTE 38. See p. 128.

*God's gradual method in the O. T.* The quotation is from St.
Irenaeus, *c. Haer.* iv. 13. 4. Cf. 13. 1 : 'omnia haec non contra-
rietatem et dissolutionem praeteritorum continent . . . sed pleni-
tudinem et extensionem.' Further quotations will be found in
*Lux Mundi*, Essay viii, 'The Holy Spirit and Inspiration,'
pp. 329–31.

## NOTE 39. See p. 128.

*St. Augustine on Evolution.* See *De Gen. ad litt.* v. 23 (44,
45): 'Consideremus ergo cuiuslibet arboris pulchritudinem in
robore, ramis, frondibus, pomis: haec species non utique repente
tanta ac talis est exorta, sed quo etiam ordine novimus. Sur-
rexit enim a radice, quam terrae primum germen infixit; atque
inde omnia illa formata et distincta creverunt. Porro illud
germen ex semine: in semine ergo illa omnia fuerunt primitus,
non mole corporeae magnitudinis, sed vi potentiaque causali . . .
Sicut autem in ipso grano invisibiliter erant omnia simul quae
per tempora in arborem surgerent: ita ipse mundus cogitandus

est, cum Deus simul omnia creavit, habuisse simul omnia quae
in illo et cum illo facta sunt, quando factus est dies ; non solum
caelum cum sole et luna et sideribus, quorum species manet
motu rotabili, et terram et abyssos ; ... sed etiam illa quae aqua
et terra produxit potentialiter atque causaliter, prius quam per
temporum moras ita exorirentur, quomodo nobis jam nota sunt
in eis operibus, quae Deus usque nunc operatur.'

### NOTE 40.  See p. 129.

*God self-limited.*  The quotation is given at length in app.
note 14 to lect. ii.   Christian thought grasped from the first this
conception of God as not 'infinite' in the sense of indeterminate, but self-limited; see the ancient unknown teacher
already quoted by St. Irenaeus in the second century (*con.
Haer.* iv. 4. 2): 'Bene qui dixit ipsum immensum Patrem in
Filio mensuratum ; mensura enim Patris Filius, quoniam et
capit eum.'  Hardly anything has done more harm in theology
than the neglect of this thought in loose ideas of the divine
'infinity.'

### NOTE 41.  See p. 129.

*Arbitrary decrees attributed to God.*  This attribution has of
course been justified by reference to St. Paul's argument in
Rom. ix.  But St. Paul is there asserting the divine absolute-
ness, not as against man's moral freedom and responsibility,
but as against the immoral and irresponsible claim of the Jew
that God had committed Himself to his race.  God's freedom
is asserted by St. Paul as against any claim on man's part
either (1) to determine his vocation, or (2) to retain his vocation
where he fails to show the correspondence of faith.  Thus he
is in fact proving that God's elections are not arbitrary from
the moral point of view (as the Jew would have them to be), but
in accordance with the moral law of correspondence.  I have
endeavoured to draw out the continuous argument of Romans

ix–xi at length in *Studia Biblica* (Clar. Press, 1891), vol. iii. pp. 37 ff.

## NOTE 42.   See p. 132.

*The three elements in man's spirit.*   Plato in trying to describe the elements of man's nature under a figure is driven to use a trinitarian formula, *Republic* ix. 588 D : σύναπτε αὐτὰ εἰς ἓν τρία ὄντα.   The Christian fathers commonly use the human trinity in various ways as an image or figure of the divine, e. g. Greg. Nyss. *Cat. Mag.* 1–4.   See *Lux Mundi*, Essay viii, p. 336. The use of this analogy by the Fathers shows at least that they did not wish us to think of the three divine Persons as separate individuals.

## NOTE 43.   See p. 135.

*God's triune being disclosed in Christ.*   I should wish to lay great stress on the fact that the existence of the Trinity in God becomes a truth of human experience, if the claim of our Lord to oneness with God is admitted.   It is, in the light of His personality and language, no mere speculation in metaphysics, any more than, e. g., the very ' metaphysical' statements of scientific men as to the luminiferous ether.

## NOTE 44.   See p. 136.

*Unitarianism untenable.*   This has been recently exemplified again in the *Appeal to Unitarians* (the work referred to in app. note 5 on p. 238), pp. 77 ff.   Dr. Martineau himself perceives that the existence of God postulates an eternal coexistent ' object' (see *Seat of Authority*, p. 32), but this object he conceives to be space, or space and matter.

# LECTURE VI.

## NOTE 45. See p. 151.

*Johannes De Lugo, S. J., Disputationes Scholasticae de Incarnatione Dominica* (Lugd. 1633): see disp. xviii–xxi, on the subject of the knowledge of Christ; disp. xxviii, on the phrase 'servus Dei'; disp. xxxiv. sec. ii. § 47, on Christ sacrificing to Himself as God. (There is no doubt a sense in which this phrase expresses the truth. But it leaves out of sight, like so much in the same school of theology, that the divine Son was personally acting under conditions of manhood.)

## NOTE 46. See p. 160.

*Divine power shewn most chiefly in self-humiliation.* Cf. Greg. Nyss. *Cat. Mag.* 24 : πρῶτον μὲν οὖν τὸ τὴν παντοδύναμον φύσιν πρὸς τὸ ταπεινὸν τῆς ἀνθρωπότητος καταβῆναι ἰσχῦσαι, πλείονα τὴν ἀπόδειξιν τῆς δυνάμεως ἔχει ἢ τὰ μεγάλα τε καὶ ὑπερφυῆ τῶν θαυμάτων. τὸ μὲν γὰρ μέγα τι καὶ ὑψηλὸν ἐξεργασθῆναι παρὰ τῆς θείας δυνάμεως, κατὰ φύσιν πώς ἐστι καὶ ἀκόλουθον. . . . ἡ δὲ πρὸς ταπεινὸν κάθοδος περιουσία τίς ἐστι τῆς δυνάμεως, οὐδὲν ἐν τοῖς παρὰ φύσιν κωλυομένης. Hilar. Pict. *de Trin.* xi. 48 : 'quod autem se ipsum intra se vacuefaciens continuit, detrimentum non attulit potestati; cum intra hanc exinanientis se humilitatem, virtute tamen omnis exinanitae intra se usus sit potestatis.'

## NOTE 47. See p. 163.

*The conception of the Incarnation.* Our Lord is commonly represented, as living during His life on earth in the habitual exercise of a double consciousness, as acting and speaking now as God and now as man. It is true of course that as being God in manhood He *possessed* at every moment the divine, as well as the human, consciousness and nature. But in great measure, the self-sacrifice of the Incarnation seems to have lain in His refraining from the exercise of what He possessed, or from the divine mode of action, that He might live under conditions of a true manhood: cf. Westcott, *Epistle to the Hebrews*, p. 66 : 'The two natures were inseparably united in the unity of His Person. In all things He acts personally: and, as far as is revealed to us, the greatest works during His earthly life are wrought by the help of the Father through the energy of a humanity enabled to do all things in fellowship with God.'

It is not enough to recognise that our Lord was ignorant of a divine secret, in respect of His human nature, unless we recognise also that He was so truly acting under conditions of human nature as Himself to be ignorant. 'The Son' did not know.

This involves no change in God because it was simply an external exhibition of an eternal capacity for self-sacrifice in the being of God.

But, it may be asked, in what relation does this self-emptying stand to the cosmic functions of the Son, 'in whom all things consist,' who 'bears along all things by the word of his power' (Col. i. 18, Heb. i. 3) ?

To this question, it seems to me, we can give but a very hesitating and partial answer. On the one hand we cannot but recognise with theologians from St. Athanasius (*de Incarn.* 17) to Dr. Westcott (*l. c.* p. 426) that the work of the Son in nature 'was in no way interrupted by the Incarnation.' On the other hand, the Incarnation is represented as involving an act of self-sacrifice on the part of the Father in surrendering the Son (see above, p. 159), and it is described as a 'coming down from heaven' on the part of the Son. (In St. John iii. 13, the words 'which is in heaven' are, we must remember, very doubtful). It seems that the matter of real importance is that we should be boldly faithful to the language of the New Testament, and not attempt to 'describe, beyond the Scriptures, the measure or the manner ' of the divine condescension (Athan. *c. Apollinar.* ii. ad fin.). The Incarnate Son was *personally, within the sphere of the Incarnation, accepting the limitation of humanity.* See Bruce, *Humiliation of Christ* (Clark, ed. 3, 1889), pp. 187–191.

### NOTE 48.  See p. 163.

*The Fathers on the human ignorance of Christ.* The support which the Fathers give to the view maintained in the text is twofold.  (1) Many recognise a real ignorance in our Lord in respect of His humanity.  (2) Some give great reality to the idea of the self-limitation of the Son.  Thus Irenaeus recognises an occasional ' quiescence ' of the Divine Word to allow of the human trials of the Incarnate (*con. Haer.* iii. 19. 3).  Origen speaks of a self-humiliation of the Son to a ' divine folly,' i.e. to a human mode of wisdom (*Hom. in Ierem.* 8. 8).  Others, as St. Cyril and St. Hilary, supply us with admirable formulas for the ' self-emptying,' though without applying it to the limitation of knowledge.

But the study of the Fathers on this subject forces upon one the conviction that they were not facing the question exactly as it presents itself to us.

I must be content for the moment to refer to the quotations from the Fathers given by Mr. Swayne in his *Enquiry into the Nature of our Lord's Knowledge as Man* (with a preface by the Bp. of Salisbury ; Longmans, 1891).

### NOTE 49.  See p. 164.

*The protest of Theodoret.* See *Repr. xii. capp. Cyril.* in anath. iv : ' If He knew the day, and, wishing to conceal it, said He was ignorant, see what blasphemy is the result.  Truth tells a lie.'

## NOTE 50.   See p. 167.

*Christ could have sinned, if He had willed.*   So St. Augustine, *Op. Imperf. c. Jul.* iv. 48 : 'Christus hanc cupiditatem vitiorum et sentire posset, si haberet; et habere, si vellet; sed absit ut vellet.' Cf. Anselm, *Cur Deus Homo*, ii. 10 : 'Possumus igitur dicere de Christo quia potuit mentiri, si subaudiatur, si vellet.' [Boethius] *c. Eut. et Nest.* c. 8.

## NOTE 51.   See p. 167.

*Man not originally perfect.* In answer to the question whether Adam was formed perfect or imperfect [τέλειος ἤ ἀτελής], Clement replies : 'They shall learn from us that he was not perfect in respect of his creation, but in a fit condition to receive virtue.' Clem. Alex. *Strom.* vi. 12. 96 ; cf. Iren. *c. Haer.* iv. 38.

# LECTURE VII.

## NOTE 52.   See p. 179.

*We know in part and prophesy in part.* The commentary of Estius on these words (1 Cor. xiii. 9) is noteworthy :—

'Itaque sensus esse videtur: Donum scientiae ac prophetiae nobis datur ob imperfectionem huius saeculi, quia per scientiam homines spiritualium rudes ac rebus sensibilibus dediti ab ipsis sensibilibus ad capienda fidei mysteria veluti manu ducendi sunt, per donum autem prophetiae de reconditis scripturarum sensibus instituendi. Quorum neutrum agetur futuro saeculo, ubi perfecta erunt omnia. . . . Consequens item est, *etiam Christum Dominum, in hac vita conversantem, cognovisse et prophetasse ex parte, sensu videlicet iam explicato.*'

That our Lord is content to use popular language, by way

of metaphor, without criticism or correction, is nowhere more
apparent than when He speaks of the unclean spirits ' passing
through waterless places, seeking rest' (St. Matt. xii. 43; cf.
Tobit viii. 3). But to regard our Lord's language about angels
and devils as not more than metaphorical, is only possible on
principles which might equally be used to evacuate all His
language of meaning.

### NOTE 53. See p. 185.

*St. Augustine on Purgatory.* See *De Civ. Dei*, xxi. 26. 4 :

' Post istius sane corporis mortem, donec ad illum veniatur,
qui post resurrectionem corporum futurus est damnationis et
remunerationis ultimus dies, si hoc temporis intervallo spiritus
defunctorum ejusmodi ignem dicuntur perpeti, quem non
sentiant illi qui non habuerunt tales mores et amores in hujus
corporis vita, ut eorum ligna, foenum, stipula consumatur; alii
vero sentiant qui ejusmodi secum aedificia portaverunt, sive ibi
tantum, sive et hic et ibi, sive ideo hic ut non ibi, saecularia,
quamvis a damnatione venialia concremantem ignem transitoriae
tribulationis inveniant; non redarguo, quia forsitan verum est.'

### NOTE 54. See p. 186.

*No new doctrines in the Church.* For Card. Newman's final
mind on this subject see above, app. note 25, p. 252. It is
worth while calling attention to the language used in the
formal ' *Declaration of the Catholic Bishops, the Vicars apostolic
and their coadjutors in Great Britain*' in 1826. (London,
Keating & Brown, 1826.) See sec. ii. p. 7. ' On the spiritual
authority of the apostles and their successors, who were divinely
commissioned to promulgate and teach the law of Christ to all
nations ; and on the uniform and universal testimony, belief, and
practice of all Christian Churches from the beginning, the certitude of the Catholic is grounded, that all the doctrines which he
believes, as articles of Catholic faith, and all the sacred precepts

and rites, which he observes, as the ordinances of Christ, were really revealed and instituted by Almighty God; and are the same as were originally delivered by Christ to His apostles, and by them promulgated over all nations.' This is simply the old Catholic rule of faith, and to bring recent Roman dogmas under it is simply to play fast and loose with history.

### NOTE 55. See p. 196.

*Our Lord's argument from Ps. cx.* It may prevent unnecessary controversy if I explain—

(1) That there is no question being raised as to the existence in the Old Testament of that doctrine of a Divine Messiah, to which our Lord was recalling the Pharisees: see above, pp. 192, 193.

(2) That no support is being given to the view which ascribes the bulk of the psalms to the period after the Captivity, and no objection being raised to the very early date of Ps. cx.

(3) That the view is not being maintained that the psalm was written in David's name by a later poet—a view to which the phrase in Mark xii. 37, 'David himself,' would be an objection.

(4) That it is not denied that to ascribe the psalm to David is the most obvious conclusion from our Lord's words. But the most obvious conclusion from our Lord's words is not always the truest. Our Lord does not teach in such a way as best to save us trouble: see above, pp. 180-1. In particular the most obvious interpretation of Mark x. 18—that which makes our Lord repudiate identity in moral goodness with God—is not the truest. Single passages must be interpreted in harmony with the whole.

(5) That if I am challenged to show why the principle of interpretation here admitted might not be used to 'explain away' any part of our Lord's teaching, I should reply: (*a*) a question, such as our Lord is here asking, can never be treated as if it were on a level with a positive statement; (*b*) the drift of the question, here as in Mark x. 18, contains within itself the

warning against converting it into a positive proposition. For the positive proposition (of which opponents of the Gospels have availed themselves) would be, that Jesus Christ is not the Son of David.

# LECTURE VIII.

## NOTE 56. See p. 203.

' *The spirit* ' and ' *the letter.*' Language is constantly used which would imply that by ' the letter ' St. Paul means what is exact or ' literal,' and by ' the spirit ' what is indefinite or metaphorical. But this is not the case. St. Paul means by ' the letter ' what is *merely* external, whether the moral enactment (2 Cor. iii. 6) or the ritual ordinance (Rom. ii. 29). With ' the spirit ' he always associates the idea of vital and divine power. The contrast therefore of ' spirit ' to ' letter ' is that of communicated power to mere powerless information (2 Cor. iii. 6) or of true divine life to mere ritual conformity (Rom. ii. 29). In fact, whatever is filled with the life of God or manifests His action is spiritual, be it never so material (see 1 Cor. x. 3, 4). Nor is there any connection between the spiritual, as St. Paul uses the word, and the metaphorical.

## NOTE 57. See p. 213.

*Excommunication.* It is inseparable from the idea of a Church's healthy action that she should be exercising ' the power of the keys,' the power of including and excluding, by formal and free discipline, doctrinal and moral. That this power needs to be exercised with consideration and liberality is of course true : it is also true that due checks upon its exercise need to be provided, because like every other power it may be misused. But its liability to misuse is no excuse for a churchman acquiescing in its practical disuse.

## NOTE 58. See p. 217.

*The new birth.* This doctrine is expressed most explicitly in St. John's Gospel, iii. 3–13 (cf. i. 13), and in his first Epistle, iii. 9, v. 1, 4, 18. But it is expressed also by St. Paul, Tit. iii. 9, and interpreted by all his teaching as to the bestowal of the Spirit on Christians. It is found also in St. James (i. 18) and in St. Peter (1 Pet. i. 3, 23 ; cf. 2 Pet. i. 4).

## NOTE 59. See p. 218.

*The Spirit conveying to us the life of Christ.* Cf. the Rev. H. C. G. Moule, Principal of Ridley Hall, *Veni Creator* (Hodder & Stoughton, 1890), pp. 39 f. :—

'The Spirit, as our Communion creed confesses, is the Life-giver, the Maker-alive (τὸ ζωοποιόν). But what is the life which He gives, with which He works ? I listen, and I hear another voice, which is yet as if also His, and it says, " I am the Life." " The Life Eternal is in the Son." " He that hath the Son hath the Life." I read these words in the light of what we have recollected now of the Holy Spirit's work on and in the Holy Son of Man : and I thus see in them a remembrance that what the Spirit does in His free and all-powerful work in the soul which He quickens into second life is, above all things, to bring it into contact with the Son. He roots it, He grafts it, He embodies it into the Son. He deals so with it that there is a continuity wholly spiritual indeed but none the less most real, unfigurative, and efficacious, between the Head and the limb, between the branch and the Root. He effects an influx into the regenerate man of the blessed virtues of the nature of the Second Adam, an infusion of the exalted life of Jesus Christ, through an open duct, living, and divine, into the man who is born again into Him the incarnate and glorified Son of God.'

It is, I think, worth while to quote a brilliant statement of this doctrine of the 'inward Christ' from a rare and little-read work of William Law, *The Spirit of Prayer* (7th edit. London, 1773), pp. 43–4 :—

'One would wonder how any persons, that believe the great mystery of our redemption, who adore the depths of the divine goodness, in that the Son of God, the second Person in the Trinity, became a man Himself, in order to make it possible for man by a birth from Him to enter again into the kingdom of God, should yet seek to, and contend for, not a real, but a figurative sense of a new birth of Jesus Christ. Is there any thing more inconsistent than this? Or can any thing strike more directly at the heart of the whole nature of our redemption? God became man, took upon Him a birth from fallen nature. But why was this done? Or wherein lies the adorable depth of this mystery? How does all this manifest the infinity of the divine love towards man? It is because nothing less than this mysterious Incarnation (which astonishes angels) could open a way, or begin a possibility, for fallen man to be born again from above, and made again a partaker of the divine nature. It was because man was become so dead to the kingdom of heaven, that there was no help for him through all nature. Now when all nature stood round about Adam as unable to help him, as he was to help himself, and all of them unable to help him, for this reason, because that which he had lost was the life and light of heaven, how glorious, how adorable is that mystery which enables us to say, that when man lay thus incapable of any relief from all power and possibilities of nature, that then the Son, the Word of God, entered by a birth into this fallen nature, that by this mysterious Incarnation all the fallen nature might be born again of Him according to the Spirit, in the same reality as they were born of Adam according to the flesh! Look at this mystery in this true light, in this plain sense of scripture, and then you must be forced to fall down before it, in adoration of it. For all that is great and astonishing in the goodness of God, all that is glorious and happy with regard to man, is manifestly contained in it. But tell me, I pray, what becomes of this, what is there left in any part of the mystery, if this new birth, for the sake of which God became man, is not really a new birth in the thing itself, is not, as the Scripture affirms, a real birth of the Son and Spirit of God in the soul, but something or other, this or that, which the critics say, may be called a new birth by a certain figure of speech? Is not this to give up all our redemption at once, and a turning all the mysteries of our salvation into mere empty unmeaning terms of speech?

' "I am the vine, ye are the branches." Here Christ, our second Adam, uses this similitude to teach us, that the new birth that we are to have from Him is real, in the most strict and literal sense of the words, and that there is the same near- ness of relation betwixt Him and His true disciples that there is betwixt the vine and its branches, that He does all that in us and for us which the vine does to its branches. Now the life of the vine must be really derived into the branches, they cannot be branches till the birth of the vine is brought forth in them. And therefore as sure as the birth of the vine must be brought forth in the branches, so sure is it that we must be born again of our second Adam; and that unless the life of the Holy Jesus be in us by a birth from Him, we are as dead to Him and the Kingdom of God as the branch is dead to the vine, from which it is broken off.

'Again our Blessed Saviour says, Without Me ye can do nothing. This is the only sense in which we can be said to be without Christ; when He is no longer in us, as the principle of a heavenly life, we are then without Him, and so can do nothing, that is, nothing that is good or holy. A Christ not in us, is the same thing as a Christ not ours.

'It is the language of Scripture that "Christ in us" is our "hope of glory," that Christ formed in us, living, growing, and raising His own life and spirit in us, is our only salvation. And indeed all this is plain from the nature of the thing; for since the serpent, sin, death, and hell, are all essentially within us, the very growth of our nature, must not our redemption be equally inward, an inward essential death to this state of our souls, and an inward growth of a contrary life within us? If Adam was only an outward person, if his whole nature was not our nature, born in us, and derived from him into us, it would be nonsense to say that his fall is our fall.   So, in like manner, if Christ, our second Adam, was only an outward person, if He entered not as deeply into our nature as the first Adam does, if we have not as really from Him a new inward spiritual man, as we have outward flesh and blood from Adam, what ground could there be to say that our righteousness is from Him, as our sin is from Adam?

'Let no one here think to charge me with disregard to the Holy Jesus, who was born of the Virgin Mary, or with setting up an inward saviour in opposition to that outward Christ, whose history is recorded in the Gospel.  No: it is with the utmost fulness of faith and assurance, that I ascribe all our redemption to that blessed and mysterious Person that was then born of the Virgin Mary and will assert no inward redemption, but what wholly proceeds from and is effected by that life-giving Redeemer, who died on the cross for our redemption.

'Was I to say, that a plant or vegetable must have the life, light, and virtues of the sun incorporated in it, that it has no benefit from the sun, till the sun is thus inwardly forming, generating, quickening, and raising up a life of the sun's virtues in it, would this be setting up an inward sun in opposition to the outward one?  Could any thing be more ridiculous than such a charge?  For is not all that is here said of an inward sun in the vegetable, so much said of power and virtue derived from the sun in the firmament?  So, in like manner, all that is said of an inward Christ, inwardly formed, and generated in the root of the soul, is only so much said of an inward life, brought forth by the power and efficacy of that Blessed Christ that was born of the Virgin Mary.'

### NOTE 60.   See p. 223.

*The glorified Christ* ' *quickening spirit*,' cf. app. note 32, p. 259. The phrase is applied by St. Paul to the Christ in His entire person (1 Cor. xv. 45), when he is emphasizing the permanence of

His humanity, in body and spirit.   Adam became a living soul at
his creation: Christ became life-giving spirit at His resurrection.
It is natural to connect these words (πνεῦμα ζωοποιοῦν) with
those of our Lord, as recorded by St. John vi. 63 (πνεῦμα καὶ
ζωή), and to interpret our Lord's words thus: 'The things that
I have been speaking to you of (τὰ ῥήματα ἃ ἐγὼ λελάληκα ὑμῖν),
that is, My flesh and blood, the flesh and blood of My ascended
manhood (see ver. 62), are not to be mere flesh, are not to be
what you understand by flesh at all, but are to be spirit and
life.'   There is I think no doubt that ῥήματα λαλεῖν could mean
'to speak about things': cf. St. Luke ii. 15–17; there ῥῆμα means
in one case the word uttered, and in the other case the thing
effected; and for λαλεῖν cf. St. John iii. 11.   This interpretation
is in harmony with that of St. Cyril and of St. Augustine *in loc.*

## NOTE 61.   See p. 228.

*The connection of grace with sacraments.*   We cannot avoid
asking the question: In what relation to this grace do those
stand who are outside the action of the sacraments?   The answer
to this question, so far as we can give it, lies in the recognition
that, according to the old saying, 'God is not tied to His
sacraments.'   While, on the one hand, we have no right to
expect His grace if we neglect the appointed means for its
bestowal, on the other hand we have no right to limit His
power to bestow where He sees moral worthiness in this life
or beyond it.   It will strike many as surprising that the great
Jesuit writer De Lugo should recognise, as fully as he does,
Christ's relation *in grace* to all men; see *De Myst. Incarn.* disp.
xvii. § 4.   He is, he says, the head of all men, by a certain
'influxus': 'influit in infideles per vocationes ad fidem et ad
alia pia opera.'   Thus 'infideles' are in a certain sense members
of Christ, i.e. 'cum voluntarie cooperantur cogitationi datae
per Christum ad aliquam honestam operationem.'

ALBEMARLE STREET,
*October, 1ʸ91.*

# MR. MURRAY'S

## LIST OF

# *FORTHCOMING WORKS.*

## A Dictionary of Hymnology,

### SETTING FORTH THE

## ORIGIN AND HISTORY OF THE CHRISTIAN HYMNS OF ALL AGES AND NATIONS,

### WITH SPECIAL REFERENCE TO THOSE CONTAINED IN THE HYMN-BOOKS OF ENGLISH-SPEAKING COUNTRIES, AND NOW IN COMMON USE;

TOGETHER WITH BIOGRAPHICAL AND CRITICAL NOTICES OF THEIR AUTHORS AND TRANSLATORS, AND HISTORICAL ARTICLES ON NATIONAL AND DENOMINATIONAL HYMNODY, BREVIARIES, MISSALS, PRIMERS, PSALTERS, SEQUENCES, &c., &c.

**Edited by JOHN JULIAN, M.A.,**
Vicar of Wincobank, Sheffield.

1600 pp. *Medium 8vo.* [ *Just r.a.l)*

## My Canadian Journal.

1872—1878.

### EXTRACTS FROM MY HOME LETTERS WRITTEN WHILE LORD DUFFERIN WAS GOVERNOR-GENERAL.

**By the MARCHIONESS OF DUFFERIN AND AVA.**

*With Portraits, Map and Illustrations, from Sketches by* Lord DUFFERIN. *Crown 8vo*

## THE BAMPTON LECTURES FOR 1891.

# The Incarnation of the Son of God.

### By Rev. CHARLES GORE, M.A.,

Editor of "Lux Mundi."
Principal of Pusey House, and Fellow of Trinity College, Oxford.

*8vo.*                                              [*Ready.*

———— ♦♦ ————

# Critical Studies of the Works of Italian Painters.

### By GIOVANNI MORELLI (Ivan Lermollieff).

TRANSLATED FROM THE GERMAN.

VOL. I.—THE GALLERIES OF MUNICH AND DRESDEN.
VOL. 2.—THE BORGHESE AND DORIA PAMPHILI GALLERIES IN ROME.

*With Illustrations.  2 vols.  8vo.*

"Signor Morelli's revised work on the Italian pictures in the Galleries of Munich and Dresden is a Manual for the guidance of all interested in the Old Italian Masters ; it teems with information.  In it he lays down a system for the young student to pursue."—*Quarterly Review, July*, 1891.

—♦♦—

# Winter Journeys in Persia and Kurdistan;

## WITH A SUMMER IN THE UPPER KARUN REGION,

### AND A VISIT TO THE RAYAH NESTORIANS.

### By MRS. BISHOP (Miss ISABELLA BIRD).

*With Maps and 60 Illustrations.  2 vols.  Crown 8vo.*

"Mrs. Bishop, or Miss Bird, as she is better known, has already shown conclusively of what a woman is capable in the way of pluck and endurance.  The paper which she read on the Tuesday following, was quite the most interesting contribution that was made this year to the Geographical Section of the British Association.  But then, Mrs. Bishop brings very different qualifications from that of being a mere woman, to fit her for her self-imposed task, and dangerous, even foolhardy, as her last expedition may seem, it was undertaken with a definite and useful purpose, and has led to excellent results.  Mrs. Bishop is a very old and experienced traveller, to whom science owes a considerable debt of gratitude, and who has never been deterred from any undertaking by its discomforts or its dangers ; and yet we do not remember ever having heard that she laid claim to, or received, any special consideration on account of her sex,"—*Spectator.*

# Lux Mundi. *CHEAPER EDITION.*

## A SERIES OF STUDIES IN THE RELIGION OF THE INCARNATION.

BY VARIOUS WRITERS.

**Edited by Rev. CHARLES GORE, M.A.,**
Principal of Pusey House, and Fellow of Trinity College, Oxford.

*Fifteenth Thousand. Crown 8vo. 6s.* [*Ready.*

——◆◆——

# Jasmin:

## BARBER, POET, PHILANTHROPIST.

**By SAMUEL SMILES, LL.D.,**
Author of the "Lives of the Engineers," "Self-Help," &c.

*Post 8vo.*

"Il rasait bien, il chantait mieux. . . . Si la France possédait dix poètes comme Jasmin, dix poètes de cette influence, elle n'aurait pas à craindre de révolutions."—SAINTE-BEUVE.

◆◆——

# Japanese Letters.

## EASTERN IMPRESSIONS OF WESTERN MEN AND MANNERS,

AS CONTAINED IN THE CORRESPONDENCE OF

TOKIWARA AND YASHIRI.

**Edited by Commander HASTINGS BERKELEY, R.N.**

*Crown 8vo.*

◆◆

# Studies in the Art of Ratcatching.

## A MANUAL FOR SCHOOLS.

**By H. C. BARKLEY,**
Author of "My Boyhood," "Between the Danube and the Black Sea," &c.

*Post 8vo.*

# The Combat with Suffering.

### By Major E. GAMBIER PARRY.

*Fcap. 8vo.*

————◆◆————

# Jamaica Revisited.

TO WHICH ARE ADDED

## PERSONAL ADVENTURES IN THE EQUATORIAL FORESTS NORTH OF THE AMAZON,

### AND IN OTHER LITTLE KNOWN REGIONS OF SOUTH AMERICA, AS ALSO IN THE WILDS OF FLORIDA.

### By H. VILLIERS-STUART,

Author of " Egypt after the War," &c.

*With Illustrations.   Royal 8vo.*

————◆◆————

# Esther Vanhomrigh.

## A NEW NOVEL.

### By MARGARET L. WOODS,

Author of " A Village Tragedy," &c.

3 *Vols.   Crown 8vo.*

————◆◆————

# Handbook of Greek Archæology,

## SCULPTURE, VASES, BRONZES, GEMS, TERRA-COTTAS, ARCHITECTURE, MURAL PAINTINGS, &c.

### By A. S. MURRAY,

Keeper of Greek and Roman Antiquities, British Museum, and Author of a " History of Greek Sculpture."

*With Illustrations.   Crown 8vo.*

"Mr. Murray, the Keeper of Greek and Roman Antiquities, is bringing out a ' Handbook of Greek Archæology.' It will deal with vases, gems, bronzes, sculptures in marble, painting, and architecture. For the chapter on ' gems ' special autogravure reproductions have been made, which are expected to add greatly to the value of the work. The book is founded upon the Rhind Lectures on Greek Archæology delivered by Mr. Murray a year or so ago at Edinburgh. It will, of course, treat the subject in a more elaborate fashion ; yet, at the same time, it will not be so severely learned that an intelligent person will not be able to read it with pleasure and profit."—*Pall Mall Gazette, Sept. 9, 1891.*

# The Psalter of 1539.

## A LANDMARK OF ENGLISH LITERATURE.

COMPRISING THE TEXT, IN BLACK LETTER TYPE.

**Edited, with Notes, by JOHN EARLE, M.A.,**
Professor of Anglo-Saxon in the University of Oxford.

*Square 8vo.*

---

# New Chapters in Greek History.

## HISTORICAL RESULTS OF RECENT EXCAVATIONS IN GREECE AND ASIA MINOR.

**By PERCY GARDNER, M.A.,**
Professor of Archæology in the University of Oxford.

*With Illustrations. 8vo.*

---

# Begun in Jest.

## A NEW NOVEL.

**By Mrs. NEWMAN.**
Author of " Her Will and Her Way," " With Costs," " The Last of the Haddons," & .

*3 Vols. Crown 8vo.*

---

# Old English Plate.

## ECCLESIASTICAL, DECORATIVE, AND DOMESTIC.

**By WILFRED J. CRIPPS, C.B.**
*Fourth and Revised Edition. With Illustrations. Medium 8vo. 21s.* [*Ready.*]

---

# Life and Career of Alexander Somerville.

## IN SCOTLAND, IRELAND, INDIA, AMERICA, AUSTRALASIA, AND THE COUNTRIES OF EUROPE.
1813-1889.

**By GEORGE SMITH, C.I.E., LL.D.,**
Author of the " Life of William Carey," &c.

*Popular Edition. With Portrait. Post 8vo. 6s.*

# Travels Amongst the Great Andes of the Equator.

## By EDWARD WHYMPER.

WITH ILLUSTRATIONS BY

BARNARD, CORBOULD, DADD, LAPWORTH, OVEREND, SKELTON, WAGNER, WILSON, WOLF, AND OTHERS.

*With 4 Maps and 140 Illustrations. Medium 8vo. 21s. nett.*

Uniform with "SCRAMBLES AMONGST THE ALPS."

"Mr. Whymper in his forthcoming work, 'Travels amongst the Great Andes,' fully recounts his experiences on the Mountains of the Equator, and describes the first ascents of Chimborazo, Cayambe, Antisana, &c. Such achievements far surpass Mr. Whymper's previous triumphs and form part of the most prolonged mountaineering journey on record. What we are able to give here may well awaken a desire in our readers to study the complete work. It is in three parts (which will be published simultaneously and sold separately). The principal volume contains the narrative, and is beautifully illustrated with one hundred and forty original engravings and four maps."—*Good Words.*

---

# Supplementary Appendix

TO

# Travels Amongst the Great Andes of the Equator.

Illustrated with Figures of new Genera and Species, drawn by

COOMBS, HERBERT, PURKISS, WILSON, AND OTHERS.

WITH CONTRIBUTIONS BY

| | |
|---|---|
| H. W. BATES, F.R.S. | F. D. GODMAN, F.R.S. |
| T. G. BONNEY, D.Sc., F.R.S. | H. S. GORHAM, F.Z.S. |
| G. A. BOULENGER. | MARTIN JACOBY. |
| PETER CAMERON. | E. J. MIERS, F.L.S., F.Z.S. |
| THE LATE DR. F. DAY, C.I.E. | A. SIDNEY OLLIFF. |
| W. L. DISTANT, F.Z.S. | O. SALVIN, F.R.S. |
| A. E. EATON, M.A. | DAVID SHARP, M.B., F.R.S. |

T. R. R. STEBBING, M.A.

And a Preface by EDWARD WHYMPER.

*With 60 Illustrations. Medium 8vo. 15s. nett.*

---

# How to Use the Aneroid Barometer.

## By EDWARD WHYMPER.

I.—COMPARISONS IN THE FIELD.  II.—EXPERIMENTS IN THE WORKSHOP. III.—UPON THE USE OF THE ANEROID BAROMETER IN DETERMINATION OF ALTITUDES.  IV.—RECAPITULATION.

*With numerous Tables. Medium 8vo. 2s. 6d. nett.*

\*\*\* *The above three Works will be sold separately.*

## A POCKET DICTIONARY OF THE

# Modern Greek and English Languages.

### AS ACTUALLY WRITTEN AND SPOKEN.

BEING A COPIOUS VOCABULARY OF ALL WORDS AND EXPRESSIONS CURRENT IN
ORDINARY READING AND IN EVERYDAY TALK, WITH ESPECIAL ILLUSTRATION,
BY MEANS OF DISTINCTIVE SIGNS, OF THE COLLOQUIAL AND POPULAR GREEK
LANGUAGE, FOR THE GUIDANCE OF STUDENTS AND TRAVELLERS THROUGH
GREECE AND THE EAST.

### By A. N. JANNARIS, Ph.D. (Germany).

Assistant Professor of Greek Literature in the National University of Greece, and Author of the
latest Ancient and Modern Greek Lexicon (the only one approved by the Greek Government), and of
various other Dictionaries and other Literary Works.

*Square Fcap. 8vo.*

———— ·◆◆ ————

# A Handbook for Japan.

### By B. H. CHAMBERLAIN,

Professor of Japanese and Philology in the Imperial University; and

### W. B. MASON,

Late of the Imperial Japanese Department of Communications.

*Third Edition* (1891), *Revised and for the most part Rewritten.*

*With 15 Maps. Post 8vo. 15s. nett.*

———— ·◆◆· ————

# John William Burgon,

### LATE DEAN OF CHICHESTER.

## A BIOGRAPHY; WITH EXTRACTS FROM HIS LETTERS AND EARLY JOURNALS.

### By EDWARD MEYRICK GOULBURN, D.D.,

Sometime Dean of Norwich.

*With Portraits. 2 Vols. 8vo.*

"Considering the marvellous personality and the endless activities of Dean Burgon, it is
extremely gratifying to know that his biography from so competent a pen as that of Dr. E. M.
Goulburn, will be in our hands within a few weeks. The work is a real biography, and not a
mere compilation of 'remains' in the shape of letters and manuscripts, mainly because Dean
Burgon never wrote letters for publication and always published what he wrote for the
printer. Readers, however, will have no reason to complain of this, for the number of good
stories and the record of witty sayings, personal reminiscences, and odd recollections with
which the book is furnished surpass the expectation even of those who knew best the
characteristic peculiarities of the late Dean of Chichester."—*Manchester Guardian.*

# The Baronetage of Great Britain;

## *A HISTORY, A CRITICISM, AND A VINDICATION.*

INCLUDING ALL ASCERTAINED FACTS AS TO THE FOUNDATION OF
THE ORDER, WITH CURIOUS PARTICULARS AS TO THE VARIED
FORTUNES OF CERTAIN TITLES AND THEIR HOLDERS,
AND THOUGHTS ON THE DEGENERACY OF THE ORDER.

### By ROBERT DENNIS.

*Square 8vo. 12s.*                              [*Ready.*

———◆◆———

# Explosives and their Powers.

*TRANSLATED and CONDENSED from the FRENCH of M. BERTHELOT.*

### By Colonel J. P. CUNDILL, R.A., H.M. Inspector of Explosives;
AND
### C. NAPIER HAKE,
Fellow of the Institute of Chemistry, Inspector of Explosives to the Government of Victoria.

*With Illustrations. 8vo.*

\*\*\* The Translation of this well-known work of the celebrated French Chemist,
M. BERTHELOT, President of the COMMISSION DES SUBSTANCES EXPLOSIVES, is
published with his sanction.

———◆◆———

### DR. WM. SMITH'S

# Young Beginner's Latin Course.—Part III.

## *EASY EXERCISES ON THE LATIN SYNTAX.*

WITH THE

PRINCIPAL RULES OF SYNTAX, QUESTIONS, VOCABULARIES, AND
AN ENGLISH-LATIN DICTIONARY TO THE EXERCISES.

*16mo. 2s.*                              [*Ready.*

"This work is the third and last of a short series, intended for the use of young beginners
in Latin. It provides a short and easy course of systematic exercises on the principal Rules
of Latin Syntax, which may be commenced as soon as the pupil has mastered the Accidence.
It claims to be the easiest exercise book on the Syntax that can be placed in the hands of beginners, and contains all that is really needful to meet the requirements of elementary examinations in
the subject, while serving as a stepping-stone to other and more advanced manuals."—*Preface.*

# Ancient and Mediæval Architecture.

## By JAMES FERGUSSON, F.R.S.

NEW AND REVISED EDITION. Edited by R. PHENÉ SPIERS, F.S.A.

*With 1000 Illustrations. 2 Vols. Medium 8vo.*

" Mr. Fergusson's beautiful and most popular books have superseded all other HISTORIES OF ARCHITECTURE. It is not only that the extraordinary abundance of his illustrations gives him a special advantage over all his rivals or predecessors, but no other writer has ever had so firm a grasp of his subject, or has been so well qualified to deal with it in all its branches."—*Saturday Review.*

# Indian and Eastern Architecture.

## By JAMES FERGUSSON, F.R.S.

*New and Cheaper Edition. With 400 Illustrations. Medium 8vo. 31s. 6d.* [*Ready.*

" At last a comprehensive and precise knowledge of Indian architecture is placed within the reach of every English reader. The endless succession of its admirably classified illustrations of themselves form a perfect study of Indian art. Their profusion, accuracy, and beauty at once arrest and rivet interest, presenting such an instructive and gorgeous panorama of the solemn temples, the stately Saracenic architecture, and ancient caverned shrines of India as could only have been produced by the labour of a lifetime. . . . Mr. Fergusson's work will mark an era in the history of the arts in Asia, and is one of the noblest tributes ever offered to the splendid civilisation of ancient India."—*Times.*

# Modern Styles of Architecture.

## By JAMES FERGUSSON, F.R.S.

*A New Edition, Revised and Enlarged.*

WITH A SPECIAL ACCOUNT OF THE RECENT PROGRESS OF ARCHITECTURE

IN AMERICA.

## By ROBERT KERR,

Professor of Architecture at King's College, London.

*With 330 Illustrations. 2 Vols. Medium 8vo. 31s. 6d.* [*Ready.*

" The volume now before us completes the history of the ' Architecture of all Countries,' which this untiring student set himself to accomplish, and it adds another proof of the learned author's indefatigability and the comprehensiveness of his research. "—*Building News.*

— -♦♦- —

# Primitive Culture.

RESEARCHES INTO THE DEVELOPMENT OF MYTHOLOGY, PHILOSOPHY, RELIGION, LANGUAGE, ART AND SCIENCE.

## By EDWARD B. TYLOR, LL.D., F.R.S.,

Keeper of the Museum, Oxford, and Author of " Researches into the Early History of Mankind."

*Third and Revised Edition. 2 Vols. 8vo.* [*Ready*

# The Student's History of the Roman Empire.

FROM THE ESTABLISHMENT OF THE EMPIRE TO THE ACCESSION OF COMMODUS, AD. 180.

*Post 8vo.*

\*\*\* This work will take up the History at the point at which Dean Liddell leaves off, and carry it down to the period at which Gibbon begins.

# Egypt under the Pharaohs.

## A HISTORY DERIVED ENTIRELY FROM THE MONUMENTS.

**By HENRY BRUGSCH BEY.**

*A New Edition, Condensed and thoroughly Revised.*

**By M. BRODRICK.**

*With Maps, Plans and Illustrations. 8vo.*

# A Plea for Liberty.

## AN ARGUMENT AGAINST SOCIALISM AND SOCIALISTIC LEGISLATION.

*ESSAYS BY VARIOUS WRITERS.*

WITH AN INTRODUCTION BY **HERBERT SPENCER.**

**Edited by THOMAS MACKAY,**

Author of "The English Poor."

*Second Edition. 8vo. 12s.*

# The Metallurgy of Iron and Steel.

**By the late JOHN PERCY, M.D., F.R.S.**

A NEW AND REVISED EDITION, WITH THE AUTHOR'S LATEST CORRECTIONS, AND BROUGHT DOWN TO THE PRESENT TIME.

**By H. BAUERMAN, F.G.S.,**

Associate of the Royal School of Mines and of the Institution of Civil Engineers.

*With Illustrations. 8vo.*

# University Extension Manuals.

THE Series of University Extension Manuals, published under the Editorship of Professor KNIGHT, of the University of St. Andrews, is primarily designed to aid the University Extension movement throughout the country, and to supply the need so widely felt by Students, of Text-books for study and reference, in connection with the authorised Courses of Lectures.

These Manuals will differ from those already in existence in that they are not intended for School use, or for Examination purposes; and that their aim is to educate, rather than to inform. The enumeration of mere details will be avoided, except in so far as they illustrate the working of general laws, and the development of principles; while the historical evolution, both of the literary and scientific subjects, will be kept in view, as well as their philosophical significance. The class for whose use the Manuals are especially designed are those whose education has been hitherto somewhat miscellaneous or fragmentary, and who are desirous of pursuing systematic study in Literature, History, Science, and Art.

The remarkable success which has attended University Extension in England and Scotland has been partly due to the combination of scientific treatment with popularity, and the union of simplicity with thoroughness. The University Extension movement, however, can only reach those resident in the larger centres of population, while all over the country there are thoughtful persons who desire the same kind of teaching; and it is for them, as well as for the Extension Lecture Students, that this Series is designed. Its aim will be to supply to the public and to the general reader, the same kind of teaching as is given in the Lectures, to reflect the spirit which has characterised the movement, and to combine as the Lectures have done, the discussion of principles as well as of facts, and of methods along with results.

The Manuals will be issued simultaneously in England and America. Volumes dealing with separate sections of Literature, Science, Philosophy, History, and Art have already been assigned to representative literary men, to University Professors, or to Extension Lectures connected with Oxford, Cambridge, London, and the Universities of Scotland and Ireland.

[*Continues*

# University Extension Manuals.

*VOLUMES ALREADY PUBLISHED.*

## The Fine Arts.
By Prof. BALDWIN BROWN, University of Edinburgh.   With Illustrations.   3s. 6d.

## English Colonization and Empire.
By A. CALDECOTT, Fellow of St. John's College, Cambridge.   Maps and Plans.   3s. 6d.

## The Use and Abuse of Money.
By Dr. W. CUNNINGHAM, Fellow of Trin. Coll., Cambridge, Professor of Economic Science, King's Coll. London.   3s.

## The Philosophy of the Beautiful.
By Professor KNIGHT, University of St. Andrews.   3s. 6d.

*IN THE PRESS AND NEARLY READY.*

## French Literature.
By H. G. KEENE, Wadham College, Oxford ; Fellow of the University of Calcutta.

## The Realm of Nature : A Manual of Physiography.
By HUGH ROBERT MILL, University of Edinburgh.   With Maps and Illustrations.   *Nearly ready.*

## The Elements of Ethics.
By JOHN H. MUIRHEAD, Balliol College, Oxford, Lecturer on Moral Science, Royal Holloway College.

## The Study of Animal Life.
By J. ARTHUR THOMSON, University of Edinburgh.

*TO BE FOLLOWED BY*

## The Daily Life of the Greeks and Romans.
By Professor W. ANDERSON, Oriel College, Oxford, and Firth College, Sheffield.

## The History of Astronomy.
By ARTHUR BERRY, Fellow of King's College, Cambridge (Senior Wrangler).

## Shakespeare, and his Predecessors in the English Drama.
By F. S. BOAS, Balliol College, Oxford.

## The English Poets, from Blake to Tennyson.
By Rev. STOPFORD A. BROOKE, Trinity College, Dublin.

[*Continued.*

# University Extension Manuals.

## Energy in Nature: An Introduction to Physical Science.
By JOHN COX, late Warden of Cavendish College, Fellow of Trinity College, Cambridge.

## Outlines of Modern Botany.
By Professor PATRICK GEDDES, University College, Dundee.

## The Jacobean Poets.
By EDMUND GOSSE, Trinity College, Cambridge.

## British Dominion in India.
By Sir ALFRED LYALL, K.C.B., K.C.S.I.

## The French Revolution.
By C. E. MALLET, Balliol College, Oxford.

## The Physiology of the Senses.
By Professor McKENDRICK, the University of Glasgow, and Dr. SNODGRASS, Physiological Laboratory, Glasgow.

## Comparative Religion.
By Professor MENZIES, University of St. Andrews.

## Logic, Inductive and Deductive.
By Professor MINTO, University of Aberdeen.

## The English Novel, from its Origin to Sir W. Scott.
By Professor RALEIGH, University College, Liverpool.

## Outlines of English Literature.
By WILLIAM RENTON, University of St. Andrews.

## Studies in Modern Geology.
By Dr. R. D. ROBERTS, Fellow of Clare College, Cambridge, Secretary to the Cambridge and London University Extension Syndicates.

## Problems of Political Economy.
By M. E. SADLER, Senior Student of Christ Church, Oxford, Secretary to the Oxford University Extension Delegacy.

## Psychology: A Historical Sketch.
By Prof. SETH, University of St. Andrews.

## Mechanics.
By Professor JAMES STUART, M.P., Trinity College, Cambridge.

## NEW HANDBOOKS AND NEW EDITIONS.

*REVISED OR RE-WRITTEN*, 1891, 1892.

"From a literary point of view, no handbooks in the market can compare with Murray's. Others may be cheaper, or more practical, but the great publisher of Albemarle Street is easily the first in all that makes the genuine book. His Guides are literature, and the literary pilgrim will find none like them."—*British Weekly.*

## India. *IN ONE VOLUME. Maps and Plans.*
A PRACTICAL GUIDE FOR TRAVELLERS THROUGH THE PRINCIPAL ROUTES IN BENGAL, BOMBAY, MADRAS, PUNJAB, &c., AND TO THE SUMMER RESORTS SIMLA, DARJEELING, MAHABALESHWAR, MATHERAN, MT. ABOO, CEYLON, &c.

## Turkey in Asia. *Revised Edition. Maps and Plans.*
CONSTANTINOPLE, THE BOSPHORUS, DARDANELLES, BROUSA, PLAIN OF TROY, CRETE, CYPRUS, SMYRNA, EPHESUS, THE SEVEN CHURCHES, COASTS OF THE BLACK SEA, ARMENIA, MESOPOTAMIA, &c.

## Holy Land. *Maps.*
SYRIA, PALESTINE, SINAI, EDOM, THE SYRIAN DESERTS, JERUSALEM, PETRA, DAMASCUS, AND PALMYRA.

## Egypt. *Maps and Plans.*
INCLUDING DESCRIPTIONS OF THE COURSE OF THE NILE THROUGH EGYPT, NUBIA, ALEXANDRIA, CAIRO, THE PYRAMIDS, THEBES, THE SUEZ CANAL, PENINSULA OF SINAI, THE OASES, THE FAYÚM, &c.

## France—Part I. *Maps and Plans.*
NORMANDY, BRITTANY, THE SEINE AND LOIRE, TOURAINE, BORDEAUX, THE GARONNE, LIMOUSIN, THE PYRENEES, &c.

## France—Part II. *Maps and Plans.*
CENTRAL FRANCE, AUVERGNE, THE CEVENNES, BURGUNDY, THE RHONE AND SAONE, PROVENCE, NIMES, ARLES, MARSEILLES, THE FRENCH ALPS, ALSACE, LORRAINE, CHAMPAGNE, &c.

## Switzerland and the Alps. *Revised Edition. Maps and Plans.* 10s.

## North Italy. *Maps and Plans.* 10s.
TURIN, MILAN, PAVIA, CREMONA, THE ITALIAN LAKES, BERGAMO, BRESCIA, VERONA, MANTUA, VICENZA, PADUA, VENICE, FERRARA, BOLOGNA, RAVENNA, RIMINI, PARMA, MODENA, PIACENZA, GENOA, AND THE RIVIERA AND ITS OFF-LYING ISLANDS.

## Eastern Counties. *Revised Edition. Maps and Plans.*
CHELMSFORD, HARWICH, COLCHESTER, MALDON, CAMBRIDGE, ELY, NEW MARKET, BURY ST. EDMUNDS, IPSWICH, WOODBRIDGE, FELIXSTOWE, LOWESTOFT, NORWICH, YARMOUTH, CROMER, &c.

## Derby, Notts, Leicester, and Stafford. *Map.*
MATLOCK, BAKEWELL, CHATSWORTH, THE PEAK, BUXTON, HARDWICK, DOVEDALE, ASHBORNE, SOUTHWELL, MANSFIELD, RETFORD, BURTON, BELVOIR, MELTON MOWBRAY, WOLVERHAMPTON, LICHFIELD, WALSALL, TAMWORTH.

## Herts, Bedford, and Hunts. *Maps.*

## Warwickshire. *Maps.*

## The English Cathedrals. *With Illustrations. One Volume.*

# MR. MURRAY'S

## LIST OF

# 𝔑𝔢𝔴 𝔞𝔫𝔡 𝔑𝔢𝔠𝔢𝔫𝔱 𝔓𝔲𝔟𝔩𝔦𝔠𝔞𝔱𝔦𝔬𝔫𝔰.

### MEMOIR OF

## *Madame Jenny Lind - Goldschmidt,*

### HER EARLY ART-LIFE AND DRAMATIC CAREER. 1820 TO 1851.

FROM ORIGINAL DOCUMENTS, LETTERS, MSS., DIARIES, &c.

**In the possession of, or collected by Mr. GOLDSCHMIDT.**

**By HENRY SCOTT HOLLAND, M.A.**
Canon and Precentor of St. Paul's, and

**W. S. ROCKSTRO,**
Author of "A General History of Music," "Life of Handel," "Mendelssohn," &c.

*Third Edition, Revised. Portraits, Appendix of Music, &c.* 2 *Vols.* 8*vo.* 32*s.*

### MEMOIRS AND LETTERS OF

## *Sidney Gilchrist Thomas,*

### INVENTOR.

**Edited by R. W. BURNIE, Barrister-at-Law.**

*With Portrait. Crown 8vo. 6s.*

" I have read through the biography of your deceased son with a profound interest. Who could fail to be moved by such a noble character, such a splendid life, of which the mere distinctions, conspicuous as they were, seem to dwindle by the side of the extraordinary moral elevation. How the interest concentrated in this short biography exceeds that commonly due to the longest and most elaborate work."—*Mr. Gladstone to Mrs. Gilchrist Thomas.*

DICTIONARY OF

# Greek and Roman Antiquities.

## INCLUDING THE LAWS, INSTITUTIONS, DOMESTIC USAGES, PAINTING, SCULPTURE, MUSIC, THE DRAMA, &c.

EDITED BY

### WILLIAM SMITH, LL.D.,

Hon. D.C.L. Oxford ; Hon. Ph.D. Leipzig ;

**WILLIAM WAYTE, M.A.,**
Late Fellow of King's College, Cambridge ;

**G. E. MARINDIN, M.A.,**
Late Fellow of King's College, Cambridge.

THIRD REVISED AND ENLARGED EDITION (2140 pp.).

*With 900 Illustrations. 2 Vols. Medium 8vo. 31s. 6d. each.*

" This year has seen also the completion of a work which may fitly receive mention here, both on account of the labours which have conspired to produce it, and on account of the wide interest which it possesses for various classes of students—I mean the third edition of Dr. William Smith's Dictionary of Greek and Roman Antiquities, edited in the first volume by Mr. Wayte, and in the second by Mr. Marindin. Forty-three years have elapsed since the last preceding edition—the second—appeared in 1848. No one who remembers how fruitful this long interval has been in fresh materials of every kind can wonder that the new issue is almost a new book. Scarcely twenty articles remain as they stood ; two-thirds have been largely altered, and one-third has been entirely rewritten."—*Professor Jebb's Address at the Annual Meeting of the* HELLENIC SOCIETY, *June 24, 1891.*

" Dr. Smith's Dictionary of Antiquities has been so greatly enlarged and improved, that it may be described as substantially a new book. Eight hundred pages have been added, or, to put the amount in round numbers, about two-fifths of the original bulk. And the quality of the work has been raised in a more than proportionate degree. Though during the forty-two years that passed between the publication of the second edition and of that of which we are now speaking, few additions were made to our store of classical literature, yet that literature has been more scientifically studied. It has been, in particular, illustrated from other provinces of human history, of which little was known to the last generation. And then a vast amount of absolutely new knowledge has been gained. The bulk of inscriptions known to the scholars of to-day is vastly greater than that with which the scholars of forty years ago had to be content. But of the general completeness and excellence of the work, and of the service which is rendered by its publication to classical study in this country, there can be no doubt. Dr. William Smith is to be congratulated on having lived to preside over the publication of this new edition, and on having secured the services of coadjutors so able as Mr. Wayte and Dr. Marindin (responsible respectively, under the editor-in-chief, for the first and second volumes."—*Spectator.*

\* \* \* \* \* \* \* \* \* \* \* \* \* \* \*

# Stray Verses.

1889—1890.

## By ROBERT, LORD HOUGHTON.

*Crown 8vo. 6s.*

" The volume of verses which he has just given to the world is full of promise. . . . Not only graceful and musical throughout ; it is animated by true poetic feeling, &c."—*Speaker.*

# The Queen's Commission :

## HOW TO PREPARE FOR IT, HOW TO OBTAIN IT, AND HOW TO USE IT;

### WITH PRACTICAL INFORMATION ON THE COST AND PROSPECTS OF A MILITARY CAREER.

INTENDED FOR THE USE OF CADETS AND SUBALTERNS AND THEIR PARENTS.

**By Capt. G. J. YOUNGHUSBAND,**

Of the Queen's Own Corps of Guides ; Author of " Frays and Forays."

*Crown 8vo.* 6s.

" It is difficult to imagine a better guide than this to parents who contemplate making soldiers of their sons ; *a fortiori* to their sons themselves."—*Times.*

"Such a book was much wanted, and that before us has evidently been carefully prepared by a very competent hand."—*The Queen.*

\* \* \* \* \* \* \* \* \* \* \* \* \* \* \* \* \*

# Two Visits to the West Coast of Ireland.

**By Miss BALFOUR.**

8vo. 1s.

\*.\* *See MURRAY'S MAGAZINE for AUGUST.*

\* \* \* \* \* \* \* \* \* \* \* \* \* \* \*

# A Publisher and His Friends :

## MEMOIR AND CORRESPONDENCE OF THE LATE JOHN MURRAY,

WITH AN ACCOUNT OF THE ORIGIN AND PROGRESS OF THE HOUSE, 1768-1843.

**By SAMUEL SMILES, LL.D.,**

*Third Edition, Revised. With Portraits.* 2 Vols. *Demy 8vo.* 32s.

" They may be placed side by side with the ' Life of Scott,' as books that will bear perpetual dipping into, and we could hardly bestow any higher praise."—*The Times.*

" The book should be read, leisurely and comfortably, by all who care for the literary history of England."—*Record.*

" It is difficult within the space at our command to do justice to a book so rich in the literary history of the time."—*Athenæum.*

" Entertaining these volumes certainly are ! Not Boswell, nor Southey, nor Lockhart, nor Moore, nor Sir George Trevelyan, nor Mr. Froude were more blessed in their subject. One might almost say that in the two volumes be the materials for a History of English literature for fifty years."—*Saturday Review.*

" The fulness of interesting detail contained in these volumes render it impossible to do justice to them within the ordinary limits of a review. Readers who care for the literary history of the century will not be satisfied with borrowing these memoirs of a distinguished man from the circulating library, but will be glad to have a copy on their shelves."—*Spectator.*

THE

# Early Political Life of Sir Robert Peel.

## AS SECRETARY FOR IRELAND, 1812–18,

## AND SECRETARY OF STATE, 1822–27.

PUBLISHED BY HIS TRUSTEES.

Viscount HARDINGE and Right Hon. ARTHUR WELLESLEY PEEL.

### Edited by CHARLES STUART PARKER, M.P.

*With Portrait.  8vo.  16s.*

" We are by no means sure that the delay in the publication of these interesting and important papers, albeit unintended and unexpected by Sir Robert Peel himself, has been any disadvantage to his memory and reputation.  The moment of publication is undoubtedly, if undesignedly, opportune. . . .  Mr. Parker, without ever obtruding himself, has greatly enhanced its interest, and illustrated its historical importance, by means of a running commentary, which for modesty, conciseness, accuracy and appositeness, is all that could be desired."
—*Times.*

♦♦♦♦♦♦♦♦♦♦♦♦♦♦♦♦♦♦♦♦♦

# Marcia.

### A New Novel by W. E. NORRIS,

Author of " Thirlby Hall," &c., &c.

*Popular Edition.  Crown 8vo.  6s.*

" Mr. Norris has the light touch of Thackeray, who guides us through three or four generations as gracefully as a well-bred man might point out the portraits of his ancestors in the family picture gallery."—*Quarterly Review.*

" The author of ' Marcia ' holds a high place among the novelists of the day.  He writes admirable English, has a keen grasp of the character, and very often there are touches in his writings of which Thackeray would not have been ashamed."—*John Bull.*

♦♦♦♦♦♦♦♦♦♦♦♦♦♦♦♦♦♦

# Impressions of a Tenderfoot,

## DURING A JOURNEY IN SEARCH OF SPORT IN THE FAR WEST.

### By LADY SEYMOUR (Mrs. ALGERNON ST. MAUR.)

*With Map and Illustrations.  Crown 8vo.  12s.*

" Mrs. St. Maur has given her readers a brightly written and fascinating account of travels in the far West.  With abundance of matter to chronicle, Mrs. St. Maur lapses but seldom into inference drawing, and the result is a book which will be read always without effort and often with keen attention."—*Morning Post.*

# London : Past and Present;

## ITS HISTORY, ASSOCIATIONS, AND TRADITIONS.

### By HENRY B. WHEATLEY, F.S.A.

*BASED ON CUNNINGHAM'S HANDBOOK.*

*Library Edition, Printed on Laid Paper.* 3 *Vols. Medium 8vo.* £3 3*s.*

"We can conceive no more welcome companion to an enlightened foreigner than this work with its laborious research, scrupulous exactness, alphabetical arrangement, and authorities from every imaginable source. As a piece of severe compact and finished structure, it is not to be surpassed."—*The Times.*

"Every spot in this thickly-peopled district has its description and anecdote ; and every page conveys some information that is curious, interesting or valuable,—communicated necessarily in the most succinct, but, at the same time, in the most authentic manner. There is nothing merely speculative and fanciful,—all is fact and substance. It will remain a lasting record of the past and present condition of our huge metropolis."—*Athenæum.*

"Mr. Wheatley's 'London Past and Present' is a kind of dictionary or cyclopædia of the streets, houses, places, squares, and public buildings of the Metropolis. Ostensibly based upon Cunningham's famous Handbook, it is in many respects an absolutely original work, and it is almost an excess of modesty which leads Mr. Wheatley to divide the credit of its production with his predecessor."—*Standard.*

●●●●●●●●●●●●●●●●●●●●●

# Lives of Twelve Good Men.

| | |
|---|---|
| MARTIN JOSEPH ROUTH. | RICHARD GRESWELL. |
| HUGH JAMES ROSE. | HENRY OCTAVIUS COXE. |
| CHARLES MARRIOTT. | HENRY LONGUEVILLE MANSEL. |
| EDWARD HAWKINS. | WILLIAM JACOBSON. |
| SAMUEL WILBERFORCE. | CHARLES PAGE EDEN. |
| RICHARD LYNCH COTTON. | CHARLES LONGUET HIGGINS. |

### By JOHN W. BURGON, B.D., Late Dean of Chichester.

*A New Edition* WITH PORTRAITS OF THE AUTHOR AND OF THE TWELVE.

*Sixth Thousand.* 8vo. 16*s.*

●●●●●●●●●●●●●●●●●

## ADVENTURES IN THE LIFE OF

# Count George Albert of Erbach.

## INCLUDING HIS SOJOURN WITH THE KNIGHTS OF MALTA,

## CAPTURE BY THE BARBARY CORSAIRS AND IMPRISONMENT IN TUNIS

## TRANSLATED FROM THE GERMAN.

### By H.R.H. PRINCESS BEATRICE.

*Second Edition. Portraits and Woodcut. Crown 8vo.* 10*s.* 6*d.*

## WORKS BY REV. DR. SALMON,

Provost of Trinity College, Dublin.

| | |
|---|---|
| ### Historical Introduction to the New Testament.<br><br>*Fifth Edition.* Crown 8vo. 9s. | ### The Infallibility of the Church.<br><br>*Second Edition.* Crown 8vo. 9s. |

********************

## Studies in European History.

### By Professor VON DÖLLINGER, D.D.,

Translated by MARGARET WARRE.

*With Portrait.* 8vo. 14s.

********************

## A History of Greek Sculpture.

### By A. S. MURRAY, LL.D., F.S.A.,

Keeper of Greek and Roman Antiquities in the British Museum.

*Revised Edition.* With 140 *Illustrations.* 2 Vols. *Medium* 8vo. 36s.

" In grasp and mastery of the subject, and clearness and attractiveness of style, the book seems to us an excellent example of what such a book should be. We beg once more to thank Mr. Murray for his interesting book—with the gratitude which consists partly in an expectation of future favours."—*Guardian.*

********************

## A Ride through Asia Minor & Armenia.

GIVING A SKETCH OF THE CHARACTERS, MANNERS AND CUSTOMS OF BOTH THE MUSSULMAN AND CHRISTIAN INHABITANTS.

### By H. C. BARKLEY,

Author of " Between the Danube and the Black Sea," and " Bulgaria before the War."

*Crown* 8vo. 10s. 6d.

" The book can be recommended as a very genuine and interesting record of intelligent personal observation in a fruitful and little-worked field."—*Athenæum.*

# An English Latin Gradus or Verse Dictionary for Schools.

INTENDED TO SIMPLIFY THE COMPOSITION OF LATIN VERSES BY
CLASSIFIED MEANINGS, SELECTED EPITHETS TO SYNONYMS, &c.

**By A. C. AINGER, M.A., and H. G. WINTLE, M.A.**

Assistant Masters at Eton College.

(450 *pp.*) *Crown 8vo.* 9*s.*

✦✦✦✦✦✦✦✦✦✦✦

# Life of a Southern Planter.

AT THE TIME OF THE AMERICAN CIVIL WAR.

**By SUSAN DABNEY SMEDES.**

*Crown 8vo.* 7*s.* 6*d.*

✦✦✦✦✦✦✦✦✦✦✦

# The Foundations of the Creed.

BEING A DISCUSSION OF THE GROUNDS UPON WHICH THE
ARTICLES OF THE APOSTLES' CREED MAY BE HELD BY
EARNEST AND THOUGHTFUL MINDS IN THE
NINETEENTH CENTURY.

**By HARVEY GOODWIN, D.D.,**

Lord Bishop of Carlisle.

*Second Edition. 8vo.* 14*s.*

" By following the lines it marks out, our younger Theologians may construct a very
popular and powerful Christian Defence."—*Church Quarterly Review.*

" A book of extreme interest, and likely to be widely read, upon a subject about which few
men are more qualified to speak."  *Record.*

" A work that deserves an honoured place in every student's library.  The massive mind
of Dr. Goodwin is well qualified to deal with the scientific defence of the truths of the
Christian religion, and his clear logical intellect never showed itself to better advantage than
in this grand and satisfactory essay.  Wisdom and love are beautifully united in the Bishop's
argument."—*Irish Ecclesiastical Gazette.*

# Our Viceregal Life in India

## DURING THE YEARS 1884—8.

### By THE MARCHIONESS OF DUFFERIN AND AVA.

*Fifth and Popular Edition.  With Map.  Crown 8vo.  7s. 6d.*

# Three Counsels of the Divine Master.

## FOR THE CONDUCT OF THE SPIRITUAL LIFE.

### By E. MEYRICK GOULBURN, D.D.
#### Late Dean of Norwich.

*Popular Edition.  Crown 8vo.  9s.*

## WORKS BY MISS CAILLARD.

### Electricity :

#### THE SCIENCE OF THE NINTH CENTURY.

*A Sketch for General Readers.*

*With Illustrations.  Crown 8vo.  7s. 6d.*

" There can be no two opinions of the merit of this work.  The subject of it has now become one of extraordinary and almost universal interest, and a manual that could put the general reader in possession of the main outlines of it must be pronounced a valuable acquisition.  This is what Miss Caillard has attempted and has effected. Difficult as the science of electricity must be to the comprehension of the uninitiated, it is capable of a popular form of exposition, and those who desire an intelligent and intelligible guide to the subject can do no better than study this compact and clearly-written book."—*The Bookseller.*

### The Invisible Powers of Nature.

SOME ELEMENTARY LESSONS IN PHYSICAL SCIENCE, HEAT, LIGHT, SOUND, GRAVITATION, SOLIDS, FLUIDS, MAGNETISM, &c.

*Crown 8vo.  6s.*

" The present work is worthy of all praise. It is evident that very great pains have been taken with it, and the descriptions are very accurate, and show considerable ingenuity and industry."—*Church Bells.*

" The young student of nature will find this a most interesting and instructive book." —*Journal of Microscopy.*

# Fortification:

## ITS PAST ACHIEVEMENTS, RECENT DEVELOPMENT, AND FUTURE PROGRESS.

### By Major G. SYDENHAM CLARKE, C.M.G.,
Royal Engineers.

*With 50 Illustrations. Medium 8vo.* 21s.

............

# A Naturalist's Voyage Round the World.

### By CHARLES DARWIN, F.R.S.

WITH 100 ILLUSTRATIONS OF THE PLACES VISITED AND DESCRIBED.

*From Sketches by* R. T. PRITCHETT. *Medium 8vo.* 21s.

\*\* *The object of this edition is to aid the author's description by actual representations of the most interesting places and objects of Natural History referred to in them. This has been effected by securing the service of an artist who has visited the countries which Darwin describes.*

............

## BAMPTON LECTURES.

| The Witness of the Psalms to Christ and Christianity. | Modern Criticism and the Fourth Gospel. |
|---|---|
| By W. ALEXANDER, D.D., Lord Bishop of Derry. | By H. W. WATKINS, D.D., Archdeacon and Canon of Durham. |
| *Third Edition. Crown 8vo.* 9s. | *8vo.* 15s. |

## WORKS BY M. PAUL DU CHAILLU.

# The Viking Age.

THE EARLY HISTORY, MANNERS, AND CUSTOMS OF THE
ANCESTORS OF THE ENGLISH-SPEAKING NATIONS.

ILLUSTRATED FROM
ANTIQUITIES DISCOVERED AND ANCIENT SAGAS AND EDDAS.

*With 13'0 Illustrations.* 2 *Vols.* 8vo. 42s.

## The Great Forest of Equatorial Africa,

AND THE COUNTRY OF THE
DWARFS.

*Popular Edition. With 90 Illustrations.*

*Post 8vo.* 7s. 6d.

## Land of the Midnight Sun.

JOURNEYS THROUGH SWEDEN, NORWAY, LAPLAND, AND FINLAND.

WITH DESCRIPTIONS OF THE MANNERS,
CUSTOMS, ETC., OF THE PEOPLE.

*Illustrations.* 2 *Vols.* 8vo. 36s.

## Travels in Australia.

AND CAMP LIFE WITH THE
ABORIGINES OF QUEENSLAND.

**By CARL LUMHOLTZ, M.A.,**
Member of the Royal Society of Science of Norway.

*Illustrations. Medium 8vo.* 24s.

## The Land of Manfred.

RAMBLES IN REMOTE PARTS
OF SOUTHERN ITALY.

**By JANET ROSS,**
Author of "Three Generations of Englishwomen."

*Illustrations. Crown 8vo.* 10s. 6d.

# The Student's Commentary on the Holy Bible.

ABRIDGED FROM THE SPEAKER'S COMMENTARY.

**By Rev. JOHN M. FULLER, M.A.,**
Professor of Ecclesiastical History, King's College, London.

6 *Vols. Crown 8vo.* 7s. 6d. each.

I. GENESIS TO DEUTERONOMY.
II. JOSHUA TO ESTHER.
III. JOB TO ECCLESIASTES.

IV. ISAIAH TO MALACHI.
V. GOSPELS AND ACTS.
VI. EPISTLES AND REVELATION.

"There can be no question that the Speaker's Commentary has marked an era in Biblical literature, as the most successful of all scientific expositions of the Bible yet given to the public, and in this abridgment we are glad to see the essential portion of the great original faithfully preserved."—*English Churchman.*

## NEW NOVELS.

### By HON. EMILY LAWLESS.

AUTHOR OF "HURRISH," ETC.

| | |
|---|---|
| **Plain Frances Mowbray** | **Major Lawrence, F.L.S.** |
| AND OTHER TALES. | A NOVEL. |
| *Post 8vo.* 6s. | *Post 8vo.* 6s. |

••••••••••••••••••

| | |
|---|---|
| **Miss Blake of Monkshalton.** | **Comedy of a Country House.** |
| By **ISABELLA O. FORD.** | By **JULIAN STURGIS,** |
| | Author of "John a Dreams," "John Maidment," &c. |
| *Post 8vo.* 5s. | *Crown 8vo.* 6s. |

••••••••••••••••••

## *Virgil in English Verse.*

### ECLOGUES, AND ÆNEID, BOOKS I.—VI.

### By the Rt. Hon. SIR CHARLES BOWEN,

Lord Justice of Appeal, F.R.S., Hon. D.C.L. of the University of Oxford, Fellow and now Visitor of Balliol College.

*2nd Edition. Frontispiece. 8vo.* 12s.

••••••••••••••••••

### ROBINSON'S GARDEN CYCLOPÆDIA.

| | |
|---|---|
| 1.—*English Flower Garden:* | 2.—*The Vegetable Garden:* |
| STYLE, POSITION, AND ARRANGE-MENT, WITH A DESCRIPTION OF ALL THE BEST PLANTS, AND DIREC-TIONS FOR THEIR CULTURE. | DESCRIPTIONS AND CULTURE OF THE GARDEN VEGETABLES CULTIVATED IN EUROPE AND AMERICA. |
| *With Illustrations. 8vo.* 15s. | *With Illustrations. 8vo.* 15s. |

## The Country Banker:

*HIS CLIENTS, CARES, & WORKS.*

From Forty Years' Experience.

**By GEORGE RAE,**

Author of "Bullion's Letters to a Bank Manager."

*Eighth Edition.   Crown 8vo.   7s. 6d.*

## A Handbook to the Death Duties.

**By SYDNEY BUXTON, M.P.,**

AND

**GEORGE STAPYLTON BARNES,**

Barrister-at-Law.

*Post 8vo.   3s. 6d.*

●●●●●●●●●●●●●●●●●●●●

## BY THE DUKE OF ARGYLL, K.G.

### The Reign of Law.

*Nineteenth Edition.   Crown 8vo.   5s.*

### The Unity of Nature.

*Third Edition.   8vo.   12s.*

●●●●●●●●●●●●●●●●●●

"The old Lord Treasurer Burleigh, if any one came to the Lords of the Council for a license to travel, he would first examine him of England; and if he found him ignorant, would bid him stay at home and know his own country first."—*The Compleat Gentleman, by Henry Peacham,* 1622.

## ENGLAND AND WALES.

# Murray's Handbook for Travellers in England and Wales.

## ALPHABETICALLY ARRANGED.

### WITH DESCRIPTION OF PLACES, RAILWAY STATIONS, HOTELS, ETC.

*New and revised Edition* (1890).   *One Volume, with Map.   Post 8vo.   12s.*

"MURRAY'S HANDBOOKS have always been distinguished for the high quality of their literary and architectural information.  In the volume before us under each place-name is given a description of the place, railway stations, hotels, and excursions best deserving of the traveller's attention.  It will thus be seen that such information is given as will suffice for all ordinary purposes.  The book is likely to be of as much use in the library as a handy gazetteer of home travel."—*Literary World.*

# The Railways and the Traders.

## A SKETCH OF THE RAILWAY RATES QUESTION IN THEORY AND PRACTICE.

### By W. M. ACWORTH, M.A. Oxon.,
And of the Inner Temple, Barrister-at-Law.

*Second Edition. Crown 8vo. 6s. and a Popular Edition, 1s.*

"That this somewhat prosaic subject is capable of being handled in a manner at once interesting and instructive is proved by the volume before us. Indeed, no one who has read 'The Railways of England' will hesitate to follow Mr. Acworth again upon his favourite subject."—*Builder.*

### By the same Author.

| THE | THE |
|---|---|
| *Railways of England.* | *Railways of Scotland.* |
| *Fourth Edition. Illustrations. 8vo. 14s.* | *With a Map. Crown 8vo. 5s.* |

••••••••••••••••••

# The Railways of America.

## THEIR CONSTRUCTION, DEVELOPMENT, MANAGEMENT, AND APPLIANCES.

*With Maps, and 200 Illustrations. Large 8vo. 31s. 6d.*

••••••••••••••••

## SIR HENRY MAINE'S WORKS.

### [NEW AND CHEAPER EDITIONS.]

| | |
|---|---|
| 1. *Ancient Law.* 9s. | 4. *Early Law and Custom.* 9s. |
| 2. *Village Communities.* 9s. | 5. *Popular Government.* 7s. 6d. |
| 3. *Early History of Institutions.* 9s. | 6. *International Law.* 7s. 6d. |

# UNIFORM EDITIONS.

## WORKS BY CHARLES DARWIN, F.R.S.

### Life and Letters of Charles Darwin.
WITH AN AUTOBIOGRAPHICAL CHAPTER.  Edited by FRANCIS DARWIN.
*Portraits.* 3 vols. 36s.

### Journal of Researches into the Natural History and Geology of Countries visited during a Voyage Round the World.
*With* 100 *Illustrations by* PRICHETT. 21s. *Popular Edit. Woodcuts.* 3s. 6d.

### Origin of Species by Means of Natural Selection; or, The Preservation of Favoured Races in the Struggle for Life.
*Large Type Edition. Portrait.* 2 vols. 12s. *Popular Edition.* 6s.

### Various Contrivances by which Orchids are Fertilized by Insects.
*Woodcuts.* 7s. 6d.

### Variation of Animals and Plants under Domestication.
*Illustrations.* 2 vols. 15s.

### Descent of Man, and Selection in Relation to Sex.
*Illustrations. Large Type Edition.* 2 vols. 15s. *Popular Edition.* 7s. 6d.

### Expression of the Emotions in Man and Animals.
*Illustrations.* 12s.

### Insectivorous Plants.
*Illustrations.* 9s.

### Movements and Habits of Climbing Plants.
*Woodcuts.* 6s.

### Effects of Cross and Self-Fertilization in the Vegetable Kingdom.
*Illustrations.* 9s.

### Different Forms of Flowers on Plants of the same Species.
*Illustrations.* 7s. 6d.

### Life of Erasmus Darwin.
*Portrait.* 7s. 6d.

### Formation of Vegetable Mould through the Action of Worms.
*Woodcuts.* 6s.

BRADBURY, AGNEW, & CO. LIMD., PRINTERS, WHITEFRIARS.